GREAT PREACHING ON
JUDGMENT

GREAT PREACHING ON

JUDGMENT

COMPILED BY
CURTIS HUTSON

SWORD of the LORD
PUBLISHERS
P.O.BOX 1099, MURFREESBORO, TN 37133

Printed and Bound in the United States of America

Preface

A certain church in England has engraved over one of its doors an exhortation to preach the Gospel "as a dying man to dying men."

These fifteen authors are great preachers of this sort, and never more so than in these conscience-arousing, heart-searching messages.

All are full of truth, needed truth, and truly needed now. Some awful facts are to be faced in this book, but they are needed facts. The authors portray conditions as they are and destiny as it shall be.

You will see clearly when and where the judgment will be, who will be judged, and what will be the basis of the judgment.

You will learn the difference between the first and second resurrections and how there will be one thousand years between.

You will see why Christians cannot come to be judged at the great white throne judgment, but will be there already gloriously saved, in glorified bodies, to bear witness against the unsaved for their sins.

You will learn how the sins of the unsaved will become known when God's record books are opened; how secret things will be brought to light; sins of the heart that no one knew will be proclaimed from the housetop.

You will hear how, at long last, when the judgment will be finished, every unsaved person, brought out of Hell to face the record of his sins, will be sent, soul and body, into the lake of fire forever!

You will learn, perhaps to your great surprise, that there will be tears in Heaven!

Alarming, convicting is the truth that men must someday meet God.

It will be found that there is a certain amount of overlapping of chapters but the general trends of thought are extremely varied, the intricate details related without contradiction—you would not wish any one left out.

This is a book that we feel cannot fail to miss its mark. Lost people who read it will come to sudden awful conviction of their sin and the price they will have to pay for it if they do not turn to Christ. And it will have a transforming effect in the lives of God's people who anticipate that day when "we shall all appear before the judgment seat of Christ"; an effect on each to so live that we will not be ashamed before Him at His coming.

Curtis Hutson, Editor
The Sword of the Lord

Table of Contents

CURTIS HUTSON
1934-

ABOUT THE MAN:

In 1961 a mail carrier and pastor of a very small church attended a Sword of the Lord conference, got on fire, gave up his route and set out to build a great soul-winning work for God. Forrest Hills Baptist Church of Decatur, Georgia, grew from 40 people into a membership of 7,900. The last four years of his pastorate there, the Sunday school was recognized as the largest one in Georgia.

After pastoring for 21 years, Dr. Hutson—the great soul winner that he is—became so burdened for the whole nation that he entered full-time evangelism, holding great citywide-areawide-cooperative revivals in some of America's greatest churches. As many as 625 precious souls have trusted Christ in a single service. In one eight-day meeting, 1,502 salvation decisions were recorded.

As an evangelist, he is in great demand.

At the request of Dr. John R. Rice, Dr. Hutson became Associate Editor of THE SWORD OF THE LORD in 1978, serving in that capacity until the death of Dr. Rice before becoming Editor, President of Sword of the Lord Foundation, and Director of Sword of the Lord conferences.

All these ministries are literally changing the lives of thousands of preachers and laymen alike, as well as winning many more thousands to Christ.

Dr. Hutson is the author of many fine books and booklets.

I.

The Believer's Threefold Judgment

CURTIS HUTSON

Past Judgment As a Sinner
Present Judgment As a Son
Future Judgment As a Servant

The believer's judgment is threefold—past, present and future. Our past judgment, as a believer, is our judgment for sin. Our present judgment is our judgment as a son. It is a self-judgment. And our future judgment is our judgment as a servant, when all Christians shall stand before the judgment seat of Christ to have our works tried by fire, according to I Corinthians 3:11-15.

I. THE BELIEVER'S PAST JUDGMENT: AS A SINNER

The Bible teaches that every sin we have ever committed—past, present and future—was laid on Christ two thousand years ago.

"...the Lord hath laid on him the iniquity of us all."—Isa. 53:6.

"For he hath made him to be sin for us, who knew no sin; that we might be made the righteousness of God in him."—II Cor. 5:21.

"Who his own self bare our sins in his own body on the tree."—I Pet. 2:24a.

Now, friends, two thousand years ago God took all the sins you have ever committed or ever will commit and placed them on Christ, just like I lay my pencil on my Bible. "The Lord [that is, Jehovah, the Father in Heaven] hath laid on him [Jesus] the iniquity of us all" (Isa. 53:6).

It is difficult for the believer to understand how Jesus could die for his future sins. But, friends, when Jesus died, all your sins were future. God looked down through the telescope of time, saw every sin that you would ever commit, took those sins in one package and laid them on Christ. Christ actually became guilty for your sins; not that He was a sinner, but He bore your sins in His own body. While Jesus was bearing all your sins in His own body on the tree, He answered to God for them. And on the cross God actually treated Jesus just as He would have to treat the guilty sinner.

It is an interesting Bible study to read the story of the rich man in Hell, recorded in Luke 16, then the account of the crucifixion of Christ. As you go from one to the other, you discover that the experience of the rich man in Hell was a preview of Calvary and Calvary is a preview of Hell. In other words, on the cross Jesus suffered everything one would have to suffer if he died without Christ and spent eternity in Hell.

For instance, the rich man in Hell suffered the agony of separation. Abraham said to him, "Between us and you there is a great gulf fixed: so that they which would pass from hence to you cannot; neither can they pass to us, that would come from thence."

Then, on the cross, Jesus suffered the agony of separation from God. While hanging on the cross, He uttered seven things. Three utterances came before the darkness, three after the darkness, and one during the darkness. That utterance was, "My God, my God, why hast thou forsaken me?"

Jesus Christ was separated from God. Not only did the rich man suffer the agony of separation; he suffered also the agony of thirst, crying, "Send Lazarus, that he may dip the tip of his finger in water, and cool my tongue; for I am tormented in this flame."

On the cross, Jesus Christ suffered the agony of thirst. The fifth cross utterance was, "I thirst."

The man in Hell suffered the agony of darkness. We read concerning the wicked, "Bind him hand and foot, and take him away, and cast him into outer darkness; there shall be weeping and gnashing of teeth" (Matt. 22:13).

On the cross, Jesus suffered the very darkness of Hell. Between 12:00 noon and 3:00 in the afternoon, it became as black as an Egyptian midnight, so black you could feel it.

On the cross, Jesus Christ suffered everything that men will have to suffer if they die without Christ and go to Hell. Otherwise, He has not fully paid my sin debt. But He did pay it.

He not only from the cross uttered, "I thirst," and "My God, my God, why hast thou forsaken me?" but He shouted, "It is finished!" That means nothing can be added to nor taken from it; it is complete. When Jesus Christ died on the cross, He made full payment for the believer's sins. He suffered everything that we should have to suffer. He satisfied the just demands of a holy God and paid in full what we sinners owe.

I once heard a man say that nobody will ever know how much Jesus suffered on the cross except those who go to Hell. That sounded reasonable to me and I believed it. But after several years I changed my mind, because even those who go to Hell will not fully know what He suffered on the cross. Here is what I mean.

The suffering of Jesus was enough to pay in full what every sinner owes. He could justly cry out from the cross, "It is finished!" Men who go to Hell will be paying on the sin debt forever but will never suffer enough to pay in full. Men in Hell can never cry, "It is finished!" because it will never be finished.

John 3:36 says, "He that believeth not the Son shall not see life; but the wrath of God abideth on him." You cannot couple annihilation with abiding wrath. Men will be in Hell forever and ever and ever and ever paying on the sin debt, but will never get it paid completely.

On the cross, Jesus Christ paid in full what the sinner owes. The Bible says in Hebrews 9:26, "Once in the end of the world hath he appeared to put away sin by the sacrifice of himself." Since Jesus Christ died on the cross for our sins, we believers will never face God in judgment for sin. God will never again deal with me as a sinner. All His dealings will be as a son.

You say, "But there will be a judgment." Yes, there will be, "For we must all appear before the judgment seat of Christ" (II Cor. 5:10). Yes, believers will be judged, but they will not be judged for sin. The moment you trust Jesus Christ as Saviour, you are justified. "Therefore being justified by faith, we have peace with God through our Lord Jesus Christ" (Rom. 5:1).

That verse means God wipes your slate clean, and you stand before God as if you had never in your life committed a single sin. And if you were to die and go to Heaven and there remind God of some sin you had committed, He would remind you of this verse: "I, even I, am he that blotteth out thy transgressions for mine own sake, and will not remember thy sins" (Isa. 43:25). God forgets our sins.

When you trust Christ, the sin question is forever settled. Jesus Christ took care of your sins by bearing them in His own body on the tree; and God judged Jesus Christ in your place, as your Substitute. The result of that judgment was death to Jesus Christ and justification to the believer. Our judgment for sin is past.

I hear some argue, "Yes, but if we sin after we are saved, we must pay for it!"

Dear friends, if we had to pay for any sin we ever committed, whether small or great, we would have to spend eternity in Hell. God has only one payment for sin. In Genesis 2:17 He said to Adam, "In the day that thou eatest thereof thou shalt surely die." And in Ezekiel 18:4, "The soul that sinneth, it shall die." And in Romans 6:23, "The wages of sin is death." God's one and only payment for sin is death. And if we had to answer to God for any sin, no matter how small, we would have to go to Hell and stay there forever and ever. That is God's price for sin, and God never alters that price because He is immutable. He never changes; therefore, His price for sin never changes.

You ask, "What if the believer sins after he is saved? Doesn't God chastise the believer?"

Yes. "For whom the Lord loveth he chasteneth, and scourgeth every son whom he receiveth" (Heb. 12:6). But, friends, chastening is not payment for sin.

If I spanked my son for breaking a window, the spanking, or chastening, would not be payment for the window. After I had spanked him, I would take money out of my pocket and pay for the window to be replaced. And when God chastises the believer, it is not payment for sin, because Jesus Christ paid for all your sin two thousand years ago at Calvary; and, as a believer, you will never answer to God for any sin. You will be chastened; but the chastening is child training, not payment for sin.

II. THE BELIEVER'S PRESENT JUDGMENT: AS A SON

Since the believer's judgment for sin is past, does that mean he can live loosely, sinfully and immorally, and get by? Certainly not. And here is where the second phase of the believer's judgment comes in. I call it his judgment as a son, a present judgment, a self-judgment.

"For if we would judge ourselves, we should not be judged. But when

we are judged, we are chastened of the Lord, that we should not be condemned with the world." —I Cor. 11:31, 32.

Now if we judge ourselves, we will not be judged. But if we do not judge ourselves, then we are judged of God and chastened that we should not be condemned with the world. Every believer should constantly look into his life to see what is wrong, then face his sins, confess them, and obtain forgiveness and cleansing.

David prayed in Psalm 139:23, 24, "Search me, O God, and know my heart: try me, and know my thoughts: And see if there be any wicked way in me, and lead me in the way everlasting." The Scandinavian word for "search" literally means ransack. David said, "Ransack my heart. Look under every corner of the rug. Pull out every drawer in the chiffonier. See if there is secret sin in my heart or any wicked way in me."

Friends, the believer is constantly to judge himself. "But let a man examine himself" (I Cor. 11:28). The purpose of this self-examination is to face up to sin and confess it that we may obtain forgiveness and cleansing.

"My little children, these things write I unto you, that ye sin not. And if any man sin, we have an advocate with the Father, Jesus Christ the righteous: And he is the propitiation [or atoning sacrifice] for our sins: and not for our's only, but also for the sins of the whole world." —I John 2:1, 2.

We are told not to sin; but if we do sin, we have an Advocate— Jesus Christ.

"If we say that we have no sin, we deceive ourselves, and the truth is not in us. If we confess our sins, he is faithful and just to forgive us our sins, and to cleanse us from all unrighteousness." —I John 1:8, 9.

I suppose one of the most difficult things for the believer is to honestly face his sins. In reading through the Bible, I find there are at least four things Christians do about their sins. First, they blame someone else. In the beginning, God gave Adam one prohibition:

"Of every tree of the garden thou mayest freely eat. . . . But of the tree of the knowledge of good and evil, thou shalt not eat of it: for in the day that thou eatest thereof thou shalt surely die." —Gen. 2:16, 17.

Now, when Adam sinned God came on the scene. "Adam, hast thou eaten of the tree, whereof I commanded thee that thou shouldest not eat?" Immediately Adam responded, "The woman whom thou gavest to be with me, she gave me of the tree, and I did eat."

Someone rightly suggested that Adam was the world's first buckpasser. "It wasn't me; it was the woman You gave to me." He tried to excuse his sin by blaming his wife, Eve. Ultimately he blamed God because he said, "The woman whom thou gavest to be with me. . . ." When we sin, it is so easy to blame someone else.

Some time back I was preaching in a small church. My wife was with me. After the service, I realized I did not have the car keys. "Honey, do you have the car keys?" I asked.

"Oh, no. I gave them to you." She insisted that she had given me the keys. I insisted she did not. This went on back and forth, back and forth for several minutes. After a while I got out of the car, looked around and to my surprise saw the keys in the car door. I had just used them to unlock the car!

Was I embarrassed! Could I have gotten by with it, I believe I would have put the keys in her purse and accused her of misplacing them! I hated to face the fact that I was guilty.

It is difficult to say, "I have sinned." In the Bible, some blame others for their sins, while still others excuse their sins.

Take the case of Saul. Though he was instructed to slay utterly, when he came back he had some prize cattle and sheep and the king he had spared in war. When the man of God asked, "Did you obey God?" "Oh, yes!" Saul said. Then when the cattle began to low, and the sheep began to bleat, the prophet said, "What meaneth then this bleating of the sheep in mine ears, and the lowing of the oxen which I hear?" Saul tried to excuse his sin by saying, "The people spared the best of the sheep and of the oxen, to sacrifice unto the Lord thy God. . . ."

I heard about a woman who went to the preacher and said, "You must pray for me. I have a cross to bear."

"What is it?" asked the preacher.

"A bad temper," she replied.

"Nonsense," replied the preacher, "you don't have a cross to bear. You have a sin. Your husband has a cross to bear."

He was right.

There are those who blame someone else for their sin and those who excuse sin.

Then there are others who try to cover their sins. "He that coveth his sins shall not prosper" (Prov. 28:13).

How many attempts have been made to cover sin!

Not long ago I was with a church in South Carolina, and the pastor told me a funny little story that illustrates this point. A man was remodeling his home. He had a thin temporary wall in the bathroom. One day the children were wrestling and one of them fell through the wall and knocked a hole large enough for a child to walk through.

When the man came home and found the hole in the wall, he lined each of the children up and asked, "Did you knock that hole in the wall?"

"Oh, no," said the first child. He was dismissed.

To the second he asked, "Did you knock the hole in the wall?"

"Oh, no!" And he was dismissed.

And so with the other children until he came to the last little fellow, "Son, did you knock that hole in the wall?"

The little fellow who was not over two or three years old, asked, "What hole?" Man, the hole was big enough to slide the bathtub through, but that kid tried to cover it up!

When I was a child, I used to close my eyes and think no one could see me. I figured since I could not see myself, no one else could see me. We may close our eyes, but we cannot cover our sins.

Something else we can do about our sins is confess them. "If we confess our sins, he is faithful and just to forgive us our sins, and to cleanse us from all unrighteousness" (I John 1:9).

I must face my sin honestly and confess it. Maybe it is a sin of neglect. Then I say, "Dear Lord, I have failed to read my Bible as I should. You promised if I would confess it, You would forgive and cleanse me; and You cannot lie." That's confessing and claiming the forgiveness and cleansing God promises in the Bible.

God not only forgives our sin when we confess it, but He cleanses it. In other words, He does away with it. It is one thing to forgive a child for falling into the mud. It is another thing to give that child a bath and fix him back like he was before he fell into the mud. That is forgiveness **and cleansing.**

Dear friend, when you come to Christ and confess your sin, wanting forgiveness, God not only forgives but cleanses. And the Bible says He is "just to forgive us our sins, and to cleanse us." He is just to forgive us because He bore that sin in His body two thousand years ago at Calvary. He doesn't sacrifice His justice in forgiving our sins, because justice was satisfied when He died at Calvary.

Somebody said the word "forgiveness" means literally to bear the burden. If you owe a man $1,000 and he forgives the debt, it means he bears the burden. When Jesus Christ forgives your sins, He bears the burden. The sin that you might commit tomorrow—He died for that one. If you sin after you are saved, it doesn't destroy your sonship, only your fellowship. "If we walk in the light, as he is in the light, we have fellowship one with another, and the blood of Jesus Christ his Son cleanseth us from all sin" (I John 1:7). As we keep our sins confessed, we keep fellowship with Christ.

Martin Luther once said, "Keep short accounts with God." By that he meant: Don't let sin pile up in your life. Don't let a day go by without confessing every known sin for the purpose of obtaining forgiveness and cleansing.

If you go to bed night after night without confessing sin, you allow it, like a brush pile, to accumulate in your life. And it is not easy to sweep it away with one prayer meeting. Remember, God's way to obtain forgiveness and cleansing is:

1. Be honest with God about your sins.

2. Confess your sins.

3. Claim the forgiveness and cleansing that God promised (I John 1:9).

4. Rest assured that any confessed sin is forgiven and cleansed because God promised and He cannot lie (Heb. 6:18).

Now, what happens if the believer does not judge himself? Let I Corinthians 11:31, 32 answer: "If we would judge ourselves, we should not be judged. But when we are judged, we are chastened of the Lord, that we should not be condemned with the world."

"And ye have forgotten the exhortation which speaketh unto you as unto children, My son, despise not thou the chastening of the Lord, nor faint when thou art rebuked of him: For whom the Lord loveth he chasteneth, and scourgeth every son whom he receiveth. If ye endure chastening, God dealeth with you as with sons; for what son is he whom the father chasteneth not? But if ye be without chastisement, whereof all are partakers, then are ye bastards, and not sons. Furthermore we have had fathers of our flesh which corrected us, and we gave them reverence: shall we not much rather be in subjection unto the Father of spirits, and live? For they verily for a few days chastened us after

their own pleasure; but he for our profit, that we might be partakers of his holiness. Now no chastening for the present seemeth to be joyous, but grievous: nevertheless afterward it yieldeth the peaceable fruit of righteousness unto them which are exercised thereby." —Heb. 12:5-11.

There are now several hundred denominations, sects, cults or religious groups in America, all teaching something different. However, in the final analysis, there are only two plans of salvation taught by men. The first is, God saves a man; the second is, man saves himself. Those who believe that God saves a man teach salvation by grace through faith in Christ. Jesus Christ made full payment for man's sins, and all we need do is trust Him for salvation.

Those who teach that man saves himself say that he saves himself by performing works before salvation in order to earn it, or performing works after salvation in order to keep it.

Those who teach salvation by grace are sometimes accused of giving a license to sin. The accusers evidently are not familiar with the Bible teaching of chastisement.

There are but three possible plans God could have in dealing with believers who sin. First, He could punish them beyond this life by sending them to Hell. But that would contradict the clear promises of God, "He that believeth on the Son hath everlasting life" (John 3:36). And, "He that heareth my word, and believeth on him that sent me, hath everlasting life, and shall not come into condemnation; but is passed from death unto life" (John 5:24).

The second possible plan for dealing with those who sin after they are saved would be to let them continue in sin and neither punish them beyond this life by sending them to Hell, nor chasten them in this life. But the Christian who sinned and was not chastened would eventually develop into the most warped and fearful character imaginable.

The third possible plan in dealing with those who sin after they are saved is to chastise them in this life so they will not be condemned with the world. This is what the Bible teaches: "We are chastened of the Lord, that we should not be condemned with the world" (I Cor. 11:32).

In this message, I will seek to set forth some simple Bible truths about Christian chastening.

1. What Is Christian Chastening?

The word "chastening" is built upon the Greek word "child." It means, "to deal with as a child" or to "child-train." The word "son" or "child" occurs six times in this passage. "If ye endure chastening, God dealeth with you as with sons" (vs. 7). "For whom the Lord loveth he chasteneth, and scourgeth every son whom he receiveth" (vs. 6).

When a person trusts Jesus Christ as Saviour, he becomes a son of God by faith. "As many as received him, to them gave he power to become the sons of God, even to them that believe on his name" (John 1:12). And, "For ye are all the children of God by faith in Christ Jesus" (Gal. 3:26).

When one is saved, God no longer deals with him as a sinner. All God's dealings from that point on are as with a son. Chastisement is not payment for sin. If I chasten my son for breaking a window, the chastisement would not be payment for the window. After I had spanked him, it would still be necessary for me to take money out of my pocket and pay for the window to be replaced.

God has only one payment for sin: "The wages of sin is death" (Rom. 6:23). If the child of God had to pay for any sin, it would be necessary to go into Hell forever. That is the payment God demands. Payment was made for our sins 2,000 years ago at Calvary. And when Christ died on the cross, He paid in full everything the believing sinner owes. That does not mean a Christian can sin and get by with it. The Bible teaches that God chastens every son He receives. And Hebrews 12:8 says, "But if ye be without chastisement, whereof all are partakers, then are ye bastards, and not sons."

Just as our earthly fathers correct us in order to build character, our Heavenly Father child-trains us to make us into the Christians He would have us be. Can you imagine what a child would become if the parents never chastened him? The Bible says in Proverbs 29:15, "A child left to himself bringeth his mother to shame." Christian chastisement is divine discipline that regulates character. It is child-training. Chastening of God's children is for correction; punishment of the unbeliever is to carry out law, for justice.

2. Who Are Chastened?

The Bible teaches that every child of God is chastened:

"For whom the Lord loveth he chasteneth, and scourgeth every son whom he receiveth. If ye endure chastening, God dealeth with you as with sons; for what son is he whom the father chasteneth not? But if

*ye be without chastisement, whereof all are partakers, then are ye
bastards, and not sons."*—Heb. 12:6-8.

Verse 6 says, ". . . and scourgeth every son whom he receiveth."
Verse 7 asks, "For what son is he whom the father chasteneth not?"
And verse 8 plainly states, "Whereof all are partakers." Here it is clear
that every child of God is chastened.

When I was a young Christian, I wondered why the wicked prospered
while seemingly the best Christians I knew had troubles. I recall singing,

**Tempted and tried we're oft made to wonder
Why it should be thus all the day long,
While there are others living about us,
Never molested tho' in the wrong.**

I was saved when I was eleven. Some other children in the
neighborhood who were not Christians cursed, smoked and did other
things I was careful not to do; but it seemed things went better for them
than for me. As a youngster I honestly questioned God, and I have
said to Him, *It doesn't pay to be a Christian. I try to do right, and I
don't seem to get along as well as some of my playmates who curse,
lie, steal and do nearly everything that is wrong.*

I now understand that there are two groups of children in the world:
"Ye are of your father the devil" (John 8:44); and, "As many as received
him, to them gave he power to become the sons of God" (John 1:12).
There are God's sons and the Devil's sons, and God doesn't whip the
Devil's children; but God will chasten believers. He leads us "in paths
of righteousness for his name's sake."

The unsaved are not chastened. If they refuse to accept Christ as
Saviour, they will be punished beyond this life, when they are sent to
Hell. The Bible says, "Fret not thyself because of him who prospereth
in his way, because of the man who bringeth wicked devices to pass. . . .
For evildoers shall be cut off" (Ps. 37:7,9).

No child of God is so good that he can evade chastisement. No
believer can get by with sin. Every sin that is not confessed and forgiven
brings the chastening hand of God upon the Christian. "He
chasteneth. . . every son whom he receiveth."

3. When Are Christians Chastened?

Christians are chastened when they tolerate known sin in their lives.
The Bible teaches that when we refuse to confess our sins in order to

obtain forgiveness and cleansing, we are judged of the Lord and chastened. "For if we would judge ourselves, we should not be judged. But when we are judged, we are chastened of the Lord, that we should not be condemned with the world" (I Cor. 11:31,32).

The believer who would live in blessed fellowship with Christ should constantly be examining himself. The purpose of this examination or judgment is to spot sin in our lives.

When we find sin, we are instructed to confess it that we may obtain forgiveness and cleansing. "If we confess our sins, he is faithful and just to forgive us our sins, and to cleanse us from all unrighteousness" (I John 1:9). When the sin is confessed, forgiven and cleansed, we continue in fellowship with Christ. "IF we walk in the light, as he is in the light, we have fellowship one with another, and the blood of Jesus Christ his Son cleanseth us from all sin" (I John 1:7).

One of two C's is always present in the believer's life: he is either changed or chastised. If the believer persists in sin, he may be sure to expect the chastening hand of God; and if one persists in sin, without chastening, the Bible makes it clear that he is not a Christian. "But if ye be without chastisement, whereof all are partakers, then are ye bastards, and not sons" (Heb. 12:8). The man who sins willfully, habitually and by preference, without chastisement, is illegitimate; he is not a son of God.

Several years ago I was conducting a revival meeting in South Georgia. During the week several members asked if I would visit a certain man in the neighborhood whom they thought was lost. When I called on the man, he was sitting on the front porch in a rocking chair. We talked a few moments and I said, "Sir, let me ask you a question. If you die today, do you know you will go to Heaven?"

To my surprise, he answered, "Yes."

Thinking he misunderstood, I continued, "Are you a Christian? Have you been born again?"

"Yes," he said, "I have accepted Jesus Christ as my Saviour."

I couldn't believe what I was hearing. Everyone in the neighborhood just knew he was unconverted. "All right," I continued, "let me read several verses from the Bible and have prayer before I leave." With an open Bible I presented clearly the plan of salvation, then asked, "Now, do you understand that you are a sinner?"

"Oh, yes," he said.

"And do you know Jesus Christ died to pay your sin-debt?"

"Yes, I understand that."

"And will you trust Him completely as your Saviour?"

"Yes," he said, "I have already done that."

Since he insisted that he was a Christian, I turned to Hebrews 12 and read verses 5 through 8. "Now, according to these verses, if you are a Christian, you will be chastised unless you honestly confess your sins and set out to live for Christ."

The dear man began to weep. "Chastised!" he said, and with that he held up the nub of one arm. "I lost this arm in a hunting accident." Pointing to the home he said, "I have lost my wife. I have lost my children. I have lost my health. Oh," said he, "I have been chastised!"

I said, "You will continue to be chastised until you get right with God. And the ultimate in Christian chastisement is premature death to the believer. 'To deliver such an one unto Satan for the destruction of the flesh, that the spirit may be saved in the day of the Lord Jesus' (I Cor. 5:5)."

In a few moments we were on our knees, and the dear man confessed his sins, claiming the forgiveness and cleansing that God promises in the Bible. He arose with a radiant face and that night was in church and came forward stating that he wanted to live for Christ and be a good Christian.

4. How Is the Christian Chastened?

Chastisement for believers who sin takes various forms. **Sometimes God uses, as a rod, the loss of health.** All sickness is not chastisement. For instance, in John 9:2, "And his disciples asked him, saying, Master, who did sin, this man, or his parents, that he was born blind?" And verse 3 continues, "Jesus answered, Neither hath this man sinned, nor his parents: but that the works of God should be made manifest in him." The blindness of this young man in John 9 was not chastening for sin, as is clearly indicated.

On the other hand, the Bible speaks of those who are sick because of certain sins: "For this cause many are weak and sickly among you, and many sleep" (I Cor. 11:30). Here the Bible teaches that some were sick because they had committed sin in connection with the Lord's Supper. The expression, "for this cause," takes us back to verse 29: "For he that eateth and drinketh unworthily, eateth and drinketh damnation to himself, not discerning the Lord's body." They were weak and sickly because they had eaten and drunk unworthily, not discerning the Lord's body.

Says James 5:14-16,

"Is any sick among you? let him call for the elders of the church; and let them pray over him, anointing him with oil in the name of the Lord: And the prayer of faith shall save the sick, and the Lord shall raise him up; and if he have committed sins, they shall be forgiven him. Confess your faults one to another, and pray one for another, that ye may be healed."

It seems that the sickness here was a result of sin. This is implied by the statement in verse 16, "Confess your faults one to another, and pray one for another, that ye may be healed." If the sins are confessed, then, of course, the person would be healed if the sickness was chastisement for unconfessed sins.

Again I say that all sickness is not chastening, but some sickness is chastisement for unconfessed sins in the believer's life.

Sometimes God uses, as a rod, the loss of property.

"I also have given you cleanness of teeth in all your cities, and want of bread in all your places: yet have ye not returned unto me, saith the Lord. And also I have withholden the rain from you, when there were yet three months to the harvest: and I caused it to rain upon one city, and caused it not to rain upon another city: one piece was rained upon, and the piece whereupon it rained not withered. So two or three cities wandered unto one city, to drink water; but they were not satisfied: yet have ye not returned unto me, saith the Lord. I have smitten you with blasting and mildew: when your gardens and your vineyards and your fig trees and your olive trees increased, the palmerworm devoured them: yet have ye not returned unto me, saith the Lord."—Amos 4:6-9.

Here the teaching is that Israel was hungry, that is, they had cleanness of teeth in all their cities and want of bread in all their places. And why were they without food? God said, "Because you have not returned unto me." The palmerworm had devoured the olive trees, the gardens, the vineyards and the fig trees. There was no water to drink, and several cities wandered into one in search of water; yet they found none. Why? God said, "Ye have not returned unto me."

The loss of property was chastisement from God because the children of Israel would not return unto Him.

In John 21, Peter became a business failure. He had quit the ministry and gone back into the fishing business. Here was an experienced fisherman. If anyone could catch fish, he could. Yet he toiled all night and caught nothing.

God made him a failure because he had backslidden and left the ministry. When he said in John 21:3, "I go a fishing," he wasn't speaking of taking a fishing trip; he was leaving the ministry to go back to his old business. And God chastened him by making him a business failure. But three chapters later, in Acts, chapter 2, Peter preached a great sermon and 3,000 souls were saved. The chastening had corrected the child of God.

Sometimes God uses as a rod the loss of joy. Consider the case of David in Psalm 51. In verse 8 he said, "Make me to hear joy and gladness; that the bones which thou hast broken may rejoice." In verse 12 he prayed, "Restore unto me the joy of thy salvation." This entire psalm is the prayer of a sinning saint. He is praying for forgiveness and cleansing. In verse 2 he cries, "Wash me throughly from mine iniquity, and cleanse me from my sin."

Sometimes God uses as a rod the loss of loved ones, as in the case of David, "Howbeit, because by this deed thou hast given great occasion to the enemies of the Lord to blaspheme, the child also that is born unto thee shall surely die" (II Sam. 12:14). Here God made it plain that, because of David's sin and because he had given occasion to the enemies of the Lord to blaspheme, the child would surely die.

In the case of Israel, God said, "I have sent among you the pestilence after the manner of Egypt: your young men have I slain with the sword" (Amos 4:10).

The loss of loved ones is not always the chastening hand of God, but many times it is.

Finally, God sometimes uses, as a rod, premature death to the believer. The ultimate in Christian chastisement is premature death to the believer. "For this cause many are weak and sickly among you, and many sleep"—are dead (I Cor. 11:30). "If any man see his brother sin a sin which is not unto death, he shall ask, and he shall give him life for them that sin not unto death. There is a sin unto death: I do not say that he shall pray for it" (I John 5:16). First Corinthians 5:5 states, "To deliver such an one unto Satan for the destruction of the flesh, that the spirit may be saved in the day of the Lord Jesus."

God the Father corrects and child-trains His children; but if other forms of chastening fail to get the desired results, the Lord will allow the believer to die a premature death.

Someone suggested that He speaks, spanks and calls Home. He speaks to the conscience; and if the believer does not make necessary corrections, He spanks, using the rod of sickness, death of loved ones or possibly loss of property. If the spanking does not produce results, then God calls the believer Home: as in the case of Moses in Deuteronomy 32:48-52:

"And the Lord spake unto Moses that selfsame day, saying, Get thee up into this mountain Abarim, unto mount Nebo, which is in the land of Moab, that is over against Jericho; and behold the land of Canaan, which I give unto the children of Israel for a possession: And die in the mount whither thou goest up, and be gathered unto thy people; as Aaron thy brother died in mount Hor, and was gathered unto his people: Because ye trespassed against me among the children of Israel at the waters of Meribah-Kadesh, in the wilderness of Zin; because ye sanctified me not in the midst of the children of Israel. Yet thou shalt see the land before thee; but thou shalt not go thither unto the land which I give the children of Israel."

I recall vividly a young father and husband who was saved under my ministry. This dear man attended church faithfully and was a good Christian, with one exception. There was a particular sin he seemingly could not overcome. He would do well for several weeks and then fall back into sin again. This happened over and over. I prayed with him numerous times.

The last time he came to see me, I said, "You had better get your house in order. The Lord has brought all kinds of chastisement upon you, with seemingly no results. I wouldn't be surprised if someone called and told me you were dead." I warned, "The ultimate chastisement is a premature death for the Christian."

A few days later his wife called to say he had been found in a motel room dead and asked if I would preach his funeral. The doctors never explained his death. But in my heart I knew what happened. He had persisted in sin; and though God had often chastened, he never made the needed correction, so God called him Home.

5. What Are the Results of Christian Chastening?

God is not a purposeless God. He never does anything without purpose. His ultimate aim for every Christian is Christlikeness. "For whom he did foreknow, he also did predestinate to be conformed to the image of his Son" (Rom. 8:29).

A visitor watched as a silversmith heated the silver in his crucible. Hotter and hotter grew the flames and all the while the silversmith was closely scanning the crucible. The visitor interrupted, "Why are you watching the silver so closely? What are you looking for?"

In an instant the silversmith replied, "I'm looking for my face. When I see my own image in the silver, then I stop. The work is done."

God is looking for a face in every child of God. It is the face of His Son. He chastens us for our own profit that we might be partakers of His holiness. "For they [earthly fathers] verily for a few days chastened us after their own pleasure; but he for our profit, that we might be partakers of his holiness" (Heb. 12:10).

The holiness mentioned here is not inward holiness. We receive the divine nature the moment we are saved. Second Peter 1:4 says, "Whereby are given unto us exceeding great and precious promises: that by these ye might be partakers of the divine nature, having escaped the corruption that is in the world through lust."

The holiness mentioned in verse 10 is outward holiness. God wants us to be like Him. He chastens us that we might be partakers of His holiness. The chastisement is always for our profit. Here the Bible says that earthly fathers sometimes chasten us for their own pleasure, but He for our profit. God never enjoys chastising the believer, but He knows we will never be all that He wants us to be without it.

Verse 11 says, "No chastening for the present seemeth to be joyous, but grievous: nevertheless afterward it yieldeth the peaceable fruit of righteousness unto them which are exercised thereby." The chastening is for our good and God's glory, that we may be more and more like Him. He is purging from us, in child-training, all that dims the image of Christ in us.

James H. McConkey said:

> Child of God, do not be associating chastening only with the word *chastise.* Couple it also with that beautiful word *chastity,* the jewel of perfect, spotless purity of heart and life. Thus chasten . . . is to make chaste, to make pure spiritually, to purge, to cleanse, to purify. That is God's great purpose in all His child-training.

Chastening produces in the believer the peaceable fruit of

righteousness. Verse 11 states, "Afterward it yieldeth the peaceable fruit of righteousness unto them which are exercised thereby."

The poet said,

It isn't raining rain for me,
It's raining daffodils;
In every dimpling drop I see
Wild flowers on the hills.

A cloud of gray engulfs the day
And overwhelms the town;
It isn't raining rain for me,
It's raining roses down.

The child of God who is being chastened may think, *It is raining hard on me today—the testings, the disappointments, the bereavements.* But it isn't raining rain for you; it is raining blessings. And out of the chastisement will come the peaceable fruit of righteousness.

6. What Should the Christian's Attitude Be Toward Chastisement?

First, may I say God does not expect us to enjoy chastening but to endure it for the sake of its reward. Verse 11 reads, "Now no chastening for the present seemeth to be joyous, but grievous: nevertheless afterward it yieldeth the peaceable fruit of righteousness unto them which are exercised thereby." Verse 5 states, "Despise not thou the chastening of the Lord." That is, we are not to think lightly or scorn to submit to the chastening of the Lord. Do not esteem lightly God's child-training. Do not look down upon it. And above all, don't allow your heart to grow hard and bitter against God because of it.

Again, verse 5 states, ". . . nor faint when thou art rebuked of him." That is, we are not to lose courage or give up. It is a mistake for the believer to throw in the towel when chastening comes. We are to bear up under it. We are not to faint. Chastening is good for us, and someday we will look back and thank God that He was thorough with us.

If one feels he is fainting, what can he do? What do you do when you are about to faint physically? You cannot do anything! You cease from your own doing, and in your faintness you lean upon the shoulder of some strong loved one or friend; and there you lie still and trust until your strength returns. So it is when we are chastened of the Lord. When it seems we can bear it no longer, we simply lean hard on Him.

In the closing months of his life, Hudson Taylor was so feeble he wrote,

I am so weak I cannot work. I cannot read my Bible. I cannot even pray. I can only lie still in God's arms like a little child and trust.

He didn't need to do anything else. Leaning on Jesus was enough.

The Bible says in Psalm 55:22, "Cast thy burden upon the Lord, and he shall sustain thee." In Hebrews 12:5-11 God gives us a threefold attitude toward child-training. First, we are not expected to enjoy chastening: "No chastening for the present seemeth to be joyous, but grievous" (vs. 11). Second, we are to despise not chastening: "My son, despise not thou the chastening of the Lord" (vs. 5). And third, we are to faint not. ". . . nor faint when thou art rebuked of him" (vs. 5).

III. THE BELIEVER'S FUTURE JUDGMENT:
AS A SERVANT

The believer's judgment as a sinner is past, and it resulted in the death of Jesus Christ and justification of the believer. His judgment as a son is present and is a self-judgment. The result of this judgment is when we confess our sins, God forgives and cleanses us; or when we fail to confess our sins, we are judged of the Lord and chastened.

The third phase of the believer's judgment is future. This is his judgment as a servant.

"For other foundation can no man lay than that is laid, which is Jesus Christ. Now if any man build upon this foundation gold, silver, precious stones, wood, hay, stubble; Every man's work shall be made manifest: for the day shall declare it, because it shall be revealed by fire; and the fire shall try every man's work of what sort it is. If any man's work abide which he hath built thereupon, he shall receive a reward. If any man's work shall be burned, he shall suffer loss: but he himself shall be saved; yet so as by fire."—I Cor. 3:11-15.

Now notice something very carefully in this passage. The Bible says nothing here about man being judged for his sins. Look at verse 13: "Every man's *work* shall be made manifest," not his sins. When a person trusts Jesus Christ as Saviour, the sin question is forever settled. This future judgment is for the believer's works. It is a judgment for our service. It is our judgment as a servant. "Every man's *work* shall be made manifest."

"If any man's *work* abide which he hath built thereupon. . ." (vs. 14). "If any man's *work* shall be burned, he shall suffer loss: but he himself shall be saved; yet so as by fire" (vs. 15).

You ask, "Do we work to be saved?" Oh, no.

D. L. Moody said,

> **I would not work my soul to save,**
> **For this my Lord hath done;**
> **But I would work like any slave,**
> **For love of His dear Son.**

"For we are his workmanship, created in Christ Jesus unto good works" (Eph. 2:10). God expects every believer to work. We are all to serve Christ. Now we don't all have the same opportunities, but God expects everyone to do something.

Somewhere I read this sign:

> I am only one, but I am one. I cannot do everything, but I can do something. What I can do, I ought to do; and what I ought to do, by the grace of God, I will do.

Now, friends, there are people you can reach with the Gospel whom I cannot reach. You have some service you can render that I cannot render. Every person should be doing what he can for the Lord. The measure of Christian service is found in that little expression in Mark 14:8, where it says of Mary of Bethany, "She hath done what she could." All God expects any of us to do is just what we can. One of the most frustrated persons in the world is the man whose ambitions exceed his abilities. Do what you can. Mary of Bethany did what she could.

Could you visit the jails? Could you distribute Bible tracts? Could you sing in the choir? Could you help keep the church building clean? Could you work as an usher? Could you drive a bus or visit on a bus route? There is some work you can do. Every believer is going to stand before God at the judgment seat of Christ and be judged as a servant. "For we must all appear before the judgment seat of Christ" (II Cor. 5:10). Your work will be tried.

Now notice something in verse 13: "The fire shall try every man's work of what *sort* it is." It says nothing about size, but it says something about sort. Quality is the important thing. The motive behind the service is important. Fire doesn't measure size; it tests quality. If He were trying for size, He would use a tape measure or scales; but it is tried by fire. The Bible says, "It shall be revealed by fire; and the fire shall try every man's *work*."

Did you know that service not motivated by love for Christ will not be rewarded at the judgment seat of Christ? The Bible says in I Corinthians 13:3, "Though I bestow all my goods to feed the poor, and though I give my body to be burned, and have not charity [or love], *it profiteth me nothing."* Paul said, "I could give all my goods to feed the poor, cash in my stocks and bonds, draw all my money out of the bank, sell all my real estate, give it all to feed the poor, be burned at the stake, and die a martyr's death; but if I have not love it profiteth me nothing."

The Lord is not only interested in what you do; He is also interested in why you do it. Did you perform that service for the glory you received? Then you have your reward. Did you make that gift to be seen of men and to receive the praise of men? Then you have your reward. Or did you do it because you love Christ? If love motivated you, then you will be rewarded at the judgment seat of Christ.

Notice what the Bible says in I Corinthians 3:14, 15:

"If any man's work abide which he hath built thereupon, he shall receive a reward. If any man's work shall be burned, he shall suffer loss: but he himself shall be saved; yet so as by fire."

This is not a judgment to determine whether a man is saved or lost. This is a judgment of works, of service, to determine the believer's reward. Notice that neither man goes to Hell from this judgment. Both are saved. One man's works abide, and he receives a reward. The other man's works are burned, and he suffers loss; but the Bible says he is saved, "yet so as by fire." Both men are saved: one is rewarded, one suffers loss.

That word "reward" means payment for service rendered. That is not Heaven. I have heard preachers say at a funeral service, "Our dearly beloved has gone to his reward." Heaven is not a reward but a gift. Salvation is also a gift. Heaven was bought and paid for at Calvary two thousand years ago. And when a man dies, he does not go to his reward, because that does not come until after the judgment seat of Christ. And this judgment will not take place until the coming of Christ.

"Therefore judge nothing before the time, until the Lord come, who both will bring to light the hidden things of darkness, and will make manifest the counsels of the hearts: and then shall every man have praise of God." —I Cor. 4:5.

The Bible says God will judge the quick (living) and the dead at His appearing (II Tim. 4:1). The bodies of Christians who have gone on to be with Christ will be raised; the living saints will be changed and caught up with them to meet the Lord in the air, then all believers will appear before the judgment seat of Christ.

Second Corinthians 5:10 tells us, "For we must all appear before the judgment seat of Christ." The little pronoun "we" is found 26 times in that 5th chapter and each time refers to believers. We—every believer— must stand before the judgment seat of Christ, and our works will be tried. If our works abide, we will receive a reward; if our works are burned, we will suffer loss; but we will be saved "yet so as by fire" (I Cor. 3:14, 15).

The Bible mentions five different crowns that will be given at the judgment seat of Christ.

The incorruptible crown:

"And every man that striveth for the mastery is temperate in all things. Now they do it to obtain a corruptible crown; but we an incorruptible."—I Cor. 9:25.

This crown is for those believers who keep their bodies under subjection, who refuse to yield to the flesh, who do not live carnally, fleshly or worldly. Such a believer will receive the incorruptible crown at the judgment seat of Christ.

The crown of rejoicing:

"For what is our hope, or joy, or crown of rejoicing? Are not even ye in the presence of our Lord Jesus Christ at his coming? For ye are our glory and joy."—I Thess. 2:19, 20.

This crown is for the soul winner. Paul says of those he had won to Christ, "You are our crown of rejoicing." This crown will only be given to those who win souls.

The crown of righteousness:

"Henceforth there is laid up for me a crown of righteousness, which the Lord, the righteous judge shall give me at that day: and not to me only, but unto all them also that love his appearing."—II Tim. 4:8.

This crown is given to those who love the second coming of Christ, those who love His appearing.

By the way, we should distinguish between our disappearing and His appearing. Some folks are anxious for Christ to come simply to get away from their troubles, from under the pressure. They love their disappearing, but I am not sure they love His appearing. The crown of righteousness is for those who love His appearing.

The crown of glory, mentioned in I Peter 5:4:

"And when the chief Shepherd shall appear, ye shall receive a crown of glory that fadeth not away."

This is the pastor or elder's crown, or for the person who surrenders himself for full-time Christian service and serves God faithfully.

"Feed the flock of God which is among you, taking the oversight thereof, not by constraint, but willingly; not for filthy lucre, but of a ready mind; Neither as being lords over God's heritage, but being ensamples to the flock. And when the chief Shepherd shall appear, ye shall receive a crown of glory that fadeth not away." —I Pet. 5:2-4.

The crown of life:

"Blessed is the man that endureth temptation: for when he is tried, he shall receive the crown of life, which the Lord hath promised to them that love him." —James 1:12.

"Fear none of those things which thou shalt suffer: behold, the devil shall cast some of you into prison, that ye may be tried; and ye shall have tribulation ten days: be thou faithful unto death, and I will give thee a crown of life." —Rev. 2:10.

The crown of life is the martyr's crown, given to those who sacrifice their lives for their testimony.

Now what will the believer do if he is rewarded with different crowns? The Bible says,

"The four and twenty elders fall down before him that sat on the throne, and worship him that liveth for ever and ever, and cast their crowns before the throne, saying, Thou art worthy, O Lord, to receive glory and honour and power: for thou hast created all things, and for thy pleasure they are and were created." —Rev. 4:10, 11.

These elders cast their crowns at the Saviour's feet. Perhaps believers, too, will stand before Christ and cast their crowns at His feet. But whatever the case may be, you will stand before the judgment seat of Christ and be judged for your work. You will be judged as a servant and either receive a reward, which will be in the form of five different crowns; or you will suffer loss. I don't believe believers will stand at the judgment seat of Christ, see their works burned, go up in smoke, and then shout and thank God for a life of unfruitful service.

Dear friends, what time you have ought to be spent wisely in serving Christ. As Mary of Bethany, do what you can. "Now, little children, abide in him; that, when he shall appear, we may have confidence, and not be ashamed before him at his coming" (I John 2:28).

Jesus is coming. If you have never trusted Him as your Saviour, then do it today. If you have trusted Him, then set out to be the best Christian you can possibly be.

JIM MERCER
1913-

ABOUT THE MAN:

Evangelist Jim Mercer was born January 21, 1913, in Hosford, Florida.

In 1934 there was a revival in Hosford, Florida, that lasted for 3½ years. The people would meet to pray and then go soul winning. Jim Mercer was the 17th man saved in that revival. He was called to preach that same day and has been an evangelist for more than 50 years.

He attended Bob Jones College in Cleveland, Tennessee.

In the 1950's he was awarded the Doctor of Divinity degree by BJU.

Ten of his sermons have been printed in THE SWORD OF THE LORD.

He and his wife have six children—two sons and four daughters.

At age 77 he is actively preaching. He describes himself as an "old-fashioned, gospel, Bible-believing preacher."

He and Mrs. Mercer now reside in Apalachicola, Florida.

II.

After Death – What?

JIM MERCER

"And as it is appointed unto men once to die, but after this the judgment."—Heb. 9:27.

Death is a part of the curse of sin. "Wherefore, as by one man sin entered into the world, and DEATH BY SIN; and so death passed upon all men, for that all have sinned" (Rom. 5:12). "Therefore as by the offence of one judgment came upon all men to condemnation . . . ." (Rom. 5:18).

Because all have sinned, all must die. "For the wages of sin is death . . ." (Rom. 6:23). We ought to face the fact of death!

Death is not a pleasant subject, but it will be profitable if we face it soberly.

It is said that "a wise man will prepare for the inevitable." What could be more inevitable than death? I KNOW THAT I AM GOING TO DIE. There is no use for me to dodge this serious fact. Unless Jesus comes for me, I must go to meet Him in death. So it is with you. One day your heart will forget to beat. Your knees will buckle under your tired body. "Tired eyelids will be pulled like purple curtains over tired eyes. Tired hands will be folded over a motionless breast." You will be dead. The hearse will back up to your door. The undertaker will notify the newspaper, and your name will be listed in the obituary column.

Now if you are wise, you will be prepared for that day. No man is ready to live until he is prepared to die.

Death is an ugly thing, but it is certain. It is our last enemy, but it is on its way to your address. Death is no respecter of persons. It lays its cold hand everywhere. It snatches the tiny baby from its warm crib. It takes the old man as he sits in the easy chair by his fireside. Death takes the young mother and leaves the baby to a faltering father's care. Sometimes death takes both parents, and the children are left to the mercy of relatives or kind friends.

God has taken people from all around you, yet your heart is still beating. Yes, it is beating now, but "like a drum pounding out your funeral march to the grave." All of us are on our way to the cemetery.

Now if the funeral were final and the grave the end of everything, what a dreary and useless existence this would be. If this life were all and a man died like a dog or a hog, you could not blame people for living like the beasts of the field. BUT THE GRAVE IS NOT ALL!

Man must live somewhere forever. Man was made in the image of God; and as long as God lives, man, too, will live. The Bible declares that beyond the grave is the judgment. The Apostle John, seeing the dramatic and exciting scene of the great white throne judgment, said:

"And I saw the dead, small and great, stand before God; and the books were opened: and another book was opened, which is the book of life: and the dead were judged out of those things which were written in the books, according to their works. And the sea gave up the dead which were in it; and death and hell delivered up the dead which were in them: and they were judged every man according to their works. And death and hell were cast into the lake of fire. This is the second death. And whosoever was not found written in the book of life was cast into the lake of fire."—Rev. 20:12-15.

"And as it is appointed unto men once to die, but after this the judgment." The unsaved must face God at the great white throne judgment. The Christian must face God at the judgment seat of Christ. Both saint and sinner must stand before God after death. The time and place and purpose of these two judgments will differ. It is not my purpose in this message to point out the fine points of Bible teaching on all the judgments. But I do want in this message to emphasize the solemn fact that we must all give an account of ourselves to God.

Daniel Webster said, "The most solemn thought ever to enter my mind is that I must give an account of myself to God."

You, too, will have to give an account of yourself to God. This is one of those times when you cannot send an agent to represent you. You must go in person. It is God's appointment for you. In that dreadful hour God will open the books and deal with you about your

Words.

Jesus said,

"But I say unto you, That EVERY IDLE WORD that men shall speak, they shall give account thereof in the day of judgment. For by thy words thou shalt be justified, and by thy words thou shalt be condemned."— Matt. 12:36,37.

Every word goes on record. It would be serious enough if only our studied prayerful words were recorded, but the Bible declares that even our idle words will be recorded!

Several years ago I received a package through the mail with a recording of a sermon I preached over the radio. I did not know that it was recorded. I do not know to this day who had it recorded or who mailed it to me. It was mailed to me with no comment. I suppose some friend did it. Anyway, it had a very sobering effect upon my life.

As I listened to this message again after several years, I began to recall the circumstances of preparation. My mind was flooded with the details and circumstances of its delivery. It was a Bible sermon. It was delivered with sincerity. I was not ashamed to own it as my own. But it caused me to think of all my utterances—public and private!

God is keeping a record, and the good things are recorded and the things that are not so good. Every foolish jest. Every whispered word. Every childish complaint. You may be solemnly certain that every oath uttered will be on your record. Every lie is kept to face you on the day God calls you to face Him. The very first lie you ever told will face you because God tells us that we all go astray, "as soon as they be born, speaking lies" (Ps. 58:3). Whether you lied to your mother as a child or whether to the government when you made out your income tax report, it makes no difference. It will be accurate. You will know that it is your very own. Lying is a terrible sin. Jesus is "the Truth," and the Antichrist is the lie!

Every dirty joke, every smutty story, every slanderous remark is on God's record books for you to face in that dreaded hour when "all earth's music is hushed" and the guilty world stands frightened before the Almighty God.

And now, what about your

Deeds?

Listen to these words:

"But after thy hardness and impenitent heart treasurest up unto thyself wrath against the day of wrath and revelation of the righteous judgment of God; Who will render to every man according to HIS DEEDS."—Rom. 2:5,6.

Every wicked act is put down under your name. Every overt action against God is recorded. Every transgression of God's law is put to your account.

Did you steal? God wrote it down! Did you cheat? God has it in the books! Did you commit adultery? God recorded it! Every foul deed done in the body is written indelibly awaiting the day for you to face the completed record. You will face the record in the very presence of God who saw you commit them. You will be without excuse! You will be forced to admit by your own testimony your guilt. And it will be too late to repent. The great white throne is not an altar of prayer! It is not a place of mercy. It is the throne of condemnation. It is the place of wrath. This is JUDGMENT DAY! In this frightful hour God will say, "Depart from me, ye cursed." When you turn from Him you will be headed to your final abode. The Bible calls it the lake of fire.

Now let's consider your

Thoughts.

Not only your words and deeds, but your thoughts are known to God. He is the great mind reader. He tells us that as a man "thinketh in his heart, so is he" (Prov. 23:7). Someone has rightly said, "Behind every wicked deed is a process of wicked thinking." A person has to think wrongly before he can act wrongly! Just before God sent the Flood and destroyed the world, He looked down from Heaven and said about man, that "every imagination of the thoughts of his heart was only evil continually" (Gen. 6:5).

Because their minds were in the gutter, their lives were in the gutter. The person who cannot control his thoughts cannot control his behavior, for out of the heart are the issues of life. Every wicked deed, then, has its origin in the brain. You had better be careful what you think. The evil idea starts in the head, goes into the heart and finally into the hand. But God judges the foul thing while it is still in the heart. Jesus tells us that, if a man looks on a woman to lust after her in his heart, he is guilty of adultery.

God will judge us as to what we really are and not what we seem to be. Man looks on the outward appearance, but God looks on the heart. It is said that a man's reputation is what people think about him; his character is what God knows about him. Most of us have a better reputation than character. What are you in the sight of God?

What if your friends knew all about you? Would they remain your friends? Now God knows all there is to know. His all-seeing eye has watched you from the cradle, and He will watch you die. He has never taken His eyes off you from the day you came into this world. Someone has said, "God watches every man as if there were only one person He had to watch."

I asked a moment ago, What are you in the sight of God? Just what do I look like to God? What am I when the bark is peeled off? With the holy eyes of God looking straight down into your soul, can you say, "All is well"?

There is so much sham and hypocrisy in the world. I am afraid there is a little humbug in the most of us. But on the day of judgment God will look beneath all the cover or crust and will point out the real man.

I believe it was Dr. Bob Jones, Sr., who said that a good test of a person's character is to find out what he would do if he knew no human being would ever find it out. What would you do if you knew beyond any shadow of doubt that only God would know? Would you tell a lie? Would you kill? Then in the eyes of God that is what you are! Then what will it be like when all the secrets are revealed!

The Secrets

Sometimes in this world the innocent are put in prison and punished while the guilty culprit goes free. Sometimes lies are told and foul deeds covered up; but in the day of judgment all the truth will come out. The secret things will be disclosed. "For God shall bring every work into judgment, with EVERY SECRET THING, whether it be good, or whether it be evil" (Eccles. 12:14).

In that day all the secrets of men's hearts shall be disclosed. Who can describe it? "Who can stand before his indignation? and who can abide in the fierceness of his anger?" (Nah. 1:6). You will be startled when God reads from the books the secrets of men's hearts. You will be more startled when God reads your own secrets—some that you have forgotten.

Have you ever noticed how strangely quiet it gets when the preacher starts talking about secret sins? There is a reason for that! Most people have some things they don't want to be known. Most of us are covering up something from somebody! But none of us have anything hidden from God. The books are going to be opened.

Would it not be interesting to open the books and read all the secrets of our neighbors? If the Federal Bureau of Investigation had access to God's record of man's secrets, all the jails would not hold the guilty that now go unpunished. How embarrassed this world would be if the contents of God's books were made known. However, even now, more is known than one would think. You might even be surprised to know just how much your own friends know about you.

Often people commit suicide in an effort to hide their sins from friends or relatives. They just can't stand to face the sad facts of a sinful life. But they must. It MUST BE FACED!

Dr. Biederwolf used to tell the story of a woman who killed her husband by driving a nail into his skull while he was sleeping under a heavy dose of sleeping pills. She pasted some wax over the nail and combed his hair so that it was not noticed. They buried the man in the community cemetery, and she buried the secret in her heart for many years to come.

But one day it became necessary to make some changes. Several graves had to be dug. When the nail was found dangling from this skull, the woman was faced with her crime. The men brought the skull to her home. When she opened the door and saw the evidence of her crime, she screamed, "My God, I'm found out at last!" And then she fainted and fell to the floor.

What will it be when millions go screaming into Hell from the judgment bar of God saying, "My God, I'm found out at last!" And it's too late! Too late to repent! Too late to get forgiveness! The day of grace is over. The door of God's mercy is shut. Never will another soul be saved. This is the day of God's wrath.

A famous evangelist had just preached his message and was on his way to his room when he suddenly noticed he was being followed by a man in soul trouble. He had a story to tell, and it could not wait.

This man said his wife died and left him with a child both blind and mentally sick. This child was a source of embarrassment and irritation to him. It was costing him a great deal of money to employ full-time help to care for the child. One day while he was at work, the Devil put into his mind a hellish plan to get her out of the way. He bought some candy and some poison and went home to do this ugly thing. His little girl ran and threw her arms around his neck, and he gave her the candy with the poison. In a moment she was on the floor writhing with agony. Soon she was dead.

This man in telling his story said, "Preacher, I'm going crazy. I can't stand it any longer! Every night when I go to bed I can see that blind child looking at me with sightless eyes through the dark."

Yes, God will bring the darkest and foulest secrets into judgment. How will it be with you?

So far in this message there is no hope for the unsaved, but only judgment and doom. "For all have sinned, and come short of the glory of God" (Rom. 3:23).

Because God is love and not willing that any should perish, He "so loved the world, that he gave his only begotten Son, that whosoever believeth in him should not perish, but have everlasting life" (John 3:16).

To those who know their sins, here now is the best news ever to fall on human ears! "Verily, verily, I say unto you, He that heareth my word, and believeth on him that sent me, hath everlasting life, and shall not come into condemnation [judgment]; but is PASSED FROM DEATH UNTO LIFE" (John 5:24). Glory be to God! If I believe on Jesus, I go straight to be with Him; and I do not stand at the judgment of the great white throne where the books are opened. When I trusted Jesus as my Saviour, He closed the books in my case.

Jesus wants to do this for you today. Just now He waits to blot out your old record completely and forever! No man can face his record and escape the lake of fire. Any man who will come to Jesus Christ and trust Him as personal Saviour can and will be saved the very moment he believes! Today is your day of opportunity.

You might say, "You make it too easy. Isn't there more for me to do to be saved?" I answer in Bible language, "Believe on the Lord Jesus Christ, and thou shalt be saved" (Acts 16:31). The reason there is no more for you to do is that Jesus did it all for you! Salvation is FREE to you, but it is not cheap. It cost God a terrible price. We are redeemed by the "precious blood of Christ."

Jesus died for our sins. He was our Substitute. He took all your sins upon Himself, and He was judged on your behalf. "Jesus paid it all; all to Him I owe."

"For by grace are ye saved through faith; and that not of yourselves:

it is the GIFT OF GOD: Not of works, lest any man should boast."—Eph. 2:8,9.

We will never be able to pay God for what He has done; but if you will just come to Him and trust Him now, it will please Him; and He will surely save you! He gives you His word that, if you hear His Word and believe on Him, you will never have to stand before Him on that awful DAY OF JUDGMENT.

Remember, Jesus said, "Him that cometh to me I will in no wise cast out" (John 6:37).

Let Jesus Blot Out All Your Sins Today

It is difficult to believe, but God says in Isaiah 43:25, "I, even I, am he that blotteth out thy transgressions for mine own sake, and will not remember thy sins." What a blessed and wonderful promise in light of the sermon you have just read by Evangelist Jim Mercer. Here God promises to blot out our transgressions for His own name's sake and will not remember our sins. I am trusting Jesus Christ as my personal Saviour. If I died and went to Heaven in the next five minutes and apologized to God for some sin I have committed, God would say, "I don't know what you are talking about." Oh, no, He is not absent-minded, but He has a divine forgetter "and will not remember thy sins."

What can you do to have your transgressions blotted out and have God forget your sins? The Bible is plain: "Believe on the Lord Jesus Christ, and thou shalt be saved" (Acts 16:31). The word *believe* means "to trust, to depend on, to rely on." The moment you trust Christ completely for salvation you are justified, cleared from all guilt, and stand before God as if you had never committed a single sin. But further still you stand before God as though you had always been righteous.

The choice is yours. Either you die without trusting Jesus Christ as Saviour or you admit that you are a sinner, believe that Jesus Christ died for you and trust Him completely for salvation. If you die without trusting Him, then someday you will stand at the great white throne judgment to answer for every sin, including idle words, deeds, thoughts and secrets. On the other hand, if you trust Jesus Christ as your Saviour, your sins are forgiven, blotted out and forgotten.

When you trust Christ as Saviour, God promises there will be no judgment for sin. Jesus said in John 5:24, "Verily, verily, I say unto you, He that heareth my word, and believeth on him that sent me, hath everlasting life, and shall not come into condemnation; but is passed from death unto life." The word *condemnation* in this verse means "judgment." Here our Lord plainly promises that the one who is trusting Him as Saviour will never come into judgment—that is, judgment for sin.

T. DEWITT TALMAGE
1832-1902

ABOUT THE MAN:

If Charles Spurgeon was the "Prince of Preachers," then T. DeWitt Talmage must be considered as one of the princes of the American pulpit. In fact, Spurgeon stated of Talmage's ministry: "His sermons take hold of my inmost soul. The Lord is with the mighty man. I am astonished when God blesses me but not surprised when He blesses him." He was probably the most spectacular pulpit orator of his time—and one of the most widely read.

Like Spurgeon, Talmage's ministry was multiplied not only from the pulpit to immense congregations, but in the printed pages of newspapers and in the making of many books. His sermons appeared in 3,000 newspapers and magazines a week, and he is said to have had 25 million readers.

And for 25 years, Talmage—a Presbyterian—filled the 4,000 to 5,000-seat auditorium of his Brooklyn church, as well as auditoriums across America and the British Isles. He counted converts to Christ in the thousands annually.

He was the founding editor of *Christian Herald,* and continued as editor of this widely circulated Protestant religious journal from 1877 until his death in 1902.

He had the face of a frontiersman and the voice of a golden bell; sonorous, dramatic, fluent, he was, first of all, an orator for God; few other evangelists had his speech. He poured forth torrents, deluges of words, flinging glory and singing phrases like a spendthrift; there was glow and warmth and color in every syllable. He played upon the heart-strings like an artist. One writer described him as the cultured Billy Sunday of his time. Many of his critics found fault with his methods; but they could not deny his mastery, nor could they successfully cloud his dynamic loyalty to his Saviour and Lord, Jesus Christ.

III.

Two Resurrections: Life or Damnation?

T. DE WITT TALMAGE

"Marvel not at this: for the hour is coming, in the which all that are in the graves shall hear his voice, And shall come forth; they that have done good, unto the resurrection of life; and they that have done evil, unto the resurrection of damnation."—John 5:28,29.

Philosophic speculation has gone through Heaven and told us there is no gold there; through Hell, and told us there is no fire there; through Christ, and told us there is no God there; and through the grave, and told us there is no resurrection, and has left hanging over all the future one great, thick London fog.

If I were to call on you to give the names of the world's great conquerors, you would say: Caesar, Alexander, Philip and the first Napoleon. You have missed the greatest! The men whose names have just been mentioned were not worthy of the name of Corporal when compared with him. He rode on the black horse that crossed the fields of Waterloo and Atlanta, and his bloody hoofs have been set on the crushed heart of the race. He has conquered every land and besieged every city, and today Paris, London, Moscow, New York and Brooklyn are going down under his fierce and long-continued assault.

That conqueror is DEATH. He carries a black flag and takes no prisoners. He digs a trench across the hemispheres and fills it with carcasses.

Herod of old slew only those of two years and under, but this monster strikes all ages. Genghis Khan sent five millions into the dust; but this, hundreds of thousands of millions. Other kings sometimes fall back and surrender territory once gained; but this king has kept all he ever won, save Christ, who escaped by omnipotent power.

What a cruel conqueror! What a bloody king! His palace is a huge sepulchre; his flowers the faded garlands that lie on coffin lids; his music the cry of desolate households; the chalice of his banquet a skull; his pleasure fountains the falling tears of a world.

But that throne shall come down; that sceptre shall break; that palace shall fall under bombardment.

"For the hour is coming, in the which all that are in the graves shall hear his voice, And shall come forth; they that have done good, unto the resurrection of life; and they that have done evil, unto the resurrection of damnation."—John 5:28,29.

Heathen philosophers guessed at the immortality of the soul, but never dreamed that the body would get up and join it. This idea is exclusively scriptural and beyond reasoning.

At the Sound of the Trumpet

Various scriptural accounts say that the work of grave breaking will begin with the blast of the trumpet. Then there will be heard the voice of the uncounted millions of the Christian dead who come rushing out of the gates of eternity, flying toward the tomb, crying, "Make way! O grave, give us back our body! We gave it you in corruption. Surrender it now in incorruption"—thousands of bodies arising from the field of Waterloo, from among the rocks of Gettysburg and from among the passes of South Mountain—from New York to Liverpool, at every few miles on the sea route, hundreds of spirits coming down to the water to meet their bodies. See that multitude!

What Will These Bodies Be?

But how will these bodies look? The bodies of the righteous, in the first place, will be *glorious*. The most perfectly formed body, indeed, is a mere skeleton to what it would have been had not sin come. God's model of a face, of a hand, of a foot, of a body, we know not. If, after an exquisite statue has been finished, you should take a chisel and clip it and chip it and set the statue in an out-of-door exposure, its beauty would nearly all be gone. The human body has been clipped and blasted and battered for thousands of years. Physical defects have been handed down from generation to generation for six thousand years, and we have inherited all the bodily infelicities of all the past.

When God, however, takes the righteous out of their graves, He will refashion, improve and adorn according to the original model until the difference between a gymnast and the emaciated wretch in the lazaretto will not be so great as that between our present bodily structures and our gloriously reconstructed forms. Then you will see the perfected eye, out of which, by waters of death, has been washed the last trace of tears and study. Then you will see the perfected hand—the knots on the knuckles of toil untied. No more stoop of the shoulders from burden-bearing and the weight of years, but all of us erect, elastic—the life of God in all the frame.

The most striking and impressive thing on earth now is a human face: Yet it is veiled in the black veil of a thousand griefs. But when God on the resurrection morn shall put aside the veil, I suppose that the face of the sun in the sky is dull and stupid compared with the outflaming glories of the countenances of the saved. I suppose that, when those faces shall turn to look toward the gate or up toward the throne, it will be like the dawn of a new morning on the bosom of everlasting day.

The body will be *immortal*. The physical system is now perpetually wasting away. Sickness and Death lurk around to see if they cannot get a pry under the tenement, and at a slight push we tumble off the embankment into the grave. But the righteous, arisen, shall have an immortal body. It will be incapable of disease. You will hear no cough or groan. There will be no miasma or fever in the air. There will be no rough steep down which to fall, no fracturing a limb.

People cross the sea for their health; but that voyage over the sea of death will cure the last Christian invalid. There grows an herb on that hill that will cure the last snake bite of earthly poison. There will be no hospital there, no dispensary, no medicines, no ambulances, no invalid chair, no crutches, no emaciation, no spectacles for poor sight, no stopping up of windows to keep out the cold blasts, but health immortal for the resurrected bodies of the righteous.

Again, the body will be *powerful*. Walking ten or fifteen miles now, we are weary. Eight hours of work make any man tired; but the resurrected body will be mighty. God always will have great projects to carry on and will want the righteous to help. Yea, in God's presence it is noonday all the time, and all Heaven is coming and going. They rest not day or night, in the lazy sense of resting. They have so many victories to celebrate! So many songs to sing! So many high days to keep! They need no sleep, for there is no call for physical renovation.

That kind of body I want. There is so much work to be done that I now begrudge the hours for sleep and necessary recreation. I sometimes have such views of the glorious work of preaching the Gospel that I wish I could tell men of Christ and Heaven, from the first day of January to the last day of December, without pausing for food or sleep or rest. Thanks be to God for the prospect of a resurrected body that will never weary and for a service of love that will never pause and never end!

Oh, glorious days of resurrection! Gladly will I fling into the grave this poor, sinful frame, if at Thy call I may rise up a body tireless and pure and glorious and immortal!

That was a blessed resurrection hymn sung at my father's burial:

> So Jesus slept: God's dying Son
> Passed through the grave, and blessed the bed.
> Rest here, blessed saint, till from His throne
> The morning break and pierce the shade.

Resurrection of Damnation

But my text speaks of *the resurrection of damnation*. The Bible says but little about it; yea, it is probable that, as the wicked are, in the last day, to be opposite in character, so will they be, in many respects, opposite in body.

Are the bodies of the righteous glorious? Those of the wicked will be repelling. You know how bad passions flatten the skull and disfigure the body. There he comes up out of the graveyard—the drunkard, the blotches on his body flaming out in worse disfigurement and his tongue bitten by an all-consuming thirst for drink—which he cannot get, for there are no cocktail lounges in Hell. There comes up the lascivious and unclean wretch, reeking with filth which made him the horror of the hospital, now wriggling across the cemetery lots—the consternation of the devils.

Here are all the faces of the unpardonable dead. The last line of attractiveness is dashed out, and the eye is wild, malignant, fierce, infernal; the cheek aflame; the mouth distorted with blasphemies. If the glance of the faces of the righteous is to be like a new morning, the glance of the faces of the lost will be like another night falling on midnight. If, after the close of a night's debauch, a man gets up and sits on the bed, sick, exhausted and horrified with the review of his past; or rouses up with delirium tremens and sees serpents crawling over him or devils dancing about him—what will be the feeling of a man who gets up out of his bed on the last morning of earth and reviews an unpardoned past? or, instead of imaginary evils crawling over him and flitting before him, finds the real frights and pains and woes of the resurrection of damnation?

Between the styles of rising, choose you. I set before you, in God's name, two resurrected bodies—the one radiant, glorious, Christlike; the other worn, blasted, infernal. I commend you to the Lord of the resurrection. Confiding in Him, Death will be to you only the black servant that opens the door, and the grave will be to you only the dressing room where you dress for glory.

It is accepting Christ as your personal Saviour that assures you of life eternal and the resurrection of life. Jesus said, "I am the resurrection, and the life: he that believeth in me, though he were dead, yet shall he live" (John 11:25). Believe then in Him—and live.

JOHN R. RICE
1895-1980

ABOUT THE MAN:

Preacher. . .evangelist. . .revivalist. . .editor. . .counsellor to thousands. . .friend to millions—that was Dr. John R. Rice, whose accomplishments were nothing short of miraculous. Known as "America's Dean of Evangelists," Dr. Rice made a mighty impact upon the nation's religious life for some sixty years, in great citywide campaigns and in Sword of the Lord Conferences.

At age nine, after hearing a sermon on "The Prodigal Son," John went forward to claim Christ as Saviour. In 1916, with only $9.35 in his pocket, he rode off on his cowpony toward Decatur Baptist College. He was now on the road to becoming a world-renowned evangelist, although he was then totally unaware of God's will for his life.

There was many a twist and turn before Rice rode through the open door into full-time preaching—the army, marriage, graduate work, more seminary, assistant pastor, pastor—then FINALLY, where God planned to use him most—in full-time evangelism.

Dr. Rice and his ministry were always colorful (born in Cooke County, in Texas, December 11, 1895, and often called "Will Rogers of the Pulpit" because of their likeness and mannerisms)—and controversial. CONTROVERSIAL—and correctly so—because of his intense stand against modernism and infidelity and his fight for the Fundamentals.

Dr. Rice lived and died a man of convictions—intense convictions. But, like many other strong fighters for the Faith, Rice was also marked with a sincere spirit of compassion. Those who knew him best knew a man who loved them. In preaching, in prayer, and in personal life, Rice wept over sinners and with saints. But there is more. . .

Less than seventy-one hours before the dawning of 1981, one of the most prolific pens in all Christendom was stilled. Dr. John R. Rice left behind a legacy in writing of more than 200 titles, with a combined circulation of over 61 million copies. And through October of 1981, a total of 24,058 precious souls reported trusting Christ through his ministries, not counting those saved in his crusades nor in foreign countries where his literature has been translated.

And who but God knows the influence of THE SWORD OF THE LORD magazine which he started and edited for forty-six years!

And while "Twentieth Century's Mightiest Pen"—and man—has been stilled, thank God the fruit remains! Though dead, he continues to speak.

IV.

Tears in Heaven

JOHN R. RICE

(Preached at Sword Conference, January 10, 1964)

Heaven—what a strange place for tears!

"And I saw a new heaven and a new earth: for the first heaven and the first earth were passed away; and there was no more sea. And I John saw the holy city, new Jerusalem, coming down from God out of heaven, prepared as a bride adorned for her husband. And I heard a great voice out of heaven saying, Behold, the tabernacle of God is with men, and he will dwell with them, and they shall be his people, and God himself shall be with them, and be their God. And God shall wipe away all tears from their eyes; and there shall be no more death, neither sorrow, nor crying, neither shall there be any more pain: for the former things are passed away."—Rev. 21:1-4.

Let us read verse 4 again:

"And God shall wipe away all tears from their eyes; and there shall be no more death, neither sorrow, nor crying, neither shall there be any more pain: for the former things are passed away."

This comes right after the story of the last judgment of the unsaved dead in chapter 20. The last verse of that chapter reads: "And whosoever was not found written in the book of life was cast into the lake of fire."

Here are people in Heaven who have just seen their loved ones go to Hell forever. God begins to wipe away their tears. God says that is the last of death, the last of crying; now He will wipe away our tears. Remember, this is after a thousand years in glorified bodies, after a thousand years of reigning with Christ on earth, and after we have gone to Heaven, that God will wipe away the tears.

You are mistaken if you think everyone in Heaven will have the same joy and happiness. We have the same salvation but not the same rewards. All in Hell are not going to have the same punishment and sorrow. The same condemnation—yes, but not the same punishment. In Hell people reap what they sow. And rewards will not be the same for those in Heaven.

Do you tobacco-chewing, cigarette-smoking, picture-show-going, lewd, drug-addicted, dirty-minded Christians who never had a family altar, never won a soul to Christ, think you will get to associate with D. L. Moody in Heaven, who won a million souls? Do you think you will be as happy as some godly soul who day and night prayed and served God and won souls? You have a sad awakening coming, if you think so. There will be tears in Heaven.

Dr. P. W. Philpott, once pastor of the famous Moody Church in Chicago and a dear man of God, said to me, "Brother John, a lot of Christians preach salvation by grace—only they preach a grace that is a disgrace, as if it doesn't matter if one sins." Now that you are saved, who cares that you live like the Devil? It doesn't matter.

It is still true that sin doesn't pay. A wasted life will not make you happy in Heaven. Let your loved ones go to Hell, and you are going to be sad about it. Up in Heaven there will be tears.

One time a mother said, "Brother Rice, I can't get my boy saved. I waited too late, waited until he was grown, until he drank and went on in sin. Now he won't listen to me. I can't get him to go to church. He is going to Hell. Brother Rice, how am I going to be happy in Heaven if my boy isn't there!"

Not knowing then the Bible answer, I did what a lot of other preachers do—I made up one! "Maybe in Heaven you won't know anything about those in Hell. You won't know about all the mistakes you made, all your failure in life."

That was not a Bible answer. I got to thinking about it: will I be more dumb in Heaven than I am now? more ignorant in Heaven than I am now?

That was not what I should have told her. If you have a chance to get somebody saved and don't do it and he goes to Hell because of your careless life and poor testimony, then you are going to rue it, weep over it up in Heaven.

Revelation 20 tells about the Christians' thousand-year reign with Christ on earth, then the last judgment of the unsaved dead and a new Heaven and a new earth. Then after all this, God begins wiping away our tears. Does that mean to wipe out the tears of the earth? No. After one has a resurrected body, the only tears he will have will be new tears in a new resurrected, glorified body. Wake in the likeness of Jesus and have a broken heart and tears? Yes.

But God will get out a big crying towel and wipe them all away. He will say, "Don't cry anymore. You have had a thousand years of heart-break over this sin." I'm glad God will say, "There will be no more death. You have seen loved ones go into the lake of fire, the second death; now, I will wipe away your tears. You can now say good-bye to sorrow."

I'm glad there is coming a time when God will wipe away tears. But remember: God has to wipe them away after a thousand years in the presence of Christ, after a thousand years and more in the resurrected body, after a thousand years in Heaven.

"That doesn't sound reasonable," you say. Then you need to be shown what the Bible says, and the Lord sent me here to do it!

I. TEARS IN HEAVEN OVER OUR SINS ON EARTH

Listen carefully. We are going to have tears in Heaven over our own sin on earth. Some of you flippantly say, "Well, when I served the Devil, I made him a good hand." You won't be bragging about it when you look Jesus Christ in the face. Don't think it won't matter then about sin. Notice this carefully here. There will be tears up in Heaven over sins on earth.

Tears of Shame

First, there will be tears of shame. Where does the Scripture say that? Look at I John 2:28, ". . . now, little children, abide in him; that, when he shall appear, we may have confidence, and not be ashamed before him at his coming."

Oh, God's children had better pause and think, for if you are to have confidence and run gladly to meet Him, then you had better abide in Him or be ashamed before Him at His coming.

Will all Christians be glad to see Jesus? No—not everyone. Many will be heartsick with fear and be sad to face Him.

So little time! The harvest will be over.
Our reaping done, we reapers taken Home.

Report our work to Jesus, Lord of harvest,
And hope He'll smile and that He'll say, "Well done!"

Many of us are going to be heartsick and ashamed before Him. He said, ". . . now, little children, abide in him; that, when he shall appear, we may have confidence, and not be ashamed before him at his coming."

I was reading again tonight in Mark, chapter 8, where Jesus said, "Whosoever will save his life shall lose it." Then He said, "Whosoever therefore shall be ashamed of me and of my words in this adulterous and sinful generation; of him also shall the Son of man be ashamed, when he cometh in the glory. . . ."

When you face Jesus Christ, all you who are ashamed of the Bible, Bible people and Bible ways, will find Jesus ashamed of you.

Why will some be ashamed when Jesus comes? Because you never stood up and talked for Him. Because you never defended the Bible. Because when you heard all that cussing, all those dirty yarns, that taking God's name in vain and running preachers down, you didn't open your mouth to protest. When Jesus comes, you will find He is ashamed of you.

Ashamed of Jesus and His work. ". . . now, little children, abide in him." Why? ". . . that, when he shall appear, we may have confidence, and not be ashamed before him at his coming." I'm not talking about whether you are saved or not, but about God's own children being heartsick and ashamed to face Jesus.

Lot Was Ashamed When His Sins Came Out

The Dead Sea now covers Sodom and Gomorrah. But suppose I could go back yonder and walk up to where children are playing. In front of the cave is an old man sitting on a log. Who is this—Lot? A couple of little boys are playing around. Yonder are two slatternly young women. A campfire is nearby.

"Well, sir, how do you do? Oh, you are Lot, the man with lots of rich cattle and sheep?"

"Yes, I am Lot, but no, my animals were destroyed when Sodom and Gomorrah burned."

"Well, Lot, your wife and your—"

"My wife turned to a pillar of salt. She was too sold on Sodom and didn't attend to her salvation."

"Well, what about your children?"

"All but two burned to death when the fire fell."

"Well, who are these?"

"My two youngest daughters."

"And who are these two little children here?"

Old Lot stammers in shame but says finally, "They are my two bastard children. I got drunk and ruined my own daughters."

Let me ask you: Does Lot stand up and brag that he is saved? Does a man, caught in his sin, think it doesn't matter? When he gets to Heaven, don't think Lot will not have a care over his sins on earth.

David Was Heartsick When His Sins Caught Up With Him

Let's go back to the palace in Jerusalem. Yonder is a man. Who is he? David, the sweet singer of Israel. Oh, I have heard of him.

"David, your psalms told me you were a man after God's own heart. David, you look unhappy."

"You would be unhappy, too, John, if this had happened to you."

"What, David?"

"I keep thinking about the baby. You know that I led Bathsheba into sin—everybody knows it. Her husband, one of my best soldiers, was my good friend. While he was in battle, I seduced his wife. When she told me she was going to have a baby, I wondered what I could do to cover my sin! Then I thought: *I will have her husband killed.* And I did."

"Then what, David?"

"Well, I thought it was over, that my sin was covered. But the baby got sick, and God said he was going to die. Nathan the prophet came and said my sin had caught up with me. He said, 'You have been forgiven; you are bound for Heaven, but the baby will die.' I fasted and prayed, but God wouldn't hear me, and my baby died. And that wasn't all."

"What else, David?"

"One of my sons—Amnon—had a cousin who was a bad influence on him. One day this cousin persuaded him to play like he was sick. He did so, and sent for his half-sister Tamar to cook for him. Then he shut the door and raped her. She tore her clothes, put dirt on her head and went and shut herself up in her brother Absalom's house."

"David, that is pretty bad."

David said, "But John, it wasn't over yet."

"What then?"

"One day Absalom had a big feast and said to his servants, 'My brother Amnon—I'll take care of him. You get things ready. Have your sharp knife ready. Somebody get a club. When they get him drunk I'll say, "Hit him, boys," and you get him.' A dozen knives were plunged into the breast of that whoremonger, my son who ruined his own sister. Another beat him over the head, while one ran and told me that the king's son had been killed, the one who ruined his own sister."

"Well, David, you sure have a lot to feel bad about."

"But," David said, "John, that isn't all."

"What else?"

"You know how heartbroken I am. My baby is dead. One of my girls has been ruined. Now my son is a murderer. Then Absalom goes out and steals the kingdom and the hearts of the people and raises them up against me. We had to run for our lives. Then at last it came to a battle. He was on his own mule, and the mule ran into an oak tree, and his hair caught in the branches, and Joab went and thrust him through with darts and killed him. They put him in a canyon and piled it high with rocks. I am heartbroken."

"David, I thought you were saved."

"Yes, John, but I have many gray hairs over my sin, and a broken heart."

You need not tell me one can sin and get by, that it won't matter. Ask David. Ask Lot. Ask any other man. Let me illustrate.

Children Who Do Wrong Are Ashamed
Before Dad and Mother

I was once in revival services on the north side of Chicago, at Lake View Free Church. Wheaton, my home town, was twenty-five miles from Chicago. One night I asked Mrs. Rice to go with me to this meeting.

She called in all our six daughters and said, "Now, girls, mother is going with daddy. I want you all to be good."

"All right, mother."

"And you big girls [Grace, Mary Lloys and Libby were called the big girls; the other three, Jessie, Joanna and Joy, were the little girls], listen. Wash the dishes. And when you finish looking at the funny-paper, pick everything up off the floor."

"All right, Mother."

"And I want Joy in bed at 8:30, Joanna and Jessie, by 9:00."

"All right, mother."

"And you big girls must be in bed by 9:30."

"Yes, mother."

We left. I preached, gave an invitation, and people were saved. Then some Swedish people invited us to their house for coffee and cake. It was late when we returned to Wheaton. About 11:00 o'clock we drove down Main Street, turned right on Franklin; and as we came in sight of that big old house at 512 Franklin Street, it was lit up like a hotel—a light in every window, and at 11:00 o'clock at night! Mrs. Rice said, "Oh, those children! Eleven o'clock and they are not even in bed!" She said, "You watch. When they hear the wheels on the gravel as we drive in the driveway, they will begin to turn out the lights and run upstairs to bed—the little brats!"

Sure enough! When we turned into the driveway, the light snapped off in the dining room, and a light off in the living room, then the light off in the stair hall and the pounding of shoes up the stairway! By the time we got upstairs a bunch of little girls were climbing into their pajamas.

Mrs. Rice said, "O my! Eleven o'clock, and you haven't even put the baby to bed! And you promised me! And you children—the paper is spread all over the floor of the living room!"

"O mother, we didn't know how late it was! Mother, I forgot. I'm sorry. I'm sorry. We won't do it anymore, mother."

Now they loved their mother, but they sure weren't glad to see her when they hadn't done right.

You too are going to be embarrassed.

Some of you old-timers and gray-heads had a mother who said, "You wait till your dad gets home, young man...!" Yes sir!

When Jesus comes, there are those who are going to be heartsick with shame.

Ashamed Before Pastor? Why Not Before Jesus?

Listen to our text again: "And now, little children, abide in him; that, when he shall appear, we may have confidence, and not be ashamed before him at his coming."

I knocked on the door at Shamrock, Texas, one winter day. People inside were smoking and gambling. I heard a scrambling. They were putting away their cards. Playing poker in the home of some of the church members! They would be terribly embarrassed for the preacher to catch them with cards.

Well, how will you feel facing Jesus Christ when you are caught up to meet Him? Embarrassed! Ashamed!

I came in front of Calvary Baptist Church in Wheaton, Illinois. A bunch of men were outside. One fellow put his hand behind him. He loved me and was so embarrassed for me to see him smoking.

You don't want the pastor to see you; but what about Jesus? Since you have been saved, how many have done things a Christian ought not do? Things you would be embarrassed about if a Christian would catch you doing it? Yes—many of you. Since you have been saved, how many have been places a Christian ought not go? Yes. How many of you, since you have been saved, have gone with some company you would be embarrassed for a good Christian to catch you with now? Yes.

You have said things, done things, been places, read books, looked at pictures, had dirty thoughts. You would be embarrassed for Jesus to suddenly catch you in that.

Well, He will. What if Jesus comes while some of you young people are out yonder in a parked car by the highway acting like lewd barnyard animals? Wouldn't you be embarrassed? Tears in Heaven over our sins on earth.

Tears of Terror

Terror in Heaven! That is the Bible word about this very matter. "Wherefore we labour [Paul says], that, whether present or absent, we may be accepted of him. For we must all appear before the judgment seat of Christ; that every one may receive the things done in his body, according to that he hath done, whether it be good or bad. Knowing therefore the terror of the Lord, we persuade men; but we are made manifest unto God; and I trust also are made manifest in your consciences" (II Cor. 5:9-11).

He said, "Whether I am here when Jesus comes or whether I have already gone to be with Him is not the point. Why do I work so hard? I have never had time to marry. I get put in jail almost everywhere I go. I work hard so that whether present when Jesus comes, or absent before that, I may be accepted."

"Why, Paul, aren't you already saved?"

"O Brother John, I didn't say that. I'm talking about whether Jesus is pleased with me and smiles and says, 'Well done.' For we must all appear before the judgment seat of Christ."

Christians, too? Yes! Nobody but Christians will be at this judgment seat. "That every one may receive the things done in his body, according to that he hath done, whether it be good or bad."

The apostle is talking by divine inspiration. What is Paul concerned about? "I'm working hard so Jesus will be pleased with me. I've got to face Him and receive the things done in the body, whether good or bad."

Now listen to the next verse: "Knowing therefore the terror of the Lord, we persuade men."

When I was a young preacher I didn't try to expound the Bible. I just took a text and made up a sermon. One time I preached to the unsaved on "The Terror of the Lord."

There is plenty in the Bible about the terror of the Lord for lost people, but this is the terror of the Lord at the judgment seat of Christ for **Christians**!

You say, "I will not be terrified of Jesus." Oh, you won't? Suppose you drive out Franklin Road tonight. You are in a hurry to get home. It is pretty late. You drive pretty fast. Suppose there is a patrol car out that way. The governor said we must tighten up. The police have orders from headquarters to give a ticket to everyone who goes five miles an hour over the limit. In fact, if the limit is sixty-five and they catch you going sixty-six, they have to write you up.

There is the flashing light and the siren. "Pull over there. Can't you read?" You stammer a bit and say, "Well-uh-uh-officer, uh- I uh-uh. . . ." Why are you so nervous? Nervous over the highway patrolman.

And you think you won't mind meeting Jesus when you have broken His rules!

"Knowing therefore the terror of the Lord, we persuade men." The Lord means that many a Christian, with knees knocking, with teeth chattering, with pale face, will look in the face of Jesus and be heartsick, ashamed and terrified over your sins.

A preacher called me in Dallas, Texas and said, "Brother Rice, pray for me."

"What is it, Alfred?"

"My sins are catching up with me."

He wasn't going to Hell. He was saved, but his sins were catching up with him. He was crying over the phone, begging me to pray for him.

Wait till you come to face Jesus Christ with a wasted life and see how you feel then. Wait till God looks at your fig tree and finds nothing but leaves and pronounces a curse on it. What then? Tears of terror in Heaven.

Tears of Loss

Wait! Tears in Heaven? Yes, tears of loss over our sins on earth. "Loss?" you say. "Why, I thought Heaven would all be gain." It will be all gain to some people, but there will be a lot of loss mixed in it for others. First Corinthians, chapter 3, tells about the tears of loss. Beginning with verse 10, Paul says,

"According to the grace of God which is given unto me, as a wise masterbuilder, I have laid the foundation, and another buildeth thereon. But let every man take heed how he buildeth thereupon. For other foundation can no man lay than that is laid, which is Jesus Christ."

Ask somebody, "Who is the foundation of the church?" and you may get the answer, "Peter." No, it is Jesus Christ. You say, "This church?" No, not your church. Some say it is the Baptist foundation. No, it is the Jesus foundation. No other foundation.

"Now if any man build upon this foundation [after you get Jesus, after you are saved] *gold, silver, precious stones, wood, hay, stubble* [three kinds that will burn]; *Every man's work shall be made manifest: for the day shall declare it, because it shall be revealed by fire; and the fire shall try every man's work of what sort it is."*—Vss. 12,13.

What is that up in Heaven? A bonfire. What for? To burn up wasted works. To burn up worthless living. To burn up all things that are of no account. Burn up all the things you did after you were saved that didn't amount to anything. Burn up the wood, hay and stubble. "Every man's work shall be made manifest." Now verse 14:

"If any man's work abide which he hath built thereupon, he shall receive a reward."

Not salvation. Everyone who is saved already has salvation. Everybody here already has the one foundation—Jesus Christ. We are not talking about burning up the foundation but about burning up the house built after you got the foundation.

Now verse 15:

"If any man's work shall be burned, he shall suffer loss: but he himself shall be saved; yet so as by fire."

Saved? Yes. Then what is the judgment for? To burn up the bad works. "If any man's work shall be burned, he shall suffer loss." Suffer loss! Two terrifying words up in Heaven—suffering and loss. Golden streets, gates of pearl, seeing Jesus' glorified body—and loss up in Heaven? It says, ". . . suffer loss"! Oh, lost opportunity! Lost opportunity!

We Will Still Know in Heaven of Those We Should Have Won

In Dallas, Texas, an old man heard me on the radio and wrote: "I am eighty years old. I have cancer and can't live long. Brother Rice, I'm not ready to die. Will you come and tell me how to be saved and pray with me?"

I put that card up, planning to see that man the next day. But I didn't. Nor the next day. That request sat up there and mocked me. After working hard and preaching daily, and with radio and mail—two weeks went by. I called Neil Pohorlok and said, "Neil, go to this sick man's house, talk and pray with him and make sure he is saved; then report to me the results of your visit."

I gave him carfare. (This was in the days of the streetcar.) He got on the car, went downtown, changed over to the south side, came to a certain street, got off and walked down to a certain number, went up to the door and knocked. Nobody answered. He knocked again; still nobody answered. He went around to the side door and knocked. A woman next door raised the window. "Are you looking for Mr. and Mrs. So-and-So? They are not there. The old man who lived with them died yesterday, and the loved ones have gone out in the country fifteen miles to the funeral. They will be back tomorrow. Anything you want me to tell them?"

"No. No, nothing to tell them. Thank you."

Neil came home and said, "Brother Rice, we went too late! The man died yesterday and is being buried today."

That is one loss I can't ever get back. Oh, I'm saved. I'm going to Heaven. But if that man doesn't get there, I'm going to be very sad about it. I hope he got saved. I hope he settled it. I hope somebody told him the way. But what if that man doesn't get to Heaven! There is no undoing that, is there?

If You Get Out of the Fire Alive but Your Family Perishes, Would You Feel Like Celebrating?

Suppose the radio and TV announced a cold wave. A certain high center up in Missouri is coming this way, and the cold air is coming down from Canada. Boy, she will be down to five above zero by morning! Good night! We had better get a good fire going! My dad used to say out in West Texas, "Son, see that bank over yonder in the North? We are going to have a blue northerner. It will freeze the horns off a billy goat before morning. So get in plenty of wood."

Suppose someone says, "We will have to have lots of fire to keep this house warm so the water won't freeze. We have to keep the fire going here." Suppose you turn the gas stove on. In the middle of the night the flames flare up and catch the window curtain. There is a bit of plastic nearby which suddenly flames up. You wake and hear something crackling. You smell smoke. Half asleep you get up from your second-floor bedroom and open the hall door. "What's happened! The house is full of smoke! Shut the door!" Well, my goodness! The house is already burning!

About that time you hear a fire siren. A ladder comes against the wall. Somebody crashes the window with a fireaxe—"Anybody in here? Get out! The roof is about to cave in! Hurry! Get out!"

You rush out; it is nearing zero. Somebody wraps a coat around you. You have one house shoe on and your pajamas. But you say, "Wait a minute! My wife and children are up there!" But you cannot get back in. Two or three hoses are streaming water on that fire; there is a crash, and the sparks fly everywhere as the roof caves in. You scream. "But my family!"

Suppose I see you the next day and say, "Say, I heard you had a fire at your house."

"Yes."

"Did you lose anything?"

"Good night! Lose anything? I lost everything!"

"Do you mean you didn't get your furniture out?"

"No!"

"Well, that's too bad. I guess all your family got out!"

"Uh-no!"

"Well, what about your wife?"

"Brother Rice, I wanted to go back for her, but I couldn't get back, and she. . . ."

"What about the children?"

"They were trapped inside, too."

Suppose I say, "I'm so glad you got out alive, brother. Let's go and celebrate. I'll buy you the best steak in town."

You answer, "I'm not hungry. I'm thinking only of my family. All gone! No one left! Please don't bother me about food."

You wouldn't be anxious for a big dinner, would you, if your wife's coffin couldn't be opened, and the charred bones of the boy were found when the fire was put out?

How Could You Be as Happy in Heaven With Your Wife in Hell?

Suppose one day when I meet you in Heaven I say, "Hello, there! You don't have your wheelchair here?"

"Bless God! No!"

"Brother, I'm glad to see you."

Suppose you say, "Well, Brother Rice, since you made so many people mad on earth, I didn't know whether you would make it to Heaven or not! I'm glad to see you, too."

Suppose I say, "Well, where is the Mrs.?"

You say, "Brother Rice, I don't know why our pastor didn't preach any plainer. My wife went to church out there. I don't know why people didn't pay her any mind, didn't talk to her about her soul. It looks like somebody would. . . ."

"What do you mean? That she was not saved?"

"Brother Rice, she isn't here!"

"Oh, that's too bad. What about your boy?"

"Brother Rice, look. He went to Sunday school. Why didn't the Sunday school teach him?"

"You mean. . . ."

"Brother Rice, he is not here!"

Well, suppose we are in Heaven, and I say, "Let's leap for joy and click our heels together, 'Glory to God! We got here!' Come on, brother, jump, holler and praise the Lord!"

You say, "With my wife and boy burning down in Hell! With my folks all gone! And you want me to jump and praise God!"

"Well, you got to Heaven, didn't you?"

"Yes, but my folks are not here."

Do you think it won't matter if your folks went to Hell? It sure will. Yes, it will. You are going to have a sad awakening one of these days up in Heaven. Tears of loss. Lost loved ones you can't do anything about, gone to Hell.

You say, "But I thought the Lord forgave sin." Yes, but there is still a law of sowing and reaping. There are still some things that won't be changed.

Saved, Forgiven, but Still With Only One Eye

Years ago there was a wicked old drinking sinner, a dirty, mean old cuss living in Evansville, Indiana. In fact, everybody called him Old Bill. I don't even know what his other name was. He wanted to be sure to get breakfast at the Evansville Rescue Mission, and he had to go to church to do it, stay all night to get his coffee, oatmeal and roll in the morning. That night he was wondrously changed.

After that he would say, "Listen! It's not Old Bill anymore. I'm New Bill. I'm under new management." So people began calling him New Bill. They would dress New Bill up and send him out to talk for the rescue mission.

Here is an interesting thing. Before, Old Bill was a drunken old sinner. He painted mailboxes for five cents apiece to get some beer. One day he and a buddy got hold of a fifth of whiskey and got in a fight, and his buddy knocked his eye out.

Now Old Bill had just one eye. But he got saved; now he is New Bill. How many eyes do you suppose he has now? Just one! Well, he is saved, isn't he? His sins are all forgiven, aren't they? He has a new heart, hasn't he? *But he still has just one eye.*

I'm just showing you that, if you let your loved ones go to Hell, they are still going to be in Hell even though you are forgiven. The Lord said to David, "Your sins are forgiven. I'm not going to let you die over this sin, but the baby will die." David was forgiven, but his baby still died, his daughter still got raped, his son still got killed, Absalom still started a rebellion.

Up in Heaven we will have tears of sorrow, tears of pain, tears of loss, tears of terror over our neglect on earth.

II. TEARS IN HEAVEN OVER LOVED ONES ON EARTH

Wait a minute! Up in Heaven we are going to have tears over our loved ones here on earth. Will we know about people down here? Oh, yes! Of that I am sure. My mother on her deathbed said, "I can see Jesus and my baby now!" I think there is a very close tie between both worlds, though we don't see it until at a time like that. Yes, they know. First Corinthians 13, verse 12, says, "For now we see through a glass, darkly; but then face to face: now I know in part; but then shall I know even as also I am known."

1. We Will Know Loved Ones in Heaven

If you get to Heaven first, you need not bother about introducing me to the Apostle Paul. I'll know him as soon as I see him. I want to shake his hand and say, "Paul, God bless you! I'm so glad to see you!" Paul will say, "John, I've been watching you for a long time. I'm glad you got here." You needn't try to introduce us then because we are going to know better than we know now.

Up in Heaven they know now what is going on. Why, the angels of God are going and coming all the time. Up in Heaven we will know what our Christian friends and loved ones are doing.

Look at Hebrews, chapter 12, verses 1 and 2: "Wherefore seeing we also are compassed about with so great a cloud [compassed, surrounded, so great a cloud, they are up here; I am up here] of witnesses." What witnesses? All those he has been naming in the 11th chapter—all those saints gone on to Heaven. ". . .we also are compassed about with so great a cloud of witnesses. . . ." He said the grandstand in Heaven is full. Boy, the Colosseum is there for the Olympic races. Now everybody. . .on your mark. . .get set. Listen, lay aside every weight and get your eyes set yonder on Jesus, the Judge at the end of the race. Paul said,

"Seeing we are compassed about with so great a cloud of witnesses, let us lay aside every weight, and the sin which doth so easily beset us, and let us run with patience the race that is set before us, Looking unto Jesus the author and finisher of our faith; who for the joy that was set before him endured the cross, despising the shame, and is set down at the right hand of the throne of God."

The Lord is saying that up in Heaven they are watching us run our race.

2. Up in Heaven They Watch Us With Great Concern

I have preached to small crowds. I have preached to people who didn't care. I have preached when nobody was saved. And I sometimes have thought, *What is the use? Nobody much is listening.*

One time when Dr. Billy McCarroll asked me to preach in the great Cicero Bible Church in Cicero, Illinois, this thing got on my heart: *Everybody in Heaven is looking on.*

You think my mother in Heaven doesn't care? She gave me to God when I was born and asked Him to make me a preacher. When John the Baptist was born, they said, "Let's name this baby after his dad and call him Zacharias"; but Zacharias called for a tablet and wrote, "His name is John." And my father heavily underlined in an old, old Bible that verse; and I know in my heart that my father decided to name me John and prayed that God would make me a preacher like John the Baptist, and he put it down in that old Bible long ago.

Oh, do you think my parents wouldn't care if I quit preaching, if I got busy making money and having fun and went into sin and let the world go to Hell? Oh, seeing you also are compassed about with so great a cloud of witnesses, run your race.

I played football. One time we played at Henrietta, Texas. We didn't have much coaching nor much reserve strength. The other team was fast and hard. I remember how out on the sidelines the students were lined up yelling, "Hold that line! Hold that line! Hold that line!" We held it. First down—they didn't make it. Second down—they made about a yard. Third down—two or three more yards. Fourth down—no gain; they must punt. Now the chant out on the sidelines again was, "Block that kick! Block that kick! Block that kick! Block that kick!" As right tackle I broke through the line, knocked the halfback down, blocked the kick and made six yards further. What a roar went up out from the crowd!

Let me tell you—on the sidelines this game in which we are now engaged is more important than any football game. All around in the great amphitheater of Heaven loved ones are looking on. What is Heaven interested in? In getting people saved.

When Jesus met Moses and Elijah up on the Mount of Transfiguration, what did they talk about? The death which He should accomplish at Jerusalem. He said, 'Boys, I am going to die and pay this debt to keep people out of Hell!' Up in Heaven their concern is for poor sinners down here. So "we also are compassed about with so great a cloud of witnesses."

All of my six girls were given to God. Grace, my oldest, played the piano for the great citywide campaign in Lewistown, Pennsylvania. There she met Allan MacMullen, and they fell in love. Allan worked in a bank. He came to talk to me. I said, "Allan, I didn't raise Grace to be a banker's wife. You and she will have to decide this matter; but if I were you, I would go to Bob Jones University, get in the preachers' classes and consider getting in the Lord's work." He did. It wasn't long till he wrote his mother, "I have got to be a preacher."

What would I think up in Heaven if my girls didn't live for God; if they thought, *Well, Daddy is an old fuddy-duddy*; if they thought, *This raising children and making them mind, keeping them separated*—what if my girls turned against all my teaching? I would be grieved if I knew about it up in Heaven.

Some time ago when living in Wheaton, Illinois, I was down in the basement. What did I see? Wedding invitations. One daughter was engaged to marry a young fellow. They were in the university together. He had plenty of money. He was going to be a preacher. They bought the rings, set the date, the wedding invitations were printed and ready to mail out. But the young fellow one day said, "I'll be glad when we are married. Then you can cut that long hair and look like other women."

Grace didn't want to look like the world. She pulled off the ring, told him good-bye, and those wedding invitations were never sent. Then God later sent along a man—the banker—who didn't mind if she looked like a Christian.

I say, what would I think up in Heaven if my girls turned away from the Lord after all the tears, all my pain, trouble and prayers?

You say mother love? Yes! Maybe a father's love doesn't show as much, but I don't think it anywhere is excelled by a mother's love.

How many of you had a good old mother, the kind of mother who, if you said a bad word, washed your mouth out with lye soap? How many of you had a dad who kept the razor strop handy? How many of you had a dad and mother who used to go to church every time the door was open? We did—prayer meeting, Sunday school, Sunday morning, Sunday night, even B.Y.P.U. We got in the wagon and everybody went. We went when it rained, when it snowed, when it was cold or hot, in harvest, in threshingtime.

What about a mother and dad like that up in Heaven—and you living carelessly and worldly? We say, "If your dad knew that, he would turn over in his grave!" He does know it, and weeps about it. "Compassed about with so great a cloud of witnesses"!

Oh, people weep in Heaven over our failures and sins! I think sometimes old Billy Sunday says up in Heaven, "Lord, don't You have any preachers down there who mean business? If I were down there, Lord, I'd give the old Devil a run for his money. All these preachers—what's the matter, Lord? Why doesn't somebody cry out against sin?" Don't you think D. L. Moody and Billy Sunday up in Heaven wish somebody would start some revivals? Up in Heaven they weep because nobody much cares.

3. In Heaven They Weep Over Unsaved Loved Ones

Up in Heaven loved ones weep over lost sinners. How do I know? Jesus said,

"What man of you, having an hundred sheep, if he lose one of them, doth not leave the ninety and nine in the wilderness, and go after that which is lost, until he find it? And when he hath found it, he layeth it on his shoulders, rejoicing. And when he cometh home, he calleth together his friends and neighbours, saying unto them, Rejoice with me; for I have found my sheep which was lost."—Luke 15:4-6.

A lost sheep pictures a lost sinner. And when the Shepherd, Jesus, searches and finds the lost sheep, He puts him on His shoulders and brings him home and invites His friends and neighbors to "rejoice with me; for I have found my sheep."

When Jesus brings the lost sheep back to Heaven, who are the friends and neighbors? Dads and mothers and kinfolks, Peter and Paul and John and all the rest. The next verse says,

"I say unto you, that likewise joy shall be in heaven over one sinner that repenteth, more than over ninety and nine just persons, which need no repentance."

And verse 10:

"Likewise, I say unto you, there is joy in the presence of the angels of God over one sinner that repenteth."

He is not talking about here on earth but up in Heaven. Up in Heaven they are rejoicing. So when a sinner is saved on earth, they know it in

Heaven! When the sinner is not saved on earth, do they know it in Heaven? Well, if they are glad when a sinner is saved, are they not sad when a sinner is lost and won't get saved?

Let me ask you this: Does the Lord Jesus feel bad when sinners just won't come? Suppose I preach my heart out, pray, cry, beg, argue and plead; but I can't get you saved. I feel bad. But how do you think Jesus feels? Well, if you were up there with Jesus and Jesus felt bad, wouldn't you feel bad, too?

Tears up in Heaven over lost sinners. Some of you are not saved. You have a mother or dad in Heaven.

How many would have to say, "If Jesus came right now, I'd be sorry. I never did get done some things I intended to do. Some things I intended to make right, I didn't. If Jesus came right suddenly and unexpectedly, I would weep over some failures and sins"?

If you are going to weep over sinners, you had better do it now.

> **Time now for warning, time now for pleading.**
> **Time now to weep, to cling to the cross.**

One day it will be too late. When you don't now take time to get souls saved, it will be too late after you get to Heaven.

Up in Heaven they weep over sinners down here; and how glad they are when somebody is saved!

> **Over the river, faces I see,**
> **Fair as the morning, looking for me;**
> **Free from their sorrow, grief and despair,**
> **Waiting and watching patiently there.**
> **Looking this way, yes, looking this way;**
> **Loved ones are waiting, looking this way;**
> **Fair as the morning, bright as the day,**
> **Dear ones in glory, looking this way.**

Up in Heaven people weep over sinners. Jesus wept when He looked on Jerusalem; I think He still weeps over Jerusalem, and over Murfreesboro.

> **Father and mother, safe in the vale,**
> **Watch for the boatman, wait for the sail,**
> **Bearing the loved ones over the tide,**
> **Into the harbor, near to their side.**
> **Looking this way, yes, looking this way;**
> **Loved ones are waiting, looking this way;**
> **Fair as the morning, bright as the day,**
> **Dear ones in glory, looking this way.**

V.

When Skeletons Come Out of Their Closets;

**When Chickens Come Home to Roost; When God's Record Books
Are Opened and Sinners Receive Their Wages; When the
Doomed and Damned Are Dragged Out of Hell to Face
Christ on the Throne; When Every Knee Shall Bow
and Every Tongue Shall Confess to God at THE
LAST JUDGMENT OF THE UNSAVED DEAD!**

JOHN R. RICE

*"And I saw the dead, small and great, stand before God; and the
books were opened: and another book was opened, which is the book
of life: and the dead were judged out of those things which were written in the books, according to their works."*—Rev. 20:12.

Men say that some things are "as certain as death." The coming of
every condemned sinner to stand in judgment before God is one of
those things. The Scripture links them together. "It is appointed unto
men once to die, but after this the judgment" (Heb. 9:27).

Man cannot get by with sin. "Be sure your sin will find you out" (Num.
32:23). With all the reaping of sorrow that sin causes, be sure that sin's
penalty has not yet been paid nor probed to the depth of its wickedness,
that the bitter, tragic, eternal, hellish fruitage of sin has not been brought
to light in this life.

Men must stand before God and be judged for their sin. Unsaved
men, condemned men, doomed men, men who will have already tasted
the torments of the damned in Hell—these all must stand before God
in judgment.

Then, out of the closet of the dead past will come the grinning, horrible
skeletons of past sins, to face and condemn every sinner. In the language

of an old proverb, skeletons must all come out of their closets; and chickens must come home to roost.

Warning after warning has fallen from the mouth of God to sinners about judgment and the result of sin. We are warned, "Be not deceived; God is not mocked: for whatsoever a man soweth, that shall he also reap" (Gal. 6:7)! We well know that man does not do all his reaping in this life. God has yet a trump card to play. He will yet call the unsaved, the unrepentant, the unregenerate to judgment, to reap what they sowed, to receive their just and public sentence and to depart to a lake of fire and a Christless, hopeless, peaceless eternity.

"The wages of sin is death," declares Romans 6:23. Does anyone doubt it? Yea, but the wages are worse than you know, the death more terrible than you dreamed—a living death, a death of condemnation and torment, a soul forsaken by the Spirit of God, his body condemned to a lake of fire! The last judgment of the unsaved dead will simply be payday for sinners.

Revelation 20 very carefully and in detail describes the last judgment of the unsaved dead. What I shall say in this message will not be imagination nor man's opinion, but all will be based on the plain Word of God. Therefore, in fear of God and for the sake of your immortal soul, I beg you, reader—you who have a soul that must spend eternity somewhere, you who are certain for Hell or Heaven, you who must give an account to God—I beg you to read most carefully and prayerfully what the Bible says about the last judgment of the unsaved dead.

The first chapter of Revelation is introduction; chapters 2 and 3 are the messages to the seven churches; then chapter 4 begins by symbolizing the rapture of the saints, a door opened in Heaven, a voice like a trumpet saying, "Come up hither," and the saints caught up to meet the Lord in the air, as John was in the Spirit caught up when he saw the "things which must be hereafter."

After picturing the rise of the Man of Sin, the plagues of the Great Tribulation and the worldwide ruin wrought under the rule of this "beast" or Antichrist, the climax comes in chapter 19 when Christ is pictured returning to earth with saints and angels, crowned with many crowns, King of kings and Lord of lords.

Then comes the mighty battle of Armageddon, when the armies of the beast, 200 million men (Rev. 9:16), are slaughtered, and only two, the Antichrist or beast himself and his false prophet, are not killed but are cast alive in their physical bodies into the lake of fire.

Now we come to chapter 20 of Revelation wherein is pictured the last judgment of the unsaved dead. Listen prayerfully, since we will refer to it repeatedly.

"And I saw an angel come down from heaven, having the key of the bottomless pit and a great chain in his hand.

"And he laid hold on the dragon, that old serpent, which is the Devil, and Satan, and bound him a thousand years,

"And cast him into the bottomless pit, and shut him up, and set a seal upon him, that he should deceive the nations no more, till the thousand years should be fulfilled: and after that he must be loosed a little season.

"And I saw thrones, and they sat upon them, and judgment was given unto them: and I saw the souls of them that were beheaded for the witness of Jesus, and for the word of God, and which had not worshipped the beast, neither his image, neither had received his mark upon their foreheads, or in their hands; and they lived and reigned with Christ a thousand years.

"But the rest of the dead lived not again until the thousand years were finished. This is the first resurrection.

"Blessed and holy is he that hath part in the first resurrection: on such the second death hath no power, but they shall be priests of God and of Christ, and shall reign with him a thousand years."

(Verses 7 to 10 tell us that, when the thousand years are expired, Satan will be loosed a little season and will cause a great rebellion, then will be cast forever into the lake of fire.)

"And I saw a great white throne, and him that sat on it, from whose face the earth and the heaven fled away; and there was found no place for them.

"And I saw the dead, small and great, stand before God; and the books were opened: and another book was opened, which is the book of life: and the dead were judged out of those things which were written in the books, according to their works.

"And the sea gave up the dead which were in it; and death and hell delivered up the dead which were in them: and they were judged every man according to their works.

"And death and hell were cast into the lake of fire. This is the second death.

"And whosoever was not found written in the book of life was cast into the lake of fire."

I believe we can understand the last judgment of the unsaved dead, pictured in Revelation, chapter 20, especially in verses 11 to 15, if we study this passage with three questions in mind. First, of the several judgments mentioned in the Bible, which is this? Second, who will be judged there? Third, how will they be judged? Remember, three words sum up the lessons we bring from God's Word about this last great judgment of the unsaved dead: *Which? Who? How?*

I. WHICH OF SEVERAL BIBLE JUDGMENTS IS THIS?

Here at the beginning of the thousand years' reign there are thrones on the earth and people reigning. Christ, of course, will reign on David's throne at Jerusalem; the apostles will sit on twelve thrones, judging the twelve tribes of Israel; and other saints of God will reign in various capacities. The saints pictured in Heaven in Revelation 5:10 praise Christ saying, "And hast made us unto our God kings and priests: and we shall reign on the earth."

With the saints of the present age, others will also reign—those converted during the Great Tribulation, after the rapture of the saints. Some who will be beheaded by the Antichrist because of their witness for Jesus and because they will not take the mark of the beast, will die; and when Jesus returns to reign, these will be resurrected and will reign "with Christ a thousand years."

Verse 5 is very important: "The rest of the dead lived not again until the thousand years were finished. This is the first resurrection." This proves there are two resurrections. The saved who will have been taken away at the rapture, caught up in the clouds to meet Christ, and who return with Christ from Heaven to reign on the earth, plus those who are converted during the Tribulation period, are all in "THE FIRST RESURRECTION." The rest of the dead, that is, the unsaved people, will be in THE SECOND RESURRECTION; but that will be a thousand years later. This distinction is clearly made here.

Saved people will be in the first resurrection; lost people in the second resurrection. The first resurrection comes before the thousand years' reign of Christ on earth, or at its beginning; the second resurrection of the unsaved dead takes place at the close of the thousand years' reign on earth. Verse 6 plainly says that it is a blessed thing to have part in the first resurrection, since none of these will go to the second death.

You may have heard talk about a "general resurrection," but the Bible never uses that term. There is no "general resurrection." There are two entirely separate resurrections, one thousand years apart in time. The first resurrection is of saved people; the second of lost people. All those in the first resurrection are saved; all those in the second resurrection are judged according to their sins and sent forever into the lake of fire.

You will notice that this is not the *only* judgment, but this is the *last* judgment. There are several judgments discussed in the Bible.

A. Judgment of Christians, Already in Resurrected, Glorified Bodies, Already in Heaven

When Christians are caught up to meet Christ in the air, then we must all stand before the judgment seat of Christ, and saved people will be rewarded according to their works. Salvation is free. Then after God gives us salvation, He, in addition, rewards us according to our works. In that judgment in Heaven none but Christians will take part.

B. The Later Judgment of Those Alive of All Nations

When Christ returns to earth and sits on the throne of His glory, all nations shall be gathered before Him, and He will separate them as a shepherd divides the sheep from the goats, described in Matthew 25:31-46. In explaining the parable of the tares (Matt. 13), Jesus mentions the same judgment. Remember that judgment is at the beginning of the thousand years' reign, a judgment of the living on earth. In that judgment will be the Gentile "sheep" (Christians), Gentile "goats" (lost people) and the "brethren" (the Jews). It will be a judgment of the people left alive on earth after the battle of Armageddon. The judgment of Matthew, chapter 25, is at the beginning of the thousand years' reign.

C. The Last Judgment of the Unsaved Dead, Who Will Be Brought Out of Hell to Receive Their Final Sentences and in Living, Resurrected Bodies Be Cast Soul and Body Into the Lake of Fire

This is the judgment to which I call your attention today. This great white throne judgment we have just read about in Revelation 20:11-15 is at the close of the thousand years' reign. They are not the same. The judgment of the living nations on earth will take place with Jesus sitting

Revelation, the last judgment of the unsaved dead, will take place away out in space, with Christ sitting upon a great white throne and with earth and heaven fled away from His face. Matthew, chapter 25, speaks of Christ judging the living; but Revelation, chapter 20, tells of the later judgment of the dead.

In the study of this judgment which we have read in Revelation, chapter 20, verses 11 to 15, the past tense is used because there John is telling us of a vision which he has already seen. But the vision is a revelation of the future. This is God's warning of the judgment yet to come when lost sinners will be dragged out of Hell to face Jesus Christ, when God's record books will be opened and when sinners will receive their wages. Sinners already condemned, already in Hell, will be called out, not to see whether they are lost, but to publicly confess their sins and have sentence passed upon them before the assembled beings of all the universe of God! This is the last judgment of the unsaved dead.

II. WHO WILL BE JUDGED HERE?

A. Not a Single Christian; Only the Unsaved

Some people believe that every soul, saved and lost—those who have trusted Christ for salvation as well as sinners—will be judged according to their works at the judgment here described. That is not true. Praise the Lord, a born-again child of God will not come to be judged and be in jeopardy of his soul!

Those who believe that men must save themselves by good works naturally believe that Heaven is attained by righteous deeds and that Hell is the penalty for those who do not live right. But the Bible never teaches any kind of salvation by works. Rather we are told, "For by grace are ye saved through faith; and that not of yourselves: it is the gift of God: Not of works, lest any man should boast" (Eph. 2:8,9).

Do you know why a Christian can never come to this judgment and be in danger of eternal damnation? The answer is this: Jesus Christ has been judged already for the sins of God's children. All who trust in Him are forgiven, and their sins are blotted out. God is a just God who must demand that sin be paid for. But since God is a just God, He cannot demand that sin be paid for twice.

If I accept the price that Jesus paid for my sins, then I shall not come into condemnation. John 5:24 says, "Verily, verily, I say unto you, He that heareth my word, and believeth on him that sent me, hath everlasting life, and shall not come into condemnation; but is passed from death unto life."

The Revised Version of the Bible makes this even clearer: "Verily, verily, I say unto you, He that heareth my word, and believeth him that sent me, hath eternal life, and cometh not into judgment, but hath passed out of death into life."

"Cometh not into judgment"! One who has trusted in Jesus Christ will never come to judgment to suffer the loss of his soul. Praise the Lord for that sweet promise!

If I should come to be judged for my deeds, I would go to Hell; for I am a sinner, and the Bible says that "the soul that sinneth, it shall die." It says that "the wages of sin is death." So I deserve death. It is only by the mercy of God that Jesus has taken my place, has been judged for my sin, and I am now forgiven. I am not condemned; I shall not come into condemnation nor into judgment.

We, then, will not be judged at the judgment of the unsaved dead.

Remember that these are the dead. For a thousand years their ashes have been trodden under foot during the reign of Christ on earth. All these in this judgment are lost people. Not a single born-again person will be judged in this judgment. It is a judgment of the "dead," and at this time all the saints of God will have been resurrected a thousand years before.

To be sure, Christians will be present as witnesses but not to be judged. Remember that Jesus said, "The men of Nineveh shall rise in judgment with this generation, and shall condemn it: because they repented at the preaching of Jonas; and, behold, a greater than Jonas is here" (Matt. 12:41). The people of Nineveh who repented and were saved will be witnesses against others. So other Christians will be present as witnesses against every sinner who rejected Christ.

I will give testimony in that day against every sinner who ever heard me preach, every careless one to whom I spoke about his soul and handed a tract. The mother in that day will be for Christ and against her own son and will witness to her tears and pleadings which he rejected. Christians will be present but will not be judged in this judgment of the unsaved dead whose spirits have been brought back from Hell and whose bodies have been brought out of the graves. This is the second resurrection, and all these will stand before God to be judged.

B. Both Small and Great Are Sinners Alike

Notice that both "the small and the great" stand before God. There will be no partiality in this court. In human courts many can hire shrewd lawyers. Sometimes a witness or a juror can be bribed. Often a witness is dead or cannot be obtained, or some evidence is overlooked. Shrewd, crooked lawyers can get a case postponed; or, by technicality, can defeat or postpone justice. But when the sinner comes out of Hell to stand before God, the great and small are alike in His terrible presence.

Sinner, you may be big or important or smart; you may have "gotten by" with sin for a long time; but I remind you that you must one day stand before God whether you are great or small!

We are told in Romans 14:11, "As I live, saith the Lord, every knee shall bow to me, and every tongue shall confess to God." In this verse, Paul is quoting from Isaiah 45:23, "Unto me every knee shall bow, every tongue shall swear." Every lost soul must appear before God in his physical body, with a knee to bow and a tongue to confess to God. This is part of the exaltation of Jesus Christ, for Philippians 2:9-11 says:

"Wherefore God also hath highly exalted him, and given him a name which is above every name: That at the name of Jesus every knee should bow, of things in heaven, and things in earth, and things under the earth; And that every tongue should confess that Jesus Christ is Lord, to the glory of God the Father."

This Scripture certainly means that every angel in Heaven, all the saved reigning with Christ on earth and all the condemned sinners in Hell, "under the earth," will be compelled to bow in humility and confess that Jesus Christ is Lord. They will not love Jesus, will not trust Him for salvation; and it will be too late for them to be saved; but the stiff knee of every rebellious and Christ-rejecting sinner will bow before Jesus Christ in humility, and every blaspheming tongue will at that time confess that Jesus Christ is the Lord and Master whom they ought to have served and loved.

C. Sinners With Physical Bodies, Literal Knees and Tongues

How terrible that will be for you, sinner, after a thousand years in the torments of Hell, to receive a physical, resurrected body and to come back to face Jesus Christ whom you have scorned, hated, despised and rejected! I can imagine that the inmates of Hell will shrink in horror from that terrible ordeal. This is the only time a sinner will ever get out of Hell. I have no doubt everyone in Hell would prefer to remain there rather than to appear before Christ, have every sin he ever did or thought revealed and be compelled to confess it!

We remember that Jesus came first to this earth as a Lamb of God, meek and lowly in heart. He was a Man of sorrows and acquainted with grief. He received the name "Jesus," for He was to "save his people from their sins." He healed, but He did not smite. He forgave, but He did not execute judgment. But Jesus will come the second time, not as Servant but as Judge, not as Prophet but as King.

I have heard that once a wild runaway horse tore down the streets of a city. In the careening buggy was a young man. He had lost the reins, so had no control over the frightened beast. Sudden death seemed to be upon him. A lawyer rushed into the street, seized the bits of the horse, held on, was dragged down the street; but he did stop and quiet the horse and save the young man's life.

A few years later, when this same young man had committed a crime and was tried for murder, he was found guilty. As he stood before the judge, the young man recognized in the judge the lawyer who had saved his life.

The judge said, "Have you anything to say for yourself before sentence is pronounced?"

The young man cried out, "Judge, don't you know me? You saved my life at the risk of your own. I appeal to you for mercy. Isn't there something you can do? Don't let them hang me, judge!"

Very sadly the judge replied, "Young man, I was once your saviour and risked my life to save you; now I am your judge and must execute the law!"

For every sinner who will be dragged out of Hell to this last judgment, Jesus died. To every one of them He was offering salvation. Their sins were paid for on the cross. We are told, "He is the propitiation for our sins: and not for our's only, but also for the sins of the whole world" (I John 2:2). At infinite cost to Himself, Jesus provided the way of escape for these sinners. He did not want them to come to this place of judgment. "As I live, saith the Lord God, I have no pleasure in the death of the wicked" (Ezek. 33:11). Again we are told that He is "not willing that any should perish, but that all should come to repentance" (II Pet. 3:9).

Jesus came into the world, not to condemn the world, but "that the world through him might be saved." All these have come to this awful moment because they would not take mercy when it was offered, would not heed when they were called, would not receive the salvation that was offered. To all these Jesus longed to be their Saviour. Since they would not receive Him as Saviour, now they must face Him as Judge.

Well I know, dear reader, that some of you never mention the name of God except with an oath; you cannot say the name of Christ or God Almighty without blasphemy. The holy God, your Creator, yet you take His name in vain! How wicked!

Again and again when I would preach on the streets, sometimes bystanders would not even remove their hats. In many a revival service wicked sinners would not even bow their heads to pray, but would often smile and whisper when Christians called on God.

Pray! No, you do not pray! You do not know what it is to bow your head over a meal and humbly thank the God who gave it. You do not kneel by your bed and ask for safekeeping during the night. You cannot even say a word of praise to God when He heals your sick wife or baby, when He gives you a new job and pours upon you a multitude of blessings. No, you do not pray!

But someday you will pray, my friend, and pray in public! You will bow the knee before God, confess your sins to Him and confess that Christ is Lord. If God cannot be glorified in your love and surrender, then He will be glorified in your damnation; for demons and sinners from Hell will bow the knee to Christ as surely as do angels and saints. The dead, small and great, must stand before God and bow the knee and confess.

The "knee" refers to the physical body; the "tongue" refers to the physical body. Resurrected sinners in bodies fresh from the graves and the sea will stand before God to be judged in the flesh for deeds done in the flesh and then to be cast, both soul and body, into Hell, the lake of fire.

D. Bodies Raised From the Sea and Graves

Does it astonish you that God could raise a physical body? Is it harder for God to assemble the dust of a body that has rotted for a thousand years, than to form the first man out of the dust of the earth? Is it too hard for God to assemble a body whose flesh has been eaten by the fish of the sea or the fowls of the air? Not if you have an infinite God, a Creator. The last grave will be opened in every cemetery. A thousand years before, the saints will have been raised and their graves left empty; now the remaining graves will give up their dead as spirits come out of Hell to possess them and be judged before God.

III. HOW WILL SINNERS BE JUDGED? ON WHAT BASIS IS THIS JUDGMENT?

A. According to Perfect Records of God

Two kinds of books are mentioned here—the record books and the Book of Life. The books are plural—"The dead were judged out of those things which were written in the *books,* according to their works." God speaks in all this passage as if it were already accomplished.

With God there is no yesterday, no tomorrow. He knows all things in the future as intimately as He knows the present. The dead are, in God's sight, already judged. But before the assembled universe they will be judged out of these books which are the records of their sins. The other book is the Book of Life, which we will mention later.

The sins which others forget, God remembers. Your works are written down. You may be sure this will be a fair judgment. All the facts will be known. The records are exact. There will be no chance for perjury. Every witness involved will be present. Every memory will be sharp and clear. Every prisoner before the bar will confess his sins. Every plea will be: "GUILTY!"

B. According to Their Works Sinners Will Get Exactly What They Deserve

Notice this: you will make your own Hell. "The wages of sin is death: but the gift of God is eternal life through Jesus Christ our Lord" (Rom. 6:23). Every man who goes to Hell makes his own way, pays for his own ticket. He is only receiving his proper wages and getting what is his due.

There will be different degrees of punishment in Hell, just as there are different degrees of sin. All go to Hell who do not accept Christ as Saviour and trust in Him, but people will be judged "according to their works." Some will suffer more than others in Hell, depending on the opportunities they rejected and the sins they committed; for Jesus said, "It shall be more tolerable for Tyre and Sidon at the day of judgment, than for you" (Matt. 11:22). It will be more bearable for some than for others.

I say, every man who goes to Hell pays his own way, for the wages of sin is death. But every man who goes to Heaven rides on a free pass furnished by Jesus Christ our Lord. In fact, all of us deserve to go to Hell, for all have sinned. But those who trust Christ escape their *wages* and get instead the *gift of God*, which is eternal life.

A tender child who comes to know himself a sinner and who rejects Christ and dies unsaved, will go to Hell. But how much heavier will be the punishment of the wicked man who, after great enlightenment, continues in sin, rejecting every offer of mercy!

"And that servant, which knew his lord's will, and prepared not himself, neither did according to his will, shall be beaten with many stripes. But he that knew not, and did commit things worthy of stripes, shall be beaten with few stripes."—Luke 12:47,48.

Men make their own Hell. There will not be one single whine about injustice at this judgment. Every man will get exactly his due. Oh, God's justice! It is not justice we need; it is MERCY! There is mercy for those who trust Christ, but only justice for those who die without repenting and come to this judgment of the unsaved dead.

God's record books will be opened, brother. Your sins will be made known. Your secret sins will come to light in that day.

C. Secret Sins Will Be Brought to Judgment

We look about us and think well of the people we see. Sometimes I have known Christians who were rebellious that sinners should go to Hell. They think of sinners about them as nice, respectable, decent people. Sometimes a mother takes sides with her unsaved boy against God. Sometimes a wife says, "Oh, my husband is the best man in the world. If he would just join the church. . . ."

But I remind you that God sees the heart. "Man looketh on the outward appearance, but the Lord looketh on the heart." And "the heart is deceitful above all things, and desperately wicked," Jeremiah 17:9 tells us.

Brother, God knows your secret sins. In some home where this sermon is read, the husband appears to be loyal and true to the wife he swore to protect, provide for and cherish. She does not know, and perhaps few others know, that he has broken his marriage vow which he made before God, made before the woman who trusted him, and made before the public. Loving wives are sometimes blind.

But, my brother, God is not! That sin is put down in His record book and one day will be read to the world, and you must confess it to Him. Your sins will find you out! Your skeletons will come out of their closets! Your chickens will come home to roost! That which is whispered in secret will be shouted from the housetop!

Oh, the torment of hidden sins! What trembling, what anxiety, what forebodings of evil, what torment of soul we have when we hide our sins, yet fear they will be discovered!

A woman wrote me from a distant state in torment of conscience over a sin committed when she was young. Later she had married, had a beautiful child, and her husband adored and trusted her. Through the years she had felt unworthy and wrote to ask me what she could not ask her pastor: should she confess to her husband the sin of her young womanhood?

In her case she had already confessed to God, and her sin was under the blood. She had been true to her husband since she married. I wrote that she was under no obligation to confess it to anybody. It was now buried in the sea of God's forgetfulness and forgiven, since she had confessed it to Him with penitent heart.

But how many thousands there are who have covered sins! Remember that the Bible says, "He that covereth his sins shall not prosper: but whoso confesseth and forsaketh them shall have mercy" (Prov. 28:13). The horrible thing about the last judgment will be that all sin will then be uncovered and secret things will be brought to light.

While I was in a revival in an Oklahoma town, a wife discovered in her husband's pocket a letter which proved he had been untrue, that he had committed adultery with another woman. Her heart was broken with grief and shame. Eventually she told him what she had found. With a horror of shame, he admitted his guilt, then said, "If you will forgive me, let us both get right with God, trust Him for salvation and then live true to each other and God." She agreed and they both were happily converted, and she told my wife the story.

That sin was uncovered and forgiven. But what about the sins hidden through all these years, unforgiven, unconfessed, unlamented? What about the sins that are kept secret now but will be revealed on the judgment day?

In a north Texas town was a groceryman of high standing in his community. He was an active church member and had the respect and af-
fection of a wide circle of friends. To the horror of his family and friends,
he was arrested, tried and proven guilty of a long series of thefts through
the years, seemingly deliberate, and was sentenced for some years in
the penitentiary. I will never forget how shocked his friends were.

Oh, the grief and shame when hidden sins come to light! And come
to light they will when God's record books are opened.

Some person who reads this stole some money when no one knew
it. Perhaps you have not been suspected at all. You are looked upon
as the soul of honor, yet you are a thief! God knows it, and one day
it will come out.

You took property that did not belong to you. Well, you had as well
make up your mind that one day, if you go on without Christ and without
having your sins forgiven, your sins will be uncovered to the whole world,
when God opens His record books!

There are many murderers abroad in the land. Many have never been
punished, and far too many have never even been tried. Some, God
knows, have never even been suspected. Yet you dealt the poison or
used the knife or pulled the trigger that sent some soul out to meet God.
Do you think you have gotten by? The eye that sees all things has
witnessed it! The book that cannot lie holds the record of it. And when
you are dragged before the mighty Judge of all the earth, your record
will be there.

Many women seem so modest, so virtuous, so kind: they would never
be suspected of murder. They pass for upright and moral mothers and
wives; and only God knows, perhaps, that they are the murderesses
of their unborn children! Little innocents who never knew the light of
day, little ones who died before they were born, yet who had a soul
given of God, little ones who ought to have been received with love
and care—these will witness at the great white throne judgment against
the red-handed murderesses—their mothers.

O God! What a reaping for your sowing! Yes, your sin will find you
out. Every skeleton will come out of the closet at the judgment of the
unsaved dead.

And how happy will be those who have turned all their sins over to
Jesus and gotten forgiveness and sweet peace! How happy will be those
whose sins are all paid for on the cross and to whom is ascribed and

imputed the righteousness of Jesus instead of our own sinful record!

D. A Judgment of Uncommitted Sin – That Is, Sins of the Heart

No human court can ever give exact justice. The trial may prove that a certain man pulled the trigger and that his bullet killed another man. But the evidence cannot show perfectly what was in his heart. Only God knows that. And so God writes down the correct record.

You never committed murder, you say? As men see it, no, but in God's sight doubtless you have. For were you not just as angry sometimes as the man who did kill another? Have you had hate or unforgiveness or grudges in your heart? Then those lead to murder and in God's sight constitute the act of murder; for in I John 3:15 we are told, "Whosoever hateth his brother IS a murderer." God's record book shows the murder that took place in your heart.

It shows not only the adultery that was physical and outward, but what took place in a lustful heart where none else sees. Jesus said,

"Ye have heard that it was said by them of old time, Thou shalt not commit adultery: But I say unto you, That whosoever looketh on a woman to lust after her hath committed adultery with her already in his heart."—Matt. 5:27,28.

The covetous is a thief, the deceiver is a liar, the hater is a murderer, the lustful is an adulterer! Many of us are like the Pharisees—outwardly whited sepulchers but inwardly full of dead men's bones and all uncleanness! Many of us have sheep's clothing, but inwardly we are ravening wolves.

If one reads this who depends on his morality, then I remind you that the Pharisees who crucified Jesus were moral, too, but oh, the wickedness of their hearts! And after you have been in Hell for over a thousand years and are dragged out to face Jesus Christ on His throne and bow the knee to Him, then the true record of your heart will be opened!

It must be apparent to all that any who come to this judgment are certain to be condemned. When it comes to any judgment passed on our own deeds, there could be only one outcome. Man is so wicked that any time he receives justice, he receives condemnation. The Scripture says, "All we like sheep have gone astray; we have turned every one to his own way; and the Lord hath laid on him the iniquity of us all" (Isa. 53:6).

We are told:

"... we have before proved both Jews and Gentiles, that they are all under sin; As it is written, There is none righteous, no, not one: There is none that understandeth, there is none that seeketh after God. They are all gone out of the way, they are together become unprofitable; there is none that doeth good, no, not one."—Rom. 3:9-12.

And again: "For there is no difference: For all have sinned, and come short of the glory of God" (Rom. 3:22,23).

And again: "If we say that we have not sinned, we make him a liar, and his word is not in us" (I John 1:10).

What chance has any sinner before God without mercy? It is written that "the soul that sinneth, it shall die" (Ezek. 18:4), and "the wages of sin is death" (Rom. 6:23). So every man, woman and child who comes to this last great judgment of the unsaved dead to be judged according to his works will meet only condemnation. This judgment is not to find out whether or not men are sinners; it is only the public and official confirmation of their guilt so that every person in Heaven and Hell will admit the justice of God.

Reader, if you come to be judged before the great white throne, then eternal torment is your portion, and there is no escape!

E. "And Whosoever Was Not Found Written in the Book of Life Was Cast Into the Lake of Fire"

Besides the record books, another book will be opened at that judgment, the Book of Life. And that is the final humiliation, the final condemnation, the final blow to every hope of every sinner at this terrible judgment before Jesus on the great white throne.

Why is it brought here, this Book of Life? Not a person here has his name written therein, so why should it be brought here? Not a word is said about any one of all the millions assembled here having his name in the Book of Life. Then what is its purpose in this judgment?

The answer is this: it is God's final answer to every plea of the sinner. When the Book of Life is closed, then mercy is gone.

It is true that people go to Hell because of their sins and that their punishment is in proportion to their guilt and according to their works. Yet in the last analysis, people do not go to Hell so much for all their lives of sin as they do for the one sin of rejecting Christ.

Every sinner deserves Hell, but a way of escape is offered in Jesus Christ. He has died for every sinner, paid every debt, offered mercy and pardon to every guilty soul. Those who come to God by faith in Christ, His crucified Son, have their names written in the Lamb's Book of Life.

The Book of Life contains not the names of good people, but the names of bad people who have been forgiven. The Book of Life does not contain the names of those who have earned Heaven, but the names of those deserving Hell but who have been freely pardoned and whose sins are under the blood of Christ!

So here the Book of Life is brought; and against every sinner after his record book is opened and he has confessed all his sins and bowed the knee to Jesus Christ, the last witness is brought out—and that is the Book of Life. They search through those pages, and their names are not there!

How solemn it must make us to realize that Heaven or Hell is not decided at the great white throne judgment but here in this life. It is only now while we live and are moved by the Spirit and led to repentance and faith in Christ that men have their names written in the Lamb's Book of Life.

Sometimes people pray, "Save us in Heaven, for Jesus' sake. Amen." But salvation is obtained in this life, not in the next. The great decision is made now while we live, not after we are dead. One who waits until the last judgment to learn whether or not he has been saved is likely due for a terrible disappointment, for salvation is a present-day matter. "He that believeth on the Son hath everlasting life: and he that believeth not the Son shall not see life; but the wrath of God abideth on him" (John 3:36).

No Present Under the Christmas Tree

When I was a small boy in West Texas, the entire community would have a Christmas tree at one of the churches. Nearly everyone would bring his presents for children, for parents, for sweetheart, for friends. Those were exciting days. We could hardly wait until the program of songs and "recitations" and speeches was over and "Santa Claus" would begin to read the names on presents taken from the tree one by one and handed out by his helpers to boys and girls. What anticipation! What thrills!

I sat many a time hoping against hope. *Could that air gun be mine?*
Was that the ball and bat and glove that I had wanted so long? A thousand hopes and fears made the suspense almost unbearable, as each
waited breathlessly for his name to be called. The packages, mysteriously
wrapped, might be almost anything glamorous and fine!

But my father was poor, and we never spent much for Christmas.
Year after year I saw the finest presents handed out to others, and I
waited while hope ebbed slowly away. If the last present was given and
some names were not called, the mock Santa Claus would reach under
the tree and get some little bag of netting holding hard candy and perhaps
an orange, and these would be handed out to the children who had
gotten no presents.

It is a faint picture, I know—for how can one picture the despair of
a lost soul! Yet it reminds me of how a poor, doomed sinner must feel
when the Book of Life—God's last witness—is brought out against him
and his despairing eyes search those holy pages; and finally, with such
sadness as none of us can ever know unless we go to Hell, he must
say, "O God! It is not there! My name is not in the Book of Life!"

Oh, if you want your name in the Book of Life, you must get it in
there now; then you will not come to this awful judgment from which
every soul, judged, returns to the lake of fire because his name is not
in the Book of Life!

Every lost sinner might well burn into his heart these words by J. A.
Brown, the sweet gospel singer:

> In a day that is not far,
> At the blazing judgment bar,
> 　　Even now the awful summons I can hear;
> I must meet the mighty God,
> I must face His holy Word,
> 　　I must stand before the judgment bar.
>
> I must meet each broken vow
> That I hold so lightly now,
> 　　Every heartache I have caused, each sigh, each tear;
> Things that time cannot erase,
> I must meet them face to face
> 　　When I stand before the judgment bar.
>
> Every secret lust and tho't
> There shall be to judgment bro't
> 　　When the Lord in all His glory shall appear;
> All the deeds of darkest night
> Shall come out to greet the light
> 　　When I stand before the judgment bar.

I must meet my cankered gold
For whose greed my life was sold.
    It shall mock me in the judgment's lurid glare,
Saying, "Ye have sold for naught
All the Saviour's blood had bo't,
    And you stand before the judgment bar."

Oh, my record will be there,
Be its pages dark or fair,
    When I stand before the judgment bar;
When the books shall open lie
In that morning by and by,
    Oh, my record! Oh, my record will be there!

Conclusion: Sinner, You Need Not Come to This Judgment

A striking and terrible thought that sinners must face God and their sins! No wonder the Scripture says, "It is appointed unto men once to die, but after this the judgment"!

But thank God, you don't have to wait for that awful day, my sinner friend. If you will trust in Christ, you can escape that judgment; for Revelation 20:6 says, "Blessed and holy is he that hath part in the first resurrection: on such the second death hath no power, but they shall be priests of God and of Christ, and shall reign with him a thousand years."

God loves you, brother! Trust Him for forgiveness and mercy today, and you will not come to this awful judgment. Christ was judged for your sins on the cross. When He cried out just before He died, "It is finished!" He meant that every sin of yours and mine was paid for— every one. And now He pleads, "Come now, and let us reason together, saith the Lord: though your sins be as scarlet, they shall be as white as snow; though they be red like crimson, they shall be as wool" (Isa. 1:18). You can have mercy instead of justice if you trust in Christ.

John 5:24 teaches us that, if you will trust in Christ, you will have no judgment, no condemnation, no second death. There Jesus said, as recorded in the American Revised Version, "Verily, verily, I say unto you, He that heareth my word, and believeth him that sent me, hath eternal life, and cometh not into judgment, but hath passed out of death into life."

"Cometh not into judgment!" That is what I need, and thank God, that is what I have!

And now let us read the last verse of the poem above, and may God grant it will be the prayer of every sinner who reads it.

Let me turn and seek the Lord,
Let me trust His holy Word,
  Let us bow and call upon Him while He's near;
Then when I my record face,
He will answer in my place!
  When I stand before the judgment bar.

Christ will answer in your place, sinner, if you trust Him. He bore your sins. He took your place. He is even now at the right hand of the Father to intercede for those who trust Him. He is one Lawyer who never loses a case, one Physician who never fails, one Friend who never turns His back on His own.

My message is done, and my heart is burdened. God will hold you to account for the way you read and the decision you make. Will you today confess your sins and trust Christ to forgive you? Will you claim Him as your Saviour? If you will, why not solemnly, with all your heart, settle the matter with God, taking Christ as your own personal Saviour?

HENRY (HARRY) ALLEN IRONSIDE
1876-1951

ABOUT THE MAN:

Few preachers had more varied ministries than this man. He was a captain in the Salvation Army, an itinerant preacher with the Plymouth Brethren, pastor of the renowned Moody Memorial Church in Chicago, and conducted Bible conferences throughout the world. Sandwiched between those major ministries, Ironside preached the Gospel on street corners, in missions, in taverns, on Indian reservations, etc.

Never formally ordained and with no experience whatever as a pastor, Ironside took over the 4,000-seat Moody Memorial Church in Chicago and often filled it to capacity for 18½ years. A seminary president once said of him, *"He has the most unique ministry of any man living."* Although he had little formal education, his tremendous mental capacity and photographic memory caused him to be called the "Archbishop of Fundamentalism."

Preaching—warm, soul-saving preaching—was his forte. Special speakers in his great church often meant nothing; the crowds came when he was there. He traveled constantly; at his prime, he averaged 40 weeks in the year on the road—always returning to Moody Memorial for Sunday services.

His pen moved, too; he contributed regularly to various religious periodicals and journals in addition to publishing 80 books and pamphlets. His writings included addresses or commentaries on the entire New Testament, all of the prophetic books of the Old Testament, and a great many volumes on specific Bible themes and subjects.

In 1951, Dr. Ironside died in Cambridge, New Zealand, and was buried there at his own request.

VI.

Crowns of Reward for Christians

(Crowns Given at the Judgment Seat of Christ)

H. A. IRONSIDE

There are two lines of truth very clearly distinguished in Scripture which are often confounded by those who do not read discriminatingly and who are not given to "rightly dividing the word of truth." I refer to the subjects, "Salvation by Grace" and "Reward for Service."

To the casual reader of the New Testament, it sometimes seems as though there is apparent contradiction, when in one place we are distinctly told that we are saved by grace alone, apart from works, whereas, in another, we are just as clearly told that we are to be rewarded according to our works.

It is only as we learn the mind of the Spirit in regard to these two very different lines of teaching that the soul is set free from self-occupation and given to know the blessedness of peace with God, on the ground of pure grace, thus leaving one free to serve in the happy knowledge that the *sin question* is forever settled, but that *service* is the outflow of a grateful heart to the One who has redeemed us, and yet that He, in His wondrous lovingkindness, takes note of everything we do for Him and will reward accordingly.

At the very outset it may be good to link together a number of Scriptures which present these various phases of truth. In Romans 4:3-5 we read:

"For what saith the scripture? Abraham believed God, and it was counted unto him for righteousness. Now to him that worketh is the reward not reckoned of grace, but of debt. But to him that worketh not, but believeth on him that justifieth the ungodly, his faith is counted for righteousness."

Here we learn that just as Abraham was accounted righteous before God on the ground of *faith alone,* so today we who believe are justified from all our ungodliness the moment we trust in Christ. Were it otherwise, were it necessary that we should prove ourselves worthy in order to be saved, our salvation would not be of grace, for we would be putting God in our debt. If salvation is a reward for service, then, clearly, God would owe it to the one who faithfully performed whatever service He demanded to save that soul in exchange for the good deeds done. This, of course, would not be grace.

How different is the principle on which we are justified! It is "to him that worketh not, but believeth on him that justifieth the ungodly." Nothing can be clearer than this, yet how many have stumbled over it!

Now let us link with this Ephesians 2:8-10:

"For by grace are ye saved through faith; and that not of yourselves: it is the gift of God: Not of works, lest any man should boast. For we are his workmanship, created in Christ Jesus unto good works, which God hath before ordained that we should walk in them."

Here again we have the precious truth manifested, that salvation is altogether of grace through faith; that is, through believing the testimony that God has given. "Faith cometh by hearing, and hearing by the word of God." Therefore even the faith by which we are saved is in no sense of ourselves; it is God's gift, for it is not until He gives a testimony that we can believe; but when that testimony comes home to us in the power of the Holy Spirit and we put our trust in it, we are saved. This leaves no place whatever for works as a procuring cause of salvation.

Were it otherwise, there would be ground for boasting. If I could obtain a place in Heaven because of my devotion to Christ down here, I would have good reason to congratulate myself for all eternity upon that very devotion which had led to so blessed a result. But no saint in Heaven will ever give himself credit for anything he has ever done. The song of all the redeemed will be, "Unto him that loveth us and hath washed us from our sins in his own blood, be glory and honour, dominion, and power and might forever and ever."

And yet, in verse 10 of our passage, we are just as distinctly told that we are created in Christ Jesus unto good works—that is, we did not enter the new creation through good works; but having been brought into this new creation by faith, it is now incumbent upon us, as obedient children, to walk in righteousness before God, living in good works which God has preappointed to characterize those who are saved.

In I Corinthians, chapter 3, the apostle tells us of the testing which evidently takes place at the judgment seat of Christ. Notice verses 11 to 15:

"For other foundation can no man lay than that is laid, which is Jesus Christ. Now if any man build upon this foundation gold, silver, precious stones, wood, hay, stubble; Every man's work shall be made manifest: for the day shall declare it, because it shall be revealed by fire; and the fire shall try every man's work of what sort it is. If any man's work abide which he hath built thereupon, he shall receive a reward. If any man's work shall be burned, he shall suffer loss: but he himself shall be saved; yet so as by fire."

According to this passage, every believer is a workman building upon the foundation already laid, which is Jesus Christ. His work may be according to the Spirit, likened unto gold, silver and costly stones, or according to the flesh and likened unto wood, hay and stubble. The day of manifestation will reveal what is of God and what is not. For that work which abides reward will be given, but that which does not abide will disappear in the cleansing fires of judgment, and for the wasted time the believer will suffer loss.

His salvation, however, is not in question. He would not appear at this scene of testing if he were not already saved. The destruction of his works does not touch this question. Though everything should be burned up, he himself shall be saved, yet so as by fire.

Another helpful passage in this connection is found in Hebrews 10:35,36:

"Cast not away therefore your confidence, which hath great recompence of reward. For ye have need of patience, that, after ye have done the will of God, ye might receive the promise."

It is to persons already saved that the exhortation comes: "Cast not away therefore your confidence, which hath great recompence of reward." This same principle was true in olden times, for we read in chapter 11, of Israel's great leader:

"By faith Moses, when he was come to years, refused to be called the son of Pharaoh's daughter; Choosing rather to suffer affliction with the people of God, than to enjoy the pleasures of sin for a season; Esteeming the reproach of Christ greater riches than the treasures in

Egypt: for he had respect unto the recompence of the reward."

There can be no question but that Moses was already a quickened soul, a child of God, in whom justifying faith dwelt, when he made his great renunciation and gave up a throne for a wilderness tent; for his eye discerned and his heart was set upon the reward in eternal ages, reserved for the one who put the testimony of God before personal comfort and convenience.

A kindred verse is found in II John 8: "Look to yourselves, that we lose not those things which we have wrought, but that we receive a full reward."

No believer can lose his salvation, for that is not in his keeping. We are told this distinctly in John 10:27-29:

"My sheep hear my voice, and I know them, and they follow me: And I give unto them eternal life; and they shall never perish, neither shall any man pluck them out of my hand. My Father, which gave them me, is greater than all; and no man is able to pluck them out of my Father's hand."

But we may lose at least a portion of our reward.

There are two verses in the book of Revelation which fit together beautifully in this connection. In chapter 3:11 the Lord announces His near return, saying, "Behold, I come quickly: hold that fast which thou hast, that no man take thy crown."

In chapter 22:12 He says, "And, behold, I come quickly; and my reward is with me, to give every man according as his work shall be."

These two verses make one thing very clear, which forms the basis of a most interesting and helpful study for our encouragement and warning. The "reward" spoken of in the latter passage is evidently synonymous with the "crown" of the other.

Anyone can readily see, by turning to the word "crown" in a critical or analytical Bible Concordance, that there are two words so translated in the New Testament. One is literally "diadem" and refers to the regal circlet worn by a king or emperor.

This is the word used in Revelation 12, 13 and 19.

In the first instance, the great red dragon, "that old serpent, which is the Devil and Satan," is seen wearing seven diadems. He is the prince of this world.

Then we see the wild beast of chapter 13—the coming prince of

Daniel 9—wearing ten diadems. This is Satan's man who will someday arise and will accept the offer that our blessed Lord indignantly spurned when shown all the kingdoms of the earth and promised their rulership if He would worship the Adversary.

In chapter 19 the descending Lord Himself comes to take the kingdom, and "upon his head are many diadems." He is to rule as King of kings and Lord of lords.

The other word—*stephanos,* from which the name "Stephen" comes—is, literally, a victor's wreath. It refers to the chaplet of laurel or other leaves placed upon the brow of the triumphant athlete in the games of old or the golden band worn upon the head of the victorious general as he marched in triumph through the city amid the plaudits of the people. Subject kings wore a crown of this character in contrast to the imperial diadem. When the soldiery mocked Jesus, they put upon Him a crown—or, *stephanos*—of thorns, the fruit of the curse. Yet He was indeed the Victor, even in the hour of His apparent defeat; and He is now "crowned with glory and honour" as He sits at the right hand of the Majesty in the heavens.

> **His be the Victor's name**
> **Who fought the fight alone,**
> **Triumphant saints no honor claim,**
> **His conquest was their own.**
> **By weakness and defeat**
> **He won the meed and crown,**
> **Trod all our foes beneath His feet**
> **By being trodden down.**

And He, the Overcomer whom the Father Himself has crowned, is the Judge of the contests in which His saints are engaged and will in due time sit upon the *Bema*—the judgment seat—and give to the overcomers the crowns they have won in the conflict with sin. We have a list of the Heroes of Faith who have fought and overcome in Hebrews 11, and in chapter 12 we read:

"Wherefore seeing we also are compassed about with so great a cloud of witnesses, let us lay aside every weight, and the sin which doth so easily beset us, and let us run with patience the race that is set before us, Looking unto Jesus the author and finisher of our faith; who for the joy that was set before him endured the cross, despising the shame, and is set down at the right hand of the throne of God."

Bless, bless the Conqueror slain;
Slain in His victory;
He lived, He died, He lives again,
For thee, His church, for thee.

We likewise are running a race and for us, as for Him, there is a crown at the end. It is of this the Apostle Paul writes when he speaks of

AN INCORRUPTIBLE CROWN

in I Corinthians 9:24. He has been speaking of service—of his own call to preach the Gospel—of the importance of faithfully fulfilling his ministry; and then he uses the striking illustration of these closing verses: "Know ye not that they which run in a race run all, but one receiveth the prize? So run, that ye may obtain."

It is not salvation of which he speaks. We do not obtain the gift of God—eternal life—by diligence or by "running." "It is not of him that willeth, nor of him that runneth, but of God that sheweth mercy" (Rom. 9:16).

But as Christians, we are running a race—we are contending in the arena—and for the victors there are fairer crowns than ever were bestowed on the winners in the Olympic games or on the battlefields of earth. Let us then see to it that we so run that we may obtain the reward.

In the next verse he goes on to remind them that "every man that striveth for the mastery is temperate in all things." The youth who would win the race is careful to subdue his natural appetites, to "train down" to the proper weight, to hold himself in check lest by self-indulgence on any line he unfit himself for the contest. "Now they do it to obtain a corruptible crown, but we an incorruptible."

In a few hours the laurel wreath will fade or the metallic circle tarnish and corrode. We are striving for an imperishable prize, a crown that is incorruptible.

All believers who die will be raised in the first resurrection to incorruptibility (as I Corinthians 15 assures us), but the incorruptible crown is the prize for faithfully running the Christian race. It is the Master's "Well done!" at the end of the course.

With such a reward in view, what an incentive I have for holy living—for self-denying devotion to Christ! Into this Paul himself fully entered:

"I therefore so run, not as uncertainly; so fight I, not as one that beateth the air: But I keep under my body, and bring it into subjection; lest that

by any means, when I have preached to others, I myself should be a castaway."

This last word is the negative form of the word that means "approved." It means therefore "disapproved" or "rejected."

The apostle covets above all else the Lord's approval. He would receive the victor's incorruptible wreath at the hands of Him who once wore the crown of thorns. With this in view he will not permit the body to be master. He will hold its tendencies in check that he may not by any possibility bring dishonor on his Lord's name through any carnal indulgence, and so miss His approbation at last.

How many a one has preached to others who has been set aside as a servant and—in some instances—proves utterly unworthy even to bear the name of Christian because he has not held his body under but has given way to fleshly lusts and passions which war against the soul.

To preach well is but to increase one's condemnation if one does not live well. Like the clean beasts of old, mouth and foot must agree, speech and walk must both be according to godliness, if one would win the crown.

The race may seem long and the way rough and difficult, but the reward is sure for him who keeps his eye on Christ and follows on in the footprints He has left on the wilderness road. To save one's life is to lose it. To lose it now for His name's sake is to keep it unto life eternal, and thus to win the incorruptible crown.

CROWN OF REJOICING

In I Thessalonians the second coming of our Lord occupies the prominent place. It may be said to be the theme of the epistle. In some aspect it is referred to in every chapter. In chapter 1 we read of the Thessalonians believed that they had "turned to God from idols to serve the living and true God, and to wait for his Son from heaven."

Waiting for the Son—and serving while they wait! What blessed and holy occupation was theirs! May it be ours too.

In chapter 3 (for I pass over chapter 2 for the moment) they were exhorted to holiness of life in view of "the coming of our Lord Jesus Christ with all his saints."

The "blessed hope" is a purifying hope and an incentive to godly living. "Every man," we are told, "that hath this hope in him [or, set on Him] purifieth himself even as he is pure."

The rapture—the order of events when the Lord descends to call away His saints—is unfolded most preciously in chapter 4, while in chapter 5 we have perfect sanctification reached at last at "the coming of our Lord Jesus Christ" (vs. 23).

But what about chapter 2? In that particular section the apostle is writing of his own service and the ministry of his fellow-laborers in view of this glorious event. He thinks of the Lord's return as the time of manifestation and reward—the time when the servant's works will all be examined and pronounced upon by the Lord Himself. It will be then that the results of his own years of toil and travail will be fully made known. Of this he is assured: the souls he has led to Christ will be a cause of thanksgiving then. So he writes—and to his own converts, be it noted—"What is our hope, or joy, or crown of rejoicing? Are not even ye in the presence of our Lord Jesus Christ at his coming? For ye are our glory and joy."

He speaks in a similar strain in Philippians 4:1, "My brethren dearly beloved and longed for, my joy and crown."

They too were the fruit of his ministry and, like the Corinthians, the seal of his apostleship in the Lord.

How sweet and tender the relationship between the minister of the Word and those he has led to Christ! And when I write "minister of the Word," I do not mean one in a clerical office or some official position, but any believer who ministers the truth of the Gospel to another and so leads him to Christ.

Those thus saved through our testimony will be to us a crown of rejoicing in that day. To see them safe in the glory, singing the praises of the Lamb who redeemed them, and then to realize that in some sense they are there because of our testimony in weakness while on earth, what a wreath of joy that will be! We shall indeed be crowned with gladness!

Rutherford knew something of this when, on looking back from his dying bed to the scene of his former labors, he gave utterance to the beautiful words which have been embalmed in poetry by Mrs. Cousins:

> Oh, Anwoth by the Solway,
>   To me thou still art dear;
> E'en from the verge of Heaven
>   I drop for thee a tear.
> Oh, if one soul from Anwoth
>   Meet me at God's right hand,

**My heaven will be two heavens
In Immanuel's land.**

Yes, one soul—saved from going down to the pit, plucked as a brand from Hell, pulled out of the fire, as Jude puts it—will be for the one used to his deliverance a veritable doubling of the joys of Heaven. What will it mean for one like Paul who won thousands to Christ? What for every God-raised-up evangelist who has been the means of the salvation of vast numbers of men and women through the preached Word?

But as intimated above, it is not only those divinely called to preach who may win this crown. We are all called to witness for Christ, to seek to win others to know Him "whom to know is life eternal." And it is written in the Word, "He that is wise winneth souls" (R.V.). Oh, to have the wisdom that will enable us to turn many to righteousness!

Soul winning is not in itself an arbitrary gift. It is something that may be cultivated by exercise and communion with God. He fits us for such blessed and honorable service.

The first requisite is to realize the need of men, their lost condition. Have you ever asked God to give you to feel the appalling need of the unsaved all around you? And has He answered by burdening you for their souls? Then continue to look to Him for the message. He will give holy boldness, tender compassion, wisdom in presenting the truth and grace to persist in spite of rebuffs. The joy of seeing one poor sinner changed into a saint will amply repay all the toil and exercise here on earth, and at the Lord's return the crown of rejoicing will be your eternal reward.

> **Go on, go on, there's all
> Eternity to rest in,
> And far too few are on the
> Active Service List;
> No labor for the Lord is
> Risky to invest in,
> But nothing will make up
> Should His "Well Done" be missed.**

And let us not forget the other side. It is written, "He that withholdeth corn, the people shall curse him." The unsaved may not relish being spoken to now. But a day will come when they will blame us if we passed them by without a warning word or a kindly message of grace. We have the food for which they are dying. We know they are doomed without the Gospel. And shall we selfishly and coldly leave them to die without an honest endeavor to awaken them to a sense of their need and make them realize a Saviour's love?

Will not the remembrance of such unfaithfulness make us "ashamed before him at his coming"?

> **Must I go and empty-handed,**
> **Thus my dear Redeemer meet?**
> **Not one sheaf with which to greet Him,**
> **Lay no trophy at His feet?**

It need not be. Each one may in his measure be a winner of souls and thus gain a crown of rejoicing in that day of all days so soon to dawn. What is needed is willingness to be used. Someone has said, "God has wonderful things to display if He could only get the show cases." Paul was such a "show case." "That in me," he says, "Jesus Christ might shew forth all longsuffering." Oh, may we too—you and I, my reader—be used to display the grace of Christ to a lost world and to attract men to Himself. Such will be our joy and crown when He returns to reckon with His servants.

CROWN OF RIGHTEOUSNESS

Second Timothy 4 is a marvelous chapter to have been penned by a worn old man in a Roman death cell, just waiting for the summons to the last act of a martyrdom that had already lasted half of an ordinary lifetime. It was probably written from an underground dungeon in the Mamertine Prison. After a few years' liberty following his first imprisonment, Paul had been re-arrested and sentenced to death for the fearful crime of preaching "another King, one Jesus"! His had been a life of almost incredible hardships for the Gospel's sake, and now his sun seemed to be setting in a night of darkness and unrelieved gloom.

But the aged apostle did not so consider it. Whatever the then-present sufferings, he saw the glory beyond. And his valedictory letter to his companion in many journeys and conflicts ends with a note of triumph such as this world has seldom heard.

"I am now ready to be offered," he exclaims—thinking of himself as a victim about to be placed on the altar of sacrifice—"and the time of my departure is at hand." The word for "departure" is *exodus*, the same word used by Peter in his second epistle (1:15), where it is translated "decease." For these men of God death was not a lapsing into unconsciousness, but a "going-out" of the body in order to be "present with the Lord."

Looking back over his long record, Paul can say without affectation, "I have fought the good fight, I have finished my course, I have kept the faith."

It was not merely that he had fought well. Undoubtedly he had. But he would leave the Lord to say that. What he says is that the fight in which he had been engaged was the good cause—in opposition to the evil. The definite article brings this out more clearly than the indefinite as in the Authorized Version.

And now what of the future? Ah, he sees all bright ahead! "Henceforth there is laid up for me a crown of righteousness, which the Lord, the righteous Judge, shall give me at that day; and not to me only, but unto all them also that love his appearing"!

May we not say that this last expression gives us the secret of Paul's devotion to the cause of righteousness? He loved—loved passionately— the glorious appearing of the Lord Jesus Christ; therefore he could count all else but dross that he might win Christ's approval in that day of manifestation.

All believers are "made the righteousness of God in Christ." To everyone who has trusted Him He is *Jehovah Tsidkenu,* "The Lord our Righteousness."

But the crown of righteousness is the reward—as distinguished from "the gift of righteousness"—which will adorn the brow of everyone who has manifested by a life of practical righteousness and devotion to the Saviour's interests in this world, that he truly loved the appearing of our Lord Jesus. "Every man that hath this hope in him [or set on Him, i.e., on the Coming One], purifieth himself even as he is pure."

Nothing is so conducive to a life of integrity before God and uprightness before men as an abiding sense in the soul of the near coming of the Lord. He who truly waits for God's Son from Heaven will be found serving the living and true God day by day.

To profess to hold the doctrine of the premillennial coming of Christ is one thing. To be really held by it is quite another. He whose life is unrighteous, whose spirit is worldly, whose outlook on life is carnal and selfish, has never yet learned to love His appearing. Nor will such ever obtain the crown of righteousness in that day. It is alone for those who, esteeming the reproach of Christ greater riches than all earth's boasted treasures, live *now* in view of *then,* because, like Moses, they "have respect unto the recompense of the reward."

Oh, how small and insignificant will the things that worldlings and carnal Christians live for, seem "in that day"! May we then truly so love His appearing as to gladly follow His steps now.

> **Unto Thee, the homeless Stranger,**
> **Outside the camp,**
> **Forth we hasten, fear no danger,**
> **Outside the camp.**
> **Thy reproach, far richer treasure**
> **Than all Egypt's boasted pleasure;**
> **Drawn by love that knows no measure,**
> **Outside the camp.**

Then when He returns, what joy unbounded will it be to receive from His pierced hand the crown of righteousness, the evidence of His approval and the recognition of a righteous life.

CROWN OF LIFE

The next victor's wreath of which I would speak is the crown of life, concerning which we read in two distinct passages. James 1:12 tells us, "Blessed is the man that endureth temptation: for when he is tried, he shall receive the crown of life, which the Lord hath promised to them that love him."

And in Revelation 2:10 the Lord comforts the church in Smyrna with the words, "Fear none of those things which thou shalt suffer: behold, the devil shall cast some of you into prison, that ye may be tried; and ye shall have tribulation ten days: be thou faithful unto death, and I will give thee a crown of life."

It is noteworthy that in each of these passages we have suffering saints in view: children of God exposed to bitter trial, even going to the length of intense, malignant persecution by Satan's emissaries. God *could* easily hinder these cruel foes; He *could* quench the fierce flames of affliction; He *could* turn back these overwhelming floods of sorrow. But He chooses rather to enable His tested ones to overcome in the day of trial than to free them from trouble. And this not because He takes any delight in the anguish of His distressed people, but because this very tribulation is a means of discipline which results in lasting blessing "to those who are exercised thereby" (Heb. 12:11).

He sits by the fining-pot and watches intently till He sees His own countenance reflected in the melted silver. He walks with His persecuted ones in the furnace, though it be heated seven times more than ordinary. And "he giveth more grace" that they who look to Him may suffer and endure.

Then when the day of manifestation comes, He will bestow with His own once-pierced hand the crown of life upon all who have fought and overcome.

When afflicted with a thorn in the flesh—"a messenger of Satan" sent to buffet him (lest he should be exalted above measure because of the abundance of the revelation he had received when caught up to the third Heaven)—Paul tells us he besought the Lord thrice that he might be delivered from the trial. But the answer came, saying in effect: I will not take the thorn out of your flesh, Paul; but I will do something even better for you than that; I will give you grace to bear it and to glorify Me in it. "My grace is sufficient for thee; for my strength is made perfect in weakness"!

And Paul at once ceases to cry out for deliverance but exclaims with chastened confidence, "Most gladly therefore will I glory in my infirmities, that the power of Christ may rest upon me."

He was but living out what he elsewhere tells his fellow-saints when he says,

"We glory in tribulation also: knowing that tribulation worketh patience; And patience, experience; and experience, hope: And hope maketh not ashamed; because the love of God is shed abroad in our hearts by the Holy Ghost which is given unto us."—Rom. 5:3-5.

Our restless hearts would feign cause us to flee from the trial, hoping for better conditions elsewhere; but we are called upon to be strong in the grace of endurance—to suffer in the flesh rather than yield to sin—to be persecuted even to death rather than to be disobedient to the heavenly vision—to be counted as the offscouring of the earth rather than to court the favor of men by unfaithfulness to Christ.

> **Should we to gain the world's applause,**
> **Or to escape its harmless frown,**
> **Refuse to countenance Thy cause**
> **   And make Thy people's lot our own,**
> **What shame would fill us in that day,**
> **When Thou Thy glory wilt display.**

How worthwhile will it all seem then, to have suffered in patience here, when we shine forth with Him when He comes, wearing the crown of life, the sign of His appreciation and approval! And if regrets are possible in Heaven, how will we regret every cowardly effort to escape reproach or every time that we, in weakness, yielded to temptation, preferring present enjoyment rather than future glory.

But the hope of the crown is not in itself incentive enough to keep us from unfaithfulness to Christ in this scene of testing. It is only as He Himself is the joy of our hearts and the present portion of our souls that we can resist the siren lures of this false world and go on in true devotedness, counting all but loss in order that He may be magnified in us. And it is as our hearts are attached to Him where He is—up there in the glory of God—that we can spurn this world's empty glory. Someone has truly said, "No one can rightly put this world beneath his feet until he has seen a better world above his head."

As we walk in the light of that world, we shall indeed be able to sing from the heart,

> **We wait for Thee, content to share**
> **In patience, days of trial;**
> **So meekly Thou the cross didst bear,**
> **Our sin, reproach, denial.**
> **How should not we receive with Thee**
> **The cup of shame and sorrow**
> **Until the promised morrow?**

That happy morn draws on apace. The only time we shall ever be permitted "to suffer for his sake," is nearly at an end! Let us then stand fast in the closing hours of the age of grace, assured that He for whom we wait is just at hand and that the joy will be His as well as ours when we receive, if faithful unto death, the crown of life.

Eternal life is the gift of God and is ours by faith upon believing. The crown of life is the reward for faithfulness, even though involving physical death.

CROWN OF GLORY

Of another crown we read in I Peter 5:1-4. He who had been specially deputed to feed the lambs and sheep of Christ's flock, writes:

"The elders which are among you I exhort, who am also an elder, and a witness of the sufferings of Christ, and also a partaker of the glory that shall be revealed; Feed the flock of God which is among you, taking the oversight thereof, not by constraint, but willingly; not for filthy

lucre, but of a ready mind; Neither as being lords over God's heritage, but being ensamples to the flock. And when the Chief Shepherd shall appear, ye shall receive a crown of glory that fadeth not away."

Every word in this stirring exhortation is of moment and may well be carefully weighed.

Note, first of all, that Peter, though one of the chiefest apostles of our Lord Jesus Christ and one to whom a special revelation and particular mission had been given, claims no authoritative place over other servants of Christ. He is "also an elder." That is, he writes of himself as a "co-presbyter"—one with his fellow-presbyters.

If Peter was the first pope, it is clear that he never knew it. He does not write as "the Holy Father" to whom others are, in duty bound, to be subject; but he exhorts his fellow-elders, as being himself one of their company.

It is true he had been privileged beyond most, if not all, of them. He had known the Lord, had companied with Him during His earthly ministry and had known Him after His resurrection. He had seen Him die—he was a witness (not a partaker) of His sufferings. He would share in the soon-coming glory.

Remembering the words of the risen Saviour, spoken so long ago that morning by the seaside, "Feed My lambs, shepherd My sheep," he passes on the exhortation to his brethren engaged in the work of ministering to the people of the Lord. Observe that he bids them, "Feed the flock of God"—not, "Fleece the flock."

Nothing can be more reprehensible than to think of a Christian church or assembly of believers as owing a living to the preacher or teacher who imparts the Word of life to them. He who thinks of the "ministry" as "one of the learned professions" and a mere means of livelihood, is on low ground indeed. The true minister of Christ is a man with a shepherd's heart who loves the flock and cares for them for the sake of Him who bought them with His blood. That they have responsibility to him is plain, but he looks not to them but to the Lord for his support.

And be it noted, the elders are not set over the flock (though indeed they are "over them in the Lord"), but they are told to "feed the flock of God which is among you." It is true they are to lead the sheep, as in Hebrews 13:17, where we read, "Obey them that have the rule over you [or, literally, that guide you], and submit yourselves: for they watch for your souls, as they that must give account, that they may do it with joy, and not with grief: for that is unprofitable for you."

In the assembly of God, if things are as they should be, there will be neither clerical pretension on the one hand nor anarchy on the other. The Christian company is a brotherhood where each should have in view the best interests of all the rest and where all the gifts given by the great Head of the church may be freely exercised for the blessing of the whole church.

To some is given in a special way the service of oversight, and such are bidden to care for the rest, not as by constraint, but willingly; that is, not as being pressed into a position from which a lowly man might well shrink but as gladly serving for Christ's sake. And although those who give their whole time to the ministry of the Word are to subsist upon what grateful saints gladly give (as unto the Lord), they are not to be controlled by covetousness, nor to serve for "filthy lucre."

Neither are they to "lord it over possessions." The word *"God's"* is in italics. The warning is really against regarding the saints as their own allotted portion.

Men speak (thoughtlessly often, no doubt) of "my church" or "my congregation"; but this is practically to deny and to forget that it is "His church" and "the congregation of the Lord," to which they may be called to minister.

It has been pointed out often that the word for *heritage* is *kleros*, from which we get our word *clergy*. And here, paradoxical as it may seem, *the laymen are the clergy!* All God's people are His clergymen, according as it is written, "The Lord's portion is his people."

What a solemn thing then to lord it over such! But how grateful such should be and how responsive to those who feed them as Christ's under-shepherds who are called upon not only to minister the Word but to be examples (or models of behavior) to the flock.

Alas, that ofttimes they find this a most thankless service. Their most earnest labors are frequently quite unappreciated; and they can say with Paul, "The more abundantly I love you, the less I [am] loved." But the "payday" is coming! When the Chief Shepherd shall be manifested, a crown of glory awaits every faithful servant who has cared for His lambs and sheep during His absence. The glory of this age passes away, but the crown of glory is unfading and eternal.

Often, down here, the faithful servant is called on to bear reproach and shame, to have his good evil spoken of and his motives impugned.

Men would crown him with thorns as they cruelly did to the Good Shepherd Himself—but even as He is now "crowned with glory and honour," so shall they who follow Him be in that day.

Go, labor on; spend and be spent;
Thy joy to do the Master's will,
It is the way the Saviour went,
Should not the saved one tread it still?

Then, when called to His judgment seat to give an account of the souls committed to his care, how will the true undershepherd rejoice as he hears, "Well done, good and faithful servant. Enter thou into the joy of thy Lord!" Then shall the unfading glory-crown encircle the head that often ached because of ingratitude and lack of appreciation here on earth, and the unchanging brilliance of the wreath that tells of divine appreciation will cover the brow that once was worn with care.

Striving Lawfully

Having noticed the various names given to the crowns of reward, I would now desire to emphasize some exhortations and warnings in regard to them which we find in the New Testament. We have already touched on the possibility of being disapproved at last if not careful to walk before God in self-judgment, keeping the physical appetites in subjection (I Cor. 9:27). And we have glanced also at II John 8: "Look to yourselves that we lose not those things which we have wrought, but that we receive a full reward."

It is self-evident then that the reward is forfeitable, though eternal life is not. How then may we, perchance, labor in vain and fail of the proffered crown?

Let us notice II Timothy 2:5. In the A.V. we read, "And if a man also strive for masteries, yet is he not crowned, except he strive lawfully."

The 1911 Version (Oxford) translates this verse as follows: "And if a man also contend in the games, yet is he not crowned if he have not observed the rules."

Here is a principle that is both important and far-reaching. The illustration is plain. In the athletic contests of the Greeks and Romans as amongst us today, there were certain recognized demands to which each contestant must conform. A youth might be strong and vigorous and display great prowess and ability; but if he failed to go by the rules of the game, he was disqualified and could not receive the victor's wreath.

At the celebrated revived Olympian games held at Stockholm, Sweden, some years ago, a young Indian, James Thorpe, excelled all others in a number of contests of strength and skill. He won many medals and was the envy of scores of white athletes, who tried in vain to defeat him. When the King of Sweden bestowed the prizes upon him, he took him by the hand and exclaimed, "You, sir, are the greatest amateur athlete in the world today!" It was a moment to be proud of, and the Indian could be excused if a feeling of gratified elation filled his breast at such a time.

But after his return to America certain men began an investigation into his past. Finally they discovered that one summer while still a student in a government school, Thorpe had played on a village baseball team for a few dollars a week. This fact disqualified him from entering an amateur contest.

When it was put before the king, he had to write to the Indian demanding the return of his trophies. The poor lad was nearly heartbroken, but he sent all back and wrote a straightforward letter in which he begged his Majesty not to think too hardly of him, reminding the king that he was "an ignorant Indian boy" who did not know he was violating any rule in entering the games after having taken money for sport.

But his ignorance of the requirements could not save him from losing his wrongly-bestowed honors. While no kindly person could feel other than sympathetic to Thorpe, yet all had to acknowledge the righteousness of the king's ruling.

And so will it be with those who are seeking after an incorruptible crown. The rewards will only be for those who "strive lawfully," who "have observed the rules" laid down in the Word of God.

There may be great self-denial, intense devotion and deep earnestness, while after all one's entire program of life and service may be thoroughly unscriptural. Therefore the need of knowing the Bible and "going by the Book."

Much that passes for Christian service today is merely fleshly activity. Much that is dignified as "church work" is thoroughly opposed to the divine revelation as to the church and its responsibilities. Much that is counted as evidence of spirituality is simply natural refinement and in no sense the result of the inworking of the Spirit of God. Much that is "highly esteemed among men" is an "abomination in the sight of God."

The service which will meet His approval and which will be rewarded at the judgment seat of Christ is that which is of the Holy Spirit in accordance with the Word of God. Nothing else will stand the test.

Men may weary themselves in seeking to "build up the cause," as it is called, and may display most commendable faithfulness to "principles" which they believe to be sound and right, only to find "in that day" that time and labor have gone for nought because they had no "thus saith the Lord" to warrant the efforts they have put forth. Our thoughts will not change God's Word.

It is of primary importance that the laborer devote much time to the prayerful conscientious study of his Bible in order that his mind may be directed by the Truth and that he may thus learn to readily detect what is contrary to sound instruction. Otherwise he may have to look back with regret on wasted energies and wasted years that might all have been devoted to the glory of Christ, but were devoted to the building up of some unscriptural system instead, and therefore will be consumed when "the fire shall try every man's work of what sort it is."

The apostle did not want to "run in vain" nor "labour in vain." Nor should we. Rather let us seek to make every day count for God as we pray, "Order my *steps* in Thy Word."

"Respect for the Reward"

But shall we work with reward in view? Is not this selfish? Is it not better to ignore this matter altogether and to work alone for Christ? These are questions often asked and not to be lightly turned aside.

Surely we would not have so many exhortations to see to it that we do not lose our reward if the Holy Spirit did not intend that we should have the crowns in view.

Of Moses we read that

"By faith [he], when he was come to years, refused to be called the son of Pharaoh's daughter; Choosing rather to suffer affliction with the people of God, than to enjoy the pleasures of sin for a season; Esteeming the reproach of Christ greater riches than the treasures in Egypt: for he HAD RESPECT unto the RECOMPENCE of the REWARD."—Heb. 11:24-26.

He weighed what Egypt could offer over against what God by His Word had promised to His people, and all Egypt's glory seemed lighter than air in comparison with the praise of God. Nor was it selfishness that thus led him to have "respect unto the recompence of the reward."

He knew that God is glorified, as His people learn to esteem His favors in the right light.

Years ago, after the present writer had been speaking along the lines of truth indicated in these papers, a modest Christian woman came up to him and asked, "Am I to understand that you are working for reward, that you are looking forward to receiving a crown?"

"Yes," was the reply; "I should rejoice indeed to be crowned by Him whose servant I am, in that day."

"Well," she exclaimed, "I am disappointed in you! I hoped you labored unselfishly out of pure love for Christ and not with any expectation of reward. For myself, I only desire to please *Him,* and I am not at all interested in the crowns."

"But, madam," she was asked, "do you recall what we are to do with the crowns if we are so happy as to win them?"

Instantly her face changed. "Oh," was the answer, "I had not thought of that. It does say somewhere—doesn't it?—that they cast their crowns at His feet!"

"Yes, that is it! And how sad it would be to have no crown in that day. You see we do not—we shall not—take any credit to ourselves for work performed, for service rendered here on earth; for when we have done all, we can but say, 'We are unprofitable servants; we have done that which it was our duty to do'; but we shall cast our crowns adoringly at His once pierced feet as we join in the song of praise, ' 'Tis Thou who art worthy, Lord Jesus. 'Tis Thou!' "

Her eyes filled with tears as she softly said, "I should indeed want a crown for that glorious occasion. I have been mistaken. I shall seek to labor for Him in view of the reward." And surely every blood-bought one instructed out of the Word will echo her sentiment.

It is good to remember how, while on earth, He was in the *habit* of saying (as the tense actually implies), "It is more blessed to give than to receive." So it will add to His joy to be able to bestow upon His victorious saints the reward which He has prepared aforehand for them. He would have each one to be numbered among those who keep the Word of His patience and overcome the world, in order that, having suffered with Him, they may reign with Him in the glory of the coming displayed kingdom.

When He comes forth to reckon with His servants and "to see what each one hath gained by trading" with the talents or pounds entrusted to him, it will be His delight to recognize what His grace has wrought in them by the power of the indwelling Holy Spirit. In honoring them He is really glorifying the Father's name and His own name.

Who in that day would be willing to miss His "Well done, good and faithful servant, enter thou into the joy of thy Lord"? And what satisfaction it will give to the one who has toiled on amid difficulty for Him in the day of His rejection when He says, "Thou hast been faithful in a few things; I will make thee ruler over many."

And yet it is not merely for crowns we labor, but that we may please Him who hath called us to be His soldiers. His approval will make up for all man's misunderstandings and persecutions. "Wherefore we labour, that, whether present or absent, we may be accepted of him."

But sometimes we fail to realize how appreciative He is of little things, of hidden devotion, of faithfulness in the daily round. We are too apt to think we must "do some great thing," serve in some public capacity, to earn the victor's wreath. But this is a mistake. He values all that is done out of love for Him, whether it be seen of men or not.

I recall a burdened little mother who said to me once:

> I cannot win a crown, for I have no opportunity to serve as I would like. In college I had dreams of a life devoted to Christ's work. I was a "student volunteer" and expected to become a missionary; but about the time I graduated, I met Charlie, and soon we were married. That ended my dreams of going out as a herald of the cross. In the years that have passed, ill health, the rearing of six children and much ill fortune financially have made it impossible for me to do anything for the Lord, and so I can never win a crown!

But I pointed out that the godly testimony of a devoted wife and mother, the rearing of a family for God, the example of a holy and consistent life—these were in the sight of God of great price; for these there is sure reward. And so indeed it is.

The busiest mother can run the Christian race and thus win the incorruptible crown.

The feeblest invalid can help to show someone the way of peace and so obtain the crown of rejoicing.

The most poverty-stricken saint can love His appearing and gain the crown of righteousness.

The humblest sufferer can be so devoted to Christ as to earn a crown of life.

And anyone who in any way ministers to the sheep or lambs of Christ's flock will surely receive the crown of glory when the Chief Shepherd shall appear.

What is needed is a heart for Christ. He will use all who are willing to let Him have His way with them. He who has saved by grace will surely reward in that day for the least service done for His own.

And now in closing may I affectionately press upon the Christian reader the Lord's own solemn warning to the Philadelphian church: "Behold, I come quickly: hold that fast which thou hast, that no man take thy crown" (Rev. 3:11).

Observe: *no* one can rob me of my salvation. Of this there is abundant evidence in Scripture. But another may take my crown if I prove faithless to the trust committed to me.

Each believer is a servant as well as a son. To each is given some special gift and some particular line of service. It may be of either a public or a private nature. But it is a stewardship committed to him of the Lord, and "it is required of stewards that a man be found faithful." If I do not exercise the ministry allotted to me, in humble dependence on the Holy Spirit that I may fulfill it faithfully, I may be set aside as a servant, and another be called to complete my work. And so I will lose my crown.

We have read of the tract distributor who, becoming discouraged because of apparent lack of appreciation, gave up his lowly service and learned twenty years after of one saved through a tract given out on the last day in which he did that work, who had taken it up himself as a ministry to needy men and after that long lapse of time met his benefactor and presented *him* with a tract. As a result a conversation sprang up which showed how the convert had taken the other's place, and the older man exclaimed with regret, "I see: I have let you take my crown!"

Let us remember, God is going to carry on His work in some way and by some instrumentality. May it be ours not to shirk responsibility but to say—and do—with Isaiah, "Here am I; send me."

ROBERT L. MOYER
1886-1944

ABOUT THE MAN:

Dr. Moyer was an evangelist from 1915-20, then became pastor of the United Brethren Church in Minneapolis. Later Dr. W. B. Riley asked him to become his assistant at First Baptist Church, Minneapolis. When Dr. Riley retired from the pastorate in 1942, Dr. Moyer then became pastor and served in that capacity until his death.

Dr. Moyer was long dean of Northwestern Bible School, and the author of several books.

Dr. H. A. Ironside said:

> Few men have the winsomeness and tenderness combined with sound scriptural teaching that characterizes the ministry of my esteemed friend and fellow-laborer, Dr. Robert L. Moyer.

VII.

The Great Tribulation

R. L. MOYER

"Will the church go through the Great Tribulation?" is a question of perennial interest and frequent discussion. Some answer emphatically, "No!" Others declare, "Yes!" Some teach that part of the church will go through all of the Tribulation; others, that all of the church will go through part of the Tribulation.

We shall answer from Scripture, although the question is stated in the theme as personal and individual: "Will YOU go through the Tribulation?"

I. TRIBULATION DESCRIBED

The Great Tribulation is a period of time still future. Alvord points out that this expression in Scripture (Rev. 7:14) might better be rendered, "The tribulation, the Great One." Scripture emphasizes the peculiarity of this period of time by declaring that nothing like it shall ever precede it or follow after it.

1. In the New Testament   *ch 4-19*

The major part of the book of Revelation is taken up with this period of time. The duration of it is stated as "forty and two months," a "thousand, two hundred and threescore days," "A time, and times, and half a time." This is three and one-half years. The description of the sufferings of that day is terrible.

It will be the day of a Devil-dominated world, when the saints who will not worship him shall be slain. The sun and the moon and the stars and the earth shall be smitten. The waters of the earth shall become as blood. Men shall gnaw their tongues with pain and blaspheme God. They will desire to die and will not be able. Their bodies will be smitten with sores and scorched with the sun. The pit of the abyss will be opened, and the world will suffer an invasion of the underworld, in the

9:7-10

form of infernal cherubim who will torment men like the torment of a scorpion. Words cannot describe the intensity of the sufferings of that day.

2. In the Old Testament

The Old Testament prophets foretell the Tribulation. Jeremiah calls it the time of "Jacob's trouble." He writes, "Alas! for that day is great, so that none is like it: it is even the time of Jacob's trouble; but he shall be saved out of it" (Jer. 30:7). It is a time of trouble and wrath upon the posterity of Jacob. Daniel declares, "There shall be a time of tribulation such as never was since there was a nation, even to that time, and at that time thy people shall be delivered" (Dan. 12:1). Joel prophesies, "The day of the Lord cometh, for it is nigh at hand; a day of darkness and gloominess. . .there hath not been ever the like" (Joel 2:1,2). Other prophets follow the same line of predictions.

Our Lord Himself specified the Tribulation: "For there shall be great tribulation, such as was not since the beginning of the world to this time, no, nor ever shall be" (Matt. 24:21).

II. PARTICIPANTS IDENTIFIED

Will YOU go through the Great Tribulation? This is a personal question, and we answer it on the supposition that the reader will be living when the Lord comes.

Will YOU go through the Great Tribulation? That all depends upon the class to which you belong. The Word of God divides the human race into three distinct classes. This threefold division is set forth in such passages as I Corinthians 10:32: "Give none offence, neither to the Jews, nor to the Gentiles, nor to the church of God."

Someone has truly said, "God, who is not a respecter of persons, is, beyond doubt, a regarder of classes." Whoever reads the Bible with careful attention cannot fail to see this truth. The Word of God is written FOR all persons, but not every part is ABOUT all persons. Whether or not you go through the Tribulation depends upon whether you are a Jew, a Gentile or a member of the body of which Christ is the Head—the church.

1. The Jew

Will YOU go through the Great Tribulation? If you are a Jew—YES!

By the Jews we mean the descendants of Abraham. A great portion of the Bible has to do with them—the nation Israel. They have a very distinct place in the plans and purposes of God. They were separated from the mass of mankind by Jehovah, who gave them specific promises never given to another nation. That nation is with us today, in unbelief. It is the miracle nation of all time and will yet be used by God to accomplish His own purpose, for "the gifts and calling of God are without repentance."

The Tribulation refers specifically to the nation of Israel, for it is very definitely called "the time of Jacob's trouble" (Jer. 30:7). The heavenly messenger told Daniel: "At that time shall Michael stand up, the great prince which standeth for the children of thy people [i.e., Daniel's people, the Jews] and there shall be a time of trouble, such as never was since there was a nation even to that same time" (12:1).

The Lord, in announcing the advent and nature of the Tribulation, used terms which could apply only to Israel, such as "let them that are in Judaea flee to the mountains"; "pray that your flight be not on the Sabbath day"; "when ye see the abomination of desolation, spoken of by Daniel, the prophet," etc. (Matt. 24:15-21; Luke 21:20). The Tribulation is the time of Israel's trouble because of her rejection of her Messiah.

Will YOU go through the Great Tribulation? If you are a Jew—Yes!

2. The Gentiles

Will YOU go through the Great Tribulation? If you are a Gentile—YES!

When God chose one nation and set that one nation over against all other nations, two classes of people were formed—the Jews and those who were not Jews—the Gentiles. God's Word always distinguishes between these two: "to the Jew first, and also to the Greek," "tribulation and anguish, upon every soul of man that doeth evil, of the Jew first, and also of the Gentile" (Rom. 1:16; 2:9). This distinction is always made in Scripture. Israel has never been "reckoned among the nations" (Num. 23:9).

The Tribulation is specially spoken of as "the time of Jacob's trouble," yet it will not be limited to Israel. It will cover the whole earth. *Flood?* The Antichrist will be the instrument of judgment in the Tribulation, and his empire will be universal, which means that the whole world will be involved. "Power was given him over all kindreds, and tongues, and nations. And all that dwell upon the earth shall worship him" (Rev. 13:7,8).

Revelation 7 makes plain the fact that many Gentiles will become

7:9,14

believers during the Tribulation period. (This is after the rapture of the church; hence, they will not be part of the body of Christ but will undoubtedly take their place among the saints of the pre-body period.)

John here sees a great unnumbered company, who have washed their robes and made them white in the blood of the Lamb. He is told that 'these are they which have come out of *the Great Tribulation'* (Rev. 7:14). They have had to pay for their faith with their lives. It is said that "they are of all nations, and kindreds, and people, and tongues" (7:9). This means, of course, that they are Gentiles, and that they have gone into the Tribulation.

Will YOU go through the Great Tribulation? If you are a Gentile—Yes!

3. The Church Exempted

Will YOU go through the Great Tribulation? If you are a member of the church, the body of Christ—NO!

The church is made up of believers on the Lord Jesus Christ, both Jews and Gentiles, who in Christ Jesus are neither Jew nor Gentile, but a new creation. Israel was the chosen nation through which all the other nations—that is, Gentiles—were to be blessed. This blessing of the nations through the Jews was to take place under the Christ, the Messiah of the Jews.

But when the Christ came, He was nailed to the cross. It was then that the sins of the whole world were laid upon Him. It was then that He who knew no sin was "smitten and afflicted of God" in the sinners' stead. It was then that He made expiation for sin. After His burial, He came forth from the dead and was preached to both Jew and Gentile; and when individuals of these two classes believed, they became members of the body of which Christ is the Head.

The church may, in fact should, suffer persecution or tribulation, in a general sense; for "all who live godly in Christ Jesus, shall suffer persecution" (II Tim. 3:12). The saints of God have always gloried in such persecution because they were "counted worthy to suffer for his name's sake."

Samuel Rutherford, in the midst of such persecution and suffering, could write,

> The Lord is with me. I care not what man can do. I burden no man, and I want nothing. No being is better provided for than I am. My chains are gilded over with gold. No pen, no words can express to you the loveliness of my only, only Lord Jesus.

There is a great difference, however, between suffering persecution for your faith at the hands of men and suffering the wrath of God in the Great Tribulation. The Tribulation is characterized as "the wine of the fierceness of the wrath of God," which is poured out upon a sinful and unrepentant world. Manifestly, the church cannot partake of this. Is the righteousness of God with which the saints are clothed so imperfect that they must pass through the fierceness of God's wrath? Did not God deal with our sins when they were laid on Christ? Would God be "faithful and righteous" if He were to plunge the church into that terrific judgment upon sin, after Christ bore her sins with their guilt and punishment? Someone has said, "Strange doctrine, indeed!" and we echo it—"Strange doctrine, indeed!" It is the doctrine of men, for there is not one syllable of Scripture to suggest it.

We are told in Romans 5:9, American Standard Version, that we are saved from "the wrath." Dr. F. E. Marsh, in commenting on this, said,

> God always protects His people before judgment comes. This is another reason why He will not allow the church to go through the Tribulation. Before the judgment of the Flood came, God took Enoch away. Lot must be safely out of Sodom before the avenging fire can fall from heaven. Noah and his family must be safe in the Ark before the waters of judgment begin their work of vengeance. The firstborn of Israel must be sheltered by the blood of the lamb before the Lord metes out judgment. The spies must be out of Jericho and Rahab's safety assured before the blast of the ram's horn proclaims the doom of the city. Surely when God says, "There is no condemnation to them who are in Christ Jesus," He means no kind of condemnation, and it would be a condemnation if a child of God were to come under the condemnation of the Great Tribulation in any way.

The two epistles to the Thessalonians deal almost entirely with the second coming of Christ. In 1:9,10 we are told that we who are saved "wait for the Lord from heaven . . . which delivereth [A.S.V.] us from the wrath to come." In 4:13-18 we are told that "the dead in Christ shall rise first: then we which are alive and remain shall be caught up together with them in the clouds, to meet the Lord in the air: and so shall we ever be with the Lord."

Following the rapture of the church, we have, in chapter 5, the Day of the Lord, which begins, as every student of the Word knows, with the Tribulation; and to emphasize the fact that the church has gone before, we are told that "God hath not appointed us to wrath, but to obtain salvation by our Lord Jesus Christ, Who died for us, that whether we wake or sleep [live or die], we should live together with him."

We submit, also, the fact that, when we are told that "the dead in Christ shall rise" and that "we which are alive and remain shall be caught up," the reference is to ALL and not to part of the church. First Corinthians 15:51-58 also refers to every believer. We need to remember that the rapture of the saints is a matter of grace and not of attainment. Our reward from the Lord depends upon our faithfulness, but our presence with the Lord depends upon His favor. Read chapter 2 of II Thessalonians in the American Standard Version. It teaches that the Antichrist, under whom the Tribulation is introduced and progresses, will not be revealed while the church is in the earth.

One thing to which we call special attention is the crushing argument that the theory of the church in the Tribulation makes us look for certain events rather than to look for our Lord. There are many events which must precede the Tribulation, such as the formation of the ten kingdoms of Daniel and Revelation and the manifestation of the Antichrist. It is true that "if the church is to go through the Tribulation, then our eyes are turned from Christ to coming events." Nowhere is the believer told the Lord comes for His people.

On the other hand, the New Testament abounds with exhortation to wait for Christ from Heaven. See such Scriptures as Romans 8:23; I Corinthians 1:7; Galatians 5:5; Philippians 3:20; I Thessalonians 1:10. Such an outlook as that of the passing through the Tribulation is never presented to the church as its objective.

Many, many other Scriptures might be introduced, had we the space, and all would be found harmonious. We quote Dr. William Evans, in closing:

> Not one single Scripture anywhere teaches that the church will go through the Tribulation. . . . Rightly interpreted, the Scripture nowhere teaches that the true church, the body of Christ, must endure the Tribulation.

Will YOU go through the Great Tribulation? If you are a member of the church, the body of Christ—NO! Ephesians tells us that God has broken down the middle wall between Jew and Gentile to make of the twain one new man. That new man is the church, made up of the saved. "If thou shalt confess with thy mouth the Lord Jesus, and shalt believe in thine heart that God hath raised him from the dead, thou shalt be saved" (Rom. 10:9).

TOM WALLACE
1930-

ABOUT THE MAN:

Dr. Tom Wallace has had a very busy and successful ministry.

After his conversion at General Motors Corporation in Wilmington, Delaware, he held noon services until he entered the ministry. And a busy, busy ministry it has been.

Dr. Wallace attended Tennessee Temple Schools and later on was on the staff of Highland Park Baptist Church, Chattanooga; pastored Baptist Bible Church, Elkton, Maryland, for 17 years. While there he founded Elkton Christian Schools; established a bus ministry with 18 routes; led the church in eight major building projects, increasing property values from $15,000 to $1,140,000; conducted two daily radio broadcasts; edited *The Visitor*, a monthly church newspaper.

Dr. Wallace served and is serving on many boards.

In 1971 he accepted the pastorate of Beth Haven Baptist Church, Louisville, Kentucky and remained there until 1986. Here many were saved. And in one year alone, he baptized more than 2,600 converts. While in Louisville, he founded Beth Haven Christian Schools and had six daily radio broadcasts.

In 1986 he went into full-time evangelism.

This warmhearted evangelist and conference speaker is widely sought after as speaker at Bible conferences, banquets, workers' meeting, soul-winning seminars, youth events, etc.

VIII.

A Thousand Years Extra in the Grave

TOM WALLACE

"But the rest of the dead lived not again until the thousand years were finished. This is the first resurrection. Blessed and holy is he that hath part in the first resurrection: on such the second death hath no power...."—Rev. 20:5,6.

Men have feared the grave since the beginning of death. The thought of dying sends a chill of terror into the soul, and the thought of lying in a coffin, worse yet.

In the misery of his suffering, Job said, "The grave is mine house: I have made my bed in the darkness" (Job 17:13).

Solomon said, "There is no work, nor device, nor knowledge, nor wisdom, in the grave, whither thou goest" (Eccles. 9:10).

But, hallelujah, there is hope! The sting has been removed. The grave has lost its victory. Man will get out of the grave. The glorious truth of the resurrection has taken the sting out of death for millions of souls.

The resurrection will not be the same for everybody. Some have already experienced resurrection; others will soon; but many will have to wait an extra thousand years to get out of their graves.

I want us to examine this Bible subject under four headings: the Resurrections of the Scripture, the Resurrection of the Saviour, the Resurrection of Saints, and the Resurrection of Sinners.

I. THE RESURRECTIONS OF THE SCRIPTURES

On eight different occasions in the Bible we read of miracle resurrections.

1. Elijah raised the widow's son. This widow had given

Elijah her last bit of meal and used the last of her oil to make him a cake. Elijah worked a miracle, and the meal barrel and the oil cruse were never empty again.

But in the midst of rejoicing and victory, the widow's son died. Elijah called out to God, and a physical resurrection took place for the first time in the history of man (I Kings 17:2).

2. Elisha raised the son of the Shunammite woman. This old couple was very gracious and kind to Elisha and his servant, Gehazi. They built a prophet's chamber onto their house. Elisha was so pleased that he prayed to God for them to be blessed with a son.

His prayer was answered. The son became the joy of their lives. One day the son died of a sunstroke, and the woman begged the prophet to pray. Elisha raised the boy from the dead and restored him to his mother (II Kings 4:35).

3. Resurrection by Elisha's bones. The Moabites were invading the land, and a man of Israel died. As they carried the man to his tomb, they saw the Moabites coming. Quickly, they threw the dead man into Elisha's cave. The Bible says that when the dead body fell on the bones of Elisha, life and breath came back into the body (II Kings 13:20).

4. Jairus' daughter raised. Jairus, a man of faith, pleaded with Jesus to come to his home and touch the body of his dead daughter that she might live. Jesus chased off the professional mourners and took the girl by the hand saying, Maid, arise"; and she did (Luke 8:54).

5. The widow's son at Nain. At the gate of the city of Nain, Jesus was filled with compassion when He saw the widow in the funeral procession of her son. In obedience to the command of Jesus, the young man arose and began to speak. What excitement must have filled the hearts of the people! What an experience for the mother! The Bible says, "And there came a fear on all: and they glorified God" (Luke 7:16).

6. Lazarus raised at Bethany. After Lazarus died, Jesus came to comfort Mary and Martha saying, "Thy brother shall rise again." Martha answered, "I know that he shall rise again in the resurrection at the last day" (John 11:24).

Jesus went to the grave and called out, "Lazarus, come forth." Jesus asked the disciples then to loose him and let him go. What a wonderful miracle for Mary, Martha, Lazarus and the world!

7. Dorcas raised by Peter. Dorcas was a wonderful woman and a disciple of the Lord. When she died, all her friends came to weep.

Peter was notified also about her death. He entered the room where her body was and asked the others to leave. He began to pray and then spoke, saying, "Tabitha, arise." And she sat up very much alive. The news spread quickly over the city of Joppa, and many were saved because of this miracle resurrection (Acts 9:42).

8. Bodies of the saints arose. When Jesus finished His seventh statement on the cross, He gave up the ghost. At that instant the veil was torn from top to bottom in the Temple, and an earthquake broke open the rocks. Many graves opened also, and the bodies of many saints arose and appeared in the city. The leader of the soldiers said, "Truly this was the Son of God" (Matt. 27:54).

Congress once issued a special edition of Thomas Jefferson's Bible. It was simply a copy of our Bible with all references to the supernatural taken out. The resurrections of the Scripture were not included in his Bible. The closing words of his "book" were: "There laid they Jesus, and rolled a great stone to the mouth of the sepulchre."

Thank God, our Bible does not stop at His death! There is another chapter in the story. He arose again!

II. THE RESURRECTION OF THE SAVIOUR

The Moslems say, "We have something you Christians do not have." "What is that?" asked a Christian of a Moslem. "We have a body, and you only have an empty tomb."

How right they are, and praise God for it! He is risen!

First, Christ's resurrection is prophesied. Job said, "For I know that my redeemer liveth, and that he shall stand at the latter day upon the earth" (Job 19:25).

David said prophetically, "For thou wilt not leave my soul in hell; neither wilt thou suffer thine Holy One to see corruption" (Ps. 16:10).

Second, Christ's resurrection was proclaimed in the New Testament. He said Himself, "Destroy this temple, and in three days I will raise it up" (John 2:19). He also said, "But after I am risen again, I will go before you into Galilee" (Matt. 26:32). After returning from the Mount of Transfiguration, He charged them not to tell what they had seen "till the Son of man were risen from the dead" (Mark 9:9).

Third, Christ's resurrection was preached by the apostles. Of the first church at Jerusalem, we read, "And with great power gave the apostles witness of the resurrection of the Lord Jesus: and great grace was upon them all" (Acts 4:33).

Peter preached to Cornelius and his loved ones, "Him God raised up the third day, and shewed him openly" (Acts 10:40).

Paul, preaching at Mars' Hill, spoke of the unknown God whom they worshiped as one that had risen from the dead (Acts 17:31). Some mocked, others were curious, but some believed.

Fourth, Christ's resurrection was proven. In Acts 1:3 we read, "He shewed himself alive...by many infallible proofs."

The resurrection is mentioned over one hundred times in the Bible.

In our courts, one witness can establish a murder charge, two witnesses are necessary to prove treason, three witnesses are needed to establish a written will; and seven, for an oral will. Many more than five hundred witnesses were called to verify the personal resurrection of Christ!

He appeared to Mary Magdalene (Mark 16:9); the other women (Matt. 28:9); two disciples (Luke 24:15); eleven disciples (Luke 24:36); Peter (I Cor. 15:5); to the ten with Thomas absent (John 20:19); to the eleven disciples (John 20:26); at the Sea of Galilee (Matt. 28:17); to James (I Cor. 15:7); at the ascension (Luke 24:50); and to Paul at his conversion (Acts 9:5).

During Napoleon's war on England, he came to the battle with Wellington at Waterloo. The battle was heavy and bloody; but eventually the shooting ceased, and the war was over.

There was no telegraph or telephone to send the news home. The only means of communication was signals from metaphor flags. As the ship approached the dock, the signal man waved out the message to the waiting people of the British Isles, W-E-L-L-I-N-G-T-O-N D-E-F-E-A-T-E-D. Just then a cloud of fog hid the signalman. The shocking news spread like fire and the gloom and despair with it.

Later when the fog lifted and the completed signal was read, "W-E-L-L-I-N-G-T-O-N D-E-F-E-A-T-E-D N-A-P-O-L-E-O-N," a cry of victory rang out through the land. The message had been changed from despair to a shout of victory by adding just one word.

The cry went out to the disciples of the Lord, "Jesus is dead and buried." A gloom and despair settled over all His followers. But then came the shout, "He is risen! He is risen!"

> **Rejoice ye Christians, everywhere!**
> **From that dark tomb so sad.**
> **Christ is risen; He's not there!**
> **Rejoice and be ye glad!**

III. THE RESURRECTION OF THE SAINTS

"Marvel not at this: for the hour is coming, in the which all that are in the graves shall hear his voice, And shall come forth; they that have done good, unto the resurrection of life. . . . "—John 5:28,29.

Before Columbus sailed across the Atlantic in 1492, the motto of Spain was: **"Nothing Beyond,"** which motto appeared on the official seal of the country. The meaning of these two words was simply that Spain was the last westward spot on the globe before the vast nothingness. When Columbus later took back gold and living natives from the New World to prove his discovery, the old motto was changed to the new one, **"More Beyond."**

There are still some people who think that the grave ends all, but we have a lively hope in Christ. There is "more beyond." There is life after death and Heaven forever for all believers.

Read what Peter said about this in I Peter 1:3-5:

"Blessed be the God and Father of our Lord Jesus Christ, which according to his abundant mercy hath begotten us again unto a lively hope by the resurrection of Jesus Christ from the dead, To an inheritance incorruptible, and undefiled, and that fadeth not away, reserved in heaven for you, Who are kept by the power of God through faith unto salvation ready to be revealed in the last time."

Jesus said, "I am the resurrection, and the life: he that believeth in me, though he were dead, yet shall he live" (John 11:25).

John said, "And this is the will of him that sent me, that every one which seeth the Son, and believeth on him, may have everlasting life: and I will raise him up at the last day" (John 6:40).

Paul said, "Knowing that he which raised up the Lord Jesus shall raise up us also by Jesus, and shall present us with you" (II Cor. 4:14).

Now the blessed part of this resurrection is that we shall be given our glorified bodies. This will take place at the rapture. At this time, "the dead in Christ shall rise" (I Thess. 4:16). Those outside of Christ, the unsaved, will remain in the grave and will not come forth for another thousand years.

An army chaplain told of accompanying a regiment of soldiers on an overnight training session. They camped in an open field and bedded down in row after row pattern. That night a light snow fell and turned to freezing rain. Each sleeping soldier snuggled in his sleeping bag formed a white, icy mound on the ground.

The chaplain arose early and, looking out across the sleeping soldiers, remarked that it looked like rows of graves. Just then the bugler blew reveille, and the men came breaking up through the snow and ice. "What a thrilling sight!" exclaimed the chaplain. "It was like witnessing the resurrection."

Someday it will happen just like that for every child of God!

IV. THE RESURRECTION OF THE SINNER

"But the rest of the dead lived not again until the thousand years were finished."—Rev. 20:5.

The people of this second resurrection will appear at the great white throne judgment, a judgment for sinners who have rejected Christ. These people were condemned already even before they died. However, the sentence will not be passed on them until after their resurrection.

The people of this resurrection will be cast into the lake of fire. The beast and false prophet will have already been cast into this same lake of fire (Rev. 19:20). Satan, the old serpent, will also be there in the fire (Rev. 20:10). The second death and eternal Hell are a part of this lake of fire (Rev. 20:14). What a sad, pitiful thing this will be for the poor sinners with no Saviour!

Then, the people of this resurrection will lie in the grave for one thousand years. During the one thousand years, the saints who are already out of the grave will be involved in the wonderful millennium period. Christ will be reigning from Jerusalem from the throne of David. We shall be kings and priests. Those who have been faithful in this life will be ruling over cities with Him and for Him.

To rule and reign with Christ during the thousand years beats lying in the grave during that time. It doesn't make sense to be lost and bound for Hell.

My friend, if you are still not saved, may I urge you to repent today and receive Christ as your Saviour. Let Him get you out of the grave a thousand years early!

R. A. TORREY
1856-1928

ABOUT THE MAN:

Torrey grew up in a wealthy home, attended Yale University and Divinity School, and studied abroad. During his early student days at Yale, young Torrey became an agnostic and a heavy drinker. But even during the days of his "wild life," he was strangely aware of a conviction that some day he was to preach the Gospel. At the end of his senior year in college, he was saved.

While at Yale Divinity School, he came under the influence of D. L. Moody. Little did Moody know the mighty forces he was setting in motion in stirring young R. A. Torrey to service!

After Moody died, Torrey took on the world-girdling revival campaigns in Australia, New Zealand, England and America.

Like many another giant for God, Torrey shone best, furthest and brightest as a personal soul winner. This one man led 100,000 to Christ in a revival that circled the globe!

Dr. Torrey's education was obtained in the best schools and universities of higher learning. Fearless, quick, imaginative and scholarly, he was a tough opponent to meet in debate. He was recognized as a great scholar, yet his ministry was marked by simplicity.

It was because of his outstanding scholastic ability and evangelistic fervor that Moody handpicked Torrey to become superintendent of his infant Moody Bible Institute. In 1912, Torrey became dean of BIOLA, where he served until 1924, pastoring the Church of the Open Door in Los Angeles from 1915-1924.

Torrey's books have probably reached more people indirectly and helped more people to understand the Bible and to have power to win souls, than the writings of any other man since the Apostle Paul, with the possible exceptions of Spurgeon and Rice. Torrey was a great Bible teacher, but most of all he was filled with the Holy Spirit.

He greatly influenced the life of Dr. John R. Rice.

IX.

The Destiny of the Christless Dead

R. A. TORREY

Most Scriptures quoted are from American Standard Version of 1901.

The first thing I wish to state is that the Bible is the sole guide to the truth on this subject. We know absolutely nothing about future punishment but what God has been pleased to tell us in the Book; just as we know absolutely nothing about the future blessedness of the saved except what God has been pleased to tell us in this Book. If you are truly logical and not merely sentimental, if you give up what the Bible teaches on the one subject, you will give up what it teaches on the other. If a man will believe that part of the Bible that he desires to believe and reject that part of the Bible that he does not desire to believe, in plain unvarnished English, he is a fool.

If the Bible is not true, we have no conclusive proof that there is either a Heaven or a Hell. And if it is true about one, it is true also about the other. Some men may be able to believe what they want to believe but to doubt or deny what they want to doubt or deny. I am not built that way. My wishes play no part in my decision. I have to be governed by my intellect; but, of course, I know that a will surrendered to the truth and to God does more than anything else to clarify the intellect.

So our whole inquiry will be, "What does the Bible teach on this subject?" Some people are always running off onto their reasoning, but speculation on this subject is necessarily entirely vain. On such a subject as this one the ounce of God's revelation is worth a thousand tons of man's speculation.

I sometimes show men what the Bible teaches on this subject and they say, "But how do you reconcile that with the love of God?" I reply, "How do you know God is love?" We owe that truth entirely to the

Bible. If the Bible is not true, we have no proof that God is love; and if you reject what the Bible teaches about future punishment and are logical, you must also give up your belief that God is love, and your whole foundation for your universalistic and kindred hope is gone.

Immeasurable Suffering for Christ-Rejecting Sinners

First, then, the Bible teaches that as a result of sin, and especially of the crowning sin of rejecting the Saviour, there is to be after death an immeasurable suffering for those who sin in this life and do not repent of their sins and accept Christ.

There is no need to dwell at length on that point. The old crude form of Universalism, that no matter how a man lives in this life he enters at once into blessedness at death, has largely disappeared, except from funeral sermons. If that were true, the kindest thing that we could do for people in the slums and other unfortunates would be to put them to death at once in some painless way.

But take one Bible statement, and this statement gives the words of Jesus: "And if thy right eye causeth thee to stumble, pluck it out, and cast it from thee: for it is profitable for thee that one of thy members should perish, and not thy whole body be cast into hell" (Matt. 5:29). Certainly these words of our Lord mean that there is to be after death, for those who sin and do not repent, such intense suffering that the greatest possible present calamity would be preferable to it.

Bodies in Hell, Too

The second thing that the Bible teaches about future punishment is that the body shall share with the soul in the suffering of the lost in the world to come. Take the verse that we have just quoted. In this Jesus Christ says, "the body"—and by the body He certainly means just what He says, "the body"—"shall be cast into hell." Take another utterance of our Lord: "And be not afraid of them that kill the body, but are not able to kill the soul: but rather fear him who is able to destroy both soul and body in hell" (Matt. 10:28).

Here is the most distinct and definite statement possible that the body as well as the soul is to suffer in the "destruction" of Hell. Neither the blessed nor the lost are to exist in the world to come as disembodied spirits. There is to be a resurrection of the just and the unjust. This our Lord definitely declares in John 5:28,29: "The hour cometh, in which all that are *in the tombs* shall hear his voice, and shall come forth; they that have done good, unto the resurrection of life; and they that have done evil, unto the resurrection of judgment." Resurrection has to do with the body and the body only. The spirit does not tumble down and decay; therefore it needs no resurrection.

The passage just quoted says, ". . . all that are in the tombs." What is "in the tombs"? The body, and the body only. The spirits of the lost at death go into Hades; the body (and the body only) into the tomb where it crumbles into dust. At the resurrection the body is raised and the spirit joins it. At death the spirits of the saved depart to be with Christ in conscious blessedness; which Paul says is very far better than the most blessed experience in the body in our present lives (Phil. 1:21-23).

The bodies of the blessed who pass away before our Lord returns crumble into dust. At the second coming of Christ the bodies of the blessed are raised and reunited with the redeemed spirits. The redeemed spirit hereafter at the second coming of Christ shall be clothed upon with a redeemed body, fit partner of the redeemed spirit that inhabits it, and partaker with it in all of its joy; and the lost spirit shall be clothed upon with a lost body, fit partner of the lost spirit that inhabits it, and partaker with it in all its misery.

While the bodily torments of Hell are not the most important feature of future punishment, while the mental agony, the agony of remorse, the agony of shame, the agony of despair, are worse, immeasurably worse; nevertheless, bodily suffering, a bodily suffering in comparison with which no pain on earth is as anything, is a feature of future punishment.

Conscious Suffering in Hell

In the third place, the Bible teaches that the sufferings of the lost will be conscious, that the lost will not be annihilated or simply exist in non-conscious existence.

This is the plain teaching of Luke 16:19-31, the story of the rich man and Lazarus in the future world. All manner of allegorizing has been used in attempting to explain away these words of our Lord, but these allegorical explanations are simply ridiculous. The same thing is clearly taught in Revelation 14:9-11 compared with Revelation 20:10.

In Revelation 14:9-11 we read,

"If any man worshippeth the beast and his image, and receiveth a

*mark on his forehead, or upon his hand, he also shall drink of the wine
of the wrath of God, which is prepared unmixed in the cup of his anger;
and he* **shall be tormented** *with fire and brimstone in the presence
of the holy angels, and in the presence of the Lamb: and the smoke
of their torment goeth up for ever and ever;* **and they have no rest
day and night,** *they that worship the beast and his image, and whoso
receiveth the mark of his name.*"

Now this certainly describes conscious suffering of the intensest kind
and cannot be fairly and honestly interpreted in any other way. In Revelation 20:10 we read, "And the devil that deceived them was cast into
the lake of fire and brimstone, where are also the beast and the false
prophet; and they shall be tormented day and night for ever and ever."

These words unmistakably speak of conscious torment! We are told
that they shall have no rest 'day nor night,' which would be impossible
language to use by any honest speaker or writer if the punishment were
unconscious.

Future Destiny Determined by Trusting
or Rejecting Christ

The fourth thing that the Bible teaches about future punishment is
that the future destiny of the individual depends entirely upon what he
does with Jesus Christ.

One passage is sufficient to show that, though a multitude might be
adduced. That passage is John 3:36: *"He that believeth on the Son
hath eternal life; but he that believeth not the Son shall not see life,
but the wrath of God abideth on him.*"

Future Punishment Endless

The fifth thing that the Bible teaches on this subject is that future
punishment is endless.

In Matthew 25:41-46 our Lord Himself is recorded as saying, "Then
shall he say also unto them on the left hand, Depart from me, ye
cursed, into the *eternal* fire which is prepared for the devil and his
angels. . . . And these [i.e., these on the left hand] shall go away into
eternal punishment: but the righteous into *eternal* life."

It is often said that the word *aionios* used in these two verses does
not *by its etymology* necessarily imply endlessness. Even were we to
admit, which we do not, that this were true, every scholar knows that

it is one of the laws of the interpretation of any book that the meaning of words in any language or any book must be determined by usage.

What is the usage in this case? This word is used seventy-two times in the New Testament. Forty-four of these seventy-two times it is used in the phrase "eternal life." That "eternal life" is endless, cannot be questioned. It is used fifteen times in connections where the idea of endlessness is absolutely necessary. This covers fifty-nine of the seventy-two instances in which the word is used. In the fifty-nine instances the thought of endlessness is absolutely necessary. In not a one of the remaining thirteen cases is it used of anything that is known to end.

If usage can determine anything, it determines to a demonstration that the usage of this word in the New Testament necessarily implies endlessness.

But that is not all. The context as well as the usage demands that in this instance, in connection with punishment, the word must imply endlessness. The context is this: "And these shall go away into *eternal* punishment: but the righteous into *eternal* life." The same Greek word is used twice. As our Lord was at least an honest man, He could not use the one word twice in the same sentence with a different meaning. And if that life into which the righteous go away is endless life, then the punishment into which the cursed go is endless also. This cannot be denied without questioning either the intelligence or honesty of the Lord Jesus.

But even that is not all. We read in the passage in Revelation 14:9-11, which we have already quoted, that the sufferings of the lost are "for ever and ever," and that throughout this "for ever and ever" they "have no rest day nor night." Here another Greek expression is used. There are two forms of this expression: "the ages of the ages"; the other is "unto the ages of the ages," the only difference between the two being the omission of the article in the latter form.

Now these expressions are used twelve times in the last book of the Bible. In eight of these twelve instances the expression refers to the duration of the existence or reign or glory of God or Christ. Once it is used of the duration of the blessed reign of the righteous. And in three remaining instances it is used of the duration of the torment of the Devil, the beast, the false prophet and the impenitent.

If we deal honestly with the words of our Lord Jesus Christ and of the inspired apostles, it is impossible to read the doctrine of endless conscious suffering of those who reject Christ out of the Bible. If anyone could produce me one single passage in the Bible that, fairly construed, according to its context and the usage of the words and grammatical construction, that clearly taught that the punishment of the wicked would not be absolutely endless and that somewhere, sometime, somehow all would repent and be saved, it would be the happiest day of my life.

But no such passage can be found. I have searched for it from the first chapter of Genesis to the last chapter of the Revelation but cannot find it; it is not there. I am thoroughly familiar with the passages that men urge. I have formerly used them myself, but they will not bear the construction that is put upon them if we deal honestly with them.

Hell or Heaven Settled on Earth

In the sixth place, the Bible teaches that the question of our eternal destiny is settled this side of the grave.

We read in II Corinthians 5:10, "For we must all be made manifest before the judgment-seat of Christ; that each one may receive *the things done in the body,* according to what he hath done, whether it be good or bad." Now of course this has to do primarily with the judgment of believers, but it shows that the eternal judgment is determined by what is done *"in the body,"* what is done this side of the grave, what is done before we shall "shuffle off this mortal coil."

In Hebrews 9:27 we read, "It is appointed unto men once to die, and after this cometh judgment." The meaning of this is plain; namely, the eternal judgment is determined before death. But our Lord Jesus says the decisive word, the word that would be decisive if it stood alone. In John 8:21, "I go my way and ye shall seek me, and shall die in your sins: whither I go, ye cannot come." Here our Lord says plainly that those who die in their sins cannot go where He does, that the destinies of the future are settled in the life that now is, settled this side the grave.

The Bible does not hold out one ray of hope to any man who dies without having accepted Jesus Christ as Saviour in the life that now is. Many there are who undertake to do this. They are taking a terrible responsibility upon themselves. They dare to do what the divinely-inspired authors of the Bible have not done. They lull men to sleep in sin and worldliness and inaction.

What shall the harvest be? Are you sure of your eternal destiny?

BASCOM RAY LAKIN
1901-1984

ABOUT THE MAN:

On June 5, 1901, a baby boy was born to Mr. and Mr. Richard Lakin in a farmhouse on Big Hurricane Creek in the hill country of Wayne County, West Virginia. Mrs. Lakin had prayed for a "preacher man" and had dedicated this baby to the Lord even before he was born.

Lakin was converted in a revival meeting at age 18. Following his conversion, he became a Baptist preacher. With a mule for transportation, he preached in small country churches in the mountains and hills of West Virginia and Kentucky. The transportation changed as well as the size of his congregations.

In 1939, he became associate pastor of Cadle Tabernacle, Indianapolis, and upon the death of Founder Cadle, became pastor of that once great edifice of evangelism that seated 10,000, and had a choir loft of 1,400. Lakin preached to over 5,000 on Sunday mornings and half that many on Sunday nights.

Cadle Tabernacle had no memberships. It was a radio-preaching center broadcasting from coast to coast. In those fourteen years there, Ray Lakin became a household word across America.

In 1952, he entered full-time evangelism. His ministry carried him around the world, resulting in an estimated 100,000 conversions, and legion the number entering the ministry.

He was the preacher's friend, the church's helper, the common man's leader, and for sixty-five years, God's mighty messenger.

He was one of the most sought-after gospel preachers in America. On March 15, 1984, the last of the old-time evangelists took off for Glory. He would soon have been 83.

X.

"...But After This the Judgment"

B. R. LAKIN

Let me open the Bible with you tonight to chapter 9 of the book of Hebrews, beginning with verse 23:

"It was therefore necessary that the patterns of things in the heavens should be purified with these; but the heavenly things themselves with better sacrifices than these. For Christ is not entered into the holy places made with hands, which are the figures of the true; but into heaven itself, now to appear in the presence of God for us: Nor yet that he should offer himself often, as the high priest entereth into the holy place every year with blood of others; For then must he often have suffered since the foundation of the world: but now once in the end of the world hath he appeared to put away sin by the sacrifice of himself. [Other men have been stoned, other men have been beaten, other men have been crucified, other men have been hounded by the godless crowd; but of no other man has it ever been said, or of no other man could it ever be said, that by his death he put away the sin of the world.] *And as it is appointed unto men once to die, but after this the judgment: So Christ was once offered to bear the sins of many; and unto them that look for him shall he appear the second time without sin unto salvation."*—Vss. 23-28.

Let me call your attention to that old familiar text, "And as it is appointed unto men once to die, but after this the judgment" (Heb. 9:27). "TO DIE" is written over the door facing of every man's soul that ever comes into this world. Only two men ever got out of this world without dying. One was Enoch, who "walked with God: and he was not; for God took him"; the other, Elijah, who went up by a whirlwind into the heavens. All others have had to die; even the Son of God Himself died upon a cross. And if Jesus tarries, each man and woman, boy and girl in this auditorium tonight, and the thousands listening by means of radio, will someday have to pass through the portals of death and out into eternity.

"TO DIE. . . ." "TO DIE. . . ." I read in the Old Testament about the men and women who lived to be eight or nine hundred years old, five hundred, six hundred; but it always wound up by saying, " . . . and he died." So tonight "TO DIE" is written over the door facing of your soul, and death comes sometimes at a most unexpected moment. The fact is, the disease that is going to take your life may already be in your body. You do not know; therefore, you ought to be ready.

You say, "Well, Dr. Lakin, I'm not afraid to die."

Sam Jones went home one day, and his wife said to him, "Sam, I want you to go see the old sheriff who is dying."

Sam said to his wife, "Honey, you know he has never believed in God. He's an infidel; he's an atheist."

"But I want you to go see him."

Sam Jones later told the story:

> I went to see him. I asked, "Sheriff, are you afraid to die?"
>
> He answered, "Sam, I've always told you that I wasn't afraid to die."
>
> I knelt down a little closer to him and asked, "But, Sheriff, what about the judgment?"
>
> He almost threw himself off the bed when he said, "My God! I hadn't thought of that!"

Listen to me, my friend. If we lived like a brute and died like a brute and they shoveled us back into the earth and that was the last of us, that wouldn't be so bad. But after that. . . *after that*. . .! And that's the thing I want to talk to you about tonight. " . . . after this *the judgment*."

There are many things about the judgment day that I do not know. There are some things that I do know about it, and I want to bring them to your attention. Remember this:

THE JUDGMENT COMES AFTER DEATH

I do not know what it is or what it is like, but the one thing is: it comes after death, and death comes sometimes when you least expect it. Some of you listening to me tonight, remember this: you are twenty-four hours nearer the judgment tonight than you were last night; you have twenty-four hours' more sin on you tonight to meet the judgment in than you had last night; and you have twenty-four hours' less chance to get ready for it tonight than you had last night. "...after this the judgment."

A friend of many years, now in Heaven, said he was preaching one night in Washington, D.C. He went back and asked a man, "Are you a Christian?"

The man shrugged his shoulders and said, "I'm all right."

That night as the man's worldly wife went out of the choir, she said, "Why did Dr. _____ want to embarrass my husband? He's all right."

About ten days later my friend was back in the city to lecture. His phone rang in the hotel, and the lady said, "Dr. _____, I want you to come quickly. My husband is dying!"

He got in a cab, rushed across the city and up to the door. The lady met him at the door and said, "Go in and pray with him."

The good doctor said, "He's all right."

She said, "Why do you say that? Why do you say that?"

He said, "Do you remember ten days ago when I tried to lead him to Jesus Christ, you haughtily said, 'He's all right'?"

"But," she said, "my God, Dr. _____, he wasn't *dying* that night!"

The preacher went on into the man's room, and the dying man said, "Pray for me, please."

My friend said, "You're all right."

"Oh," he said, "why do you mock me?"

Dr. _____ said, "Do you remember ten days ago when I tried to lead you to Christ, and you haughtily said, 'I'm all right'?"

The man said, "But I wasn't *dying* that night!"

You feel you are not dying tonight, and that's the reason you're unconcerned. Out yonder in the heavens are thousands of worlds sparkling in the sky, many of them many, many times larger than this little speck upon which we live called the Earth. When I walk out of this building and down the street, I pay very little attention to those stars. I'm not concerned about them; I am not interested in them. Why? Because they seem to be so far away.

Listen, do you know why you're not interested in death, Hell, judgment and eternity? Because they seem so far away. When you're down yonder beneath the old oxygen tent and the doctor is shaking his head and looking concerned, it will not seem so far away then.

THE JUDGMENT IS CERTAIN

If you were to cease to breathe tonight where you sit, you would not pass into the "nowhere." You would not be a nonentity; you would be *somebody,* and you would be *somewhere.*

I know people who live in sin and who live like brutes and who would like to think they would die like brutes and that would be the end of it. People living in sin tonight may scoff at the fact of the judgment, may scoff at the fact of a life beyond; but remember this: you may scoff, you may laugh, but you will never be able to laugh the fact away. You will never be able to scoff it out of this Book tonight because "For ever, O Lord, thy word is settled in heaven" (Ps. 119:89). It may not be settled in some universities and colleges and seminaries, but you put it down tonight—it is forever settled in Heaven! The stars may fall and the mountains crumble to dust and the empires cease; but Thy Word, O God, will abide forever! You will never get around it.

So the certainty of the judgment day out yonder before you is true. Why? Because God said He hath appointed, He has fixed a day in the which He is going to judge this world in righteousness. *God* hath appointed or fixed. I do not know when that day will be, but I know this: in the calendar of God, the judgment day is a future, definite, fixed event the same as Fourth of July, New Year's, Christmas or any other holiday is fixed in our calendar. God said He hath "appointed a day, in the which he will judge the world in righteousness by that man whom he hath ordained [Christ Jesus]; whereof he hath given assurance unto all men, in that he hath raised him from the dead" (Acts 17:31).

Laugh at it tonight if you will, but you will never laugh it away. Scoff at it if you will, but you will never scoff it away. It is going to stand out there—the judgment day. God said, "I have fixed it, and it is an absolute certainty."

In the days of Noah, folks must have laughed at the idea of a judgment, when Noah, that faithful preacher, went out there and said, "God is fed up with this whole mess, and the vials of His wrath have filled up and are about ready to overflow. Pretty soon God is going to pour out His wrath upon this whole earth, upon this antediluvian world; and He's going to put the waterworks to it, scrub it, scour it until it will be a fit place for decent people to live." God announced that He was going to sink it beneath the flood waters; but He said, "Noah, you build you an ark for the saving of you and your house."

Noah went out and preached that God was going to bring a judgment day. And you know what they said? Dr. Broadmouth and

Dr. Wigglejaw and Professor So-and-So down yonder in the college and the university laughed at him. People said to them, "What do you think about that kind of preaching that Brother Noah's doing?" They answered, "Well, Noah is a pretty good country preacher, but he's got a little roof trouble and his trolley's off, so don't pay him much mind."

But one day God said, "Noah, it is all over. It is time to come in." The ark had been completed, and Noah came in. But that morning when the animals started coming up out of the jungles and the forest two by two, people asked the critics, "What do you think of this?" The critics said, "It is quite a phenomenon; but it is unscientific to believe there will be any rain because only a mist has gone up from the earth."

Then God said, "Noah, take your family and go in," and he went in. Then God shut him in; and when God shut him in, the clouds began to roll up. It got dark above, and the earth trembled from beneath. Then the waters came up, and the waters came down!

And when the floods descended and the rain came, do you know what the people did? They got out their little johnboats and their little rafts and started manufacturing some sort of conveyances for themselves. Somehow they had had them all along, and their boats were just as good as Noah's ark—as long as the sun was shining. But when the test came, when the judgment came, they found theirs were inadequate.

A lot of you listening to me tonight have your little religious raft, your little raft of skepticism, your little raft of liberalism, your little evolutionistic raft—you've got it all! And you know something? As long as you're healthy and have red blood in your veins, they're just as good as the old-time religion. But, brother, when the undertaker backs the hearse up at the door, you'll want the old-time religion then because you'll want something that stands.

In the days of Lot they mocked it, too; but just as in the days of Noah the Flood came, in the days of Lot the fire fell from Heaven. And when the fire fell from Heaven and Lot and his two daughters had escaped, the cities of the plains burned up.

Every one of God's judgments, every one of God's predictions about judgments in the past have come true. And just as every one came true in the past, every one of God's predicted judgments in the future will come true, in spite of all the false hopes and false theories that are held up by all the false prophets and modernistic preachers. Every one of them will come true.

And so, my friend, remember this: the judgment day is as certain as the sun to come up in the morning—more certain.

You say, "Brother Lakin, it doesn't include me." Yes, because

THE JUDGMENT IS UNIVERSAL

You may get away from some things, but God is going to judge the *world*. I don't mean just a few people on the other side of the tracks, just a few poor, ignorant people. A preacher said to me not long ago, "I have to have a revival every now and then in my church to satisfy that class of people." He said, "The more intellectual, the more cultured in my congregation don't believe in it; but I have to do it to satisfy these others."

My friend, when judgment day comes, you are going to stand before God regardless of race or standing or culture or condition. The woman who sparkles and scintillates with diamonds and rustles in silks and satins will stand before God the same as the woman who cleans and scrubs her floors, because it will not be a class proposition. You are going to face God.

You may not think so, you may not like it, but God said you are going to stand before Him. When that time comes, you will not evade it, avoid it, nor escape it. You are going to have to stand, and you will be brought there and kept until your case is settled.

I have had people escape me while I have been preaching. I have had people get mad and leave the meeting. I have had people say, "I don't go to revivals." But I tell them, "There is one meeting you're going to attend. There is one meeting when you are going to be there."

Every unsaved man, every hypocritical church member, there is one meeting you're going to be in and that is the meeting at the judgment bar of God. You will not run out; you will not get away. You will stay there until your case is settled.

God is bringing some of you to that meeting tonight. Out yonder in Heaven when God got ready to bring you to judgment, you know what He did? He dispatched a deputy sheriff from the Glory one day and touched your hair, and it became gray. He dispatched another one day who touched your limbs, and you walked upon a cane. He dispatched another one day and touched my eyes, and I put on these glasses.

Listen to me! There is an old, gray-bearded preacher going up and down this world with a mowing scythe in one hand and an hourglass in the other, and one day he'll take you for his text. He will mow you down and drag you to the judgment bar of God. And when you come, you will have to face Him and stay until your case is settled.

You say, "Brother Lakin, I'll have to come?" It is a world judgment—a universal judgment.

IT IS A JUDGMENT OF "SECRET THINGS"

"But," you say, "what will He judge me about?"

That is the question. If you are indicted in the court, they always file what they call a Bill of Particulars. In that Bill of Particulars they list certain things with which you are charged.

When you stand before the judgment bar of Almighty God and the books are opened, you are being judged out of the things that are written in these books. You will not be judged for your state in eternity but for your standing in eternity—out of the books. He said, "...and the books were opened." Of course, there is a book also, and those that are found in the book will not be in the books, my friend. You will be judged out of the things that are written in the books; and when you come to face that, He is going to charge you on "the secret things." He said, "God shall judge the secrets of men by Jesus Christ" (Rom. 2:16). You will have to answer to God for secret things, things that are covered, things that no one knows about.

You may hide some things tonight from your husband, from your children, from your family; you may hide them from your pastor, from your church—but you will not hide them from God, because the eyes like flames of fire that "run to and fro throughout the whole earth" will uncover, reveal and bring those secret things to light.

I believe there are people tonight who would commit suicide in a moment if they only knew things that were covered up in their lives were going to be exposed. Tonight as I preach, if I could cause the three secret sins of your life to come up out of your heart and write themselves across your face, I wonder how many in this audience or the audience by radio would want a false face if that could happen?

Suppose I had the power to put your life right up there on that wall and your heart as the people think it is; then on the other hand, suppose I could put it tonight as God really knows it is—would you want to be sitting beside your wife or your husband? Boy, girl, would you want mother and father to see it tonight if I could put it up there?

Suppose I, in the next five minutes, could put the secret sins of this audience on this wall tonight. How many would grab something and rush out of this building? Suppose I could take you down into the basement of this church and there turn out the lights and on the wall flash your heart as God really knows it. I wonder what you would think about it.

In that day, "God shall judge the secrets of men by Jesus Christ." You may cover it and hide it for awhile, but ". . . be sure your sin will find you out" (Num. 32:23). If not now, then at the judgment of God.

THE JUDGMENT ISSUE: "WHAT DID YOU DO WITH JESUS?"

You say, "Brother Lakin, what could I do?" "Some men's sins are open beforehand, going before to judgment; and some men they follow after" (I Tim. 5:24). Thank God, I want to send all my sin ahead to the judgment of God and have it covered.

Martin Luther said that, while once in prayer, the Devil unrolled a great scroll to him. On it were all the sins that Luther had committed, a great long roll of sin. The Devil said, "For this you must go to Hell."

Martin Luther said, "But, Devil, there is one thing you didn't put on it: you ought to write at the top of that scroll, '. . . and the blood of Jesus Christ his Son cleanseth us from all sin' " (I John 1:7).

Thank God, I have no fear of the judgment! Why? Not because I am good or perfect or have always been sinless, but because my sins are under the blood; they are covered and cannot be seen but are blotted out of the book of God's remembrance!

You say, "Brother Lakin, I am a member of the church." That doesn't matter. You say, "I've got my name on a church book." Church books, church records will be burned. My friend, the only book that will abide is the book of life; and if your name is there, these others will not matter.

Then God said that "every idle word that men shall speak, they shall give account thereof in the day of judgment" (Matt. 12:36). Most of us talk too much and say too little. What is the most idle thing you've ever heard? It is for a man to say there is no God. "The fool hath said in his heart, There is no God" (Ps. 14:1).

You say, "Brother Lakin, what will be the final verdict?" Well, whatever it is, it is going to be eternal. It will be eternal joy and eternal happiness, eternal misery and eternal woe. The issues of the judgment day will be eternal and will be based upon this one thing: **What did you do with Jesus Christ?** In that day when God is judging you, you will stand face to face with Him; and He will ask you this one question, **"What did you do with Jesus?"**

The other day while in Jerusalem, I went over to Pilate's Hall after I had come from the Garden of Gethsemane. I walked down and across the little brook Kidron and over into the Garden of Gethsemane, and there under the old olive tree I knelt and prayed. I thought of that night when the blood was forced out of His skin. As I prayed in the Garden, I saw the crowd come, led by Judas. I saw them lay hold upon Him and take Him over to Pilate's Hall, take His garment off and slash Him with the thongs tied with bits of bone and steel until the blood ran and the gore spattered. He stood there for a moment in a crown of thorns with a seamless robe wrapped round Him. Pilate sought somehow to get Him off his hands by asking, "Whom shall I release?" They shouted, "Barabbas! Release unto us Barabbas!" Then Pilate said, "What shall I do then with Jesus which is called Christ?" And they cried, "Crucify Him! Crucify Him!"

> **Jesus is standing in Pilate's hall,**
> **Friendless, forsaken, betrayed by all;**
> **Hearken, what meaneth the sudden call,**
> **"What will you do with Jesus?"**

My friend, when you stand yonder before God, you have to answer for how you have treated His Son.

You say, "Brother Lakin, who's going to judge me?" One who knows all about you. One who knows your faults and failings. One who knows where you have been and where you are going. One who knows every thought that ever percolated through your brain. One who attends the funeral of every sparrow and counts the numbers of the hairs of your head. It is Jesus Christ, the Jesus whose deity you are denying, the Jesus whose blood you are spurning, the Jesus whose love and mercy you are rejecting—He is the One you will have to stand and face.

You have heard the story of the man standing on the street corner when a runaway team came rushing down the street. He leaped out into the street and was about to be crushed beneath their feet when a man pulled him onto the walk.

That night this one who was saved from death was arrested for some minor crime. The next morning as he was about to be sentenced, he pleaded, "But, Judge, you know me! I'm the man you saved just last night."

The judge answered him sternly: "Last night I was your saviour; today I am your judge."

Tonight Jesus is your Saviour; tomorrow He will be your Judge. That is going to be a sad day, isn't it?

That is going to be a sad day for Pontius Pilate when he stands there before Him. I have often thought of Pilate sitting on that throne. I see that man come rushing down the aisle and hand him up a little note from his wife which said, "Have thou nothing to do with that just man: for I have suffered many things this day in a dream because of him" (Matt. 27:19). But Pilate said, "Give me some water." He washed his hands, but he didn't wash his heart. Down yonder beside an imaginary stream, in the place of the damned, I see a man wash his hands and lift them; and the blood drips from his fingers again. When he stands face to face with Jesus, the Saviour says, "Pilate, you had Me before you one day. You knew I was innocent, knew I was the Son of God; but you were a politician. In order to cater to that crowd, you allowed them to take Me out yonder on that rugged hill and nail Me to a cross. Pilate, you knew it that day."

That is going to be a sad day for Judas Iscariot.

Jesus says, "Judas, remember the night you came across the little brook and over into the Garden and said, 'Hail, Master,' and kissed Me? Remember when you sold Me for thirty pieces of silver, then threw down the silver?"

I imagine yonder, tonight, walking up and down the sulfuric streets of the damned, a man throws the money down; it bounces back into his hands . . . and again it bounces back into his hands. Jesus says, "Judas, if you had only waited—even after they crucified Me; if you hadn't gone out and hanged yourself, if you hadn't gone out and committed suicide . . . if you had even waited until after I had risen from the dead and if you had stopped as I went along the road to Emmaus and come out into the middle of the road and bowed down before Me, I would have even then forgiven you and saved you and taken you to Heaven. But, Judas, you sold Me and went out and committed suicide."

It is going to be a sad day for some false preachers and prophets and professors who have damned people and robbed them of their faith. It is going to be a sad day for some mothers when they turn the street in the corners of Hell and run into a daughter who says, "You put me in the dance; you put me in the place of amusement . . .and here I am." It is going to be a sad day for some father whose son runs into him and says, "I filled a drunkard's grave because you taught me. . .you taught me." That is going to be a sad day for some, my friend.

Sit here nonchalantly tonight, but remember this—there is coming a day when you are going to stand face to face with Him.

> I dreamed that the great judgment morning
>   Had dawned, and the trumpet had blown;
> I dreamed that the nations had gathered
>   To judgment before the white throne;
> From the throne came a bright shining angel,
>   And stood on the land and the sea,
> And swore with his hand raised to Heaven,
>   That time was no longer to be.
> And O, what a weeping and wailing,
>   As the lost were told of their fate;
> They cried for the rocks and the mountains,
>   They prayed, but their prayer was too late.

I would to God I could paint you a picture of the judgment day till you would never forget it. The great hall is all filled now, and the people are waiting with expectancy. Yonder is the throne; its overwhelming splendor I can't describe. There comes One to sit upon the throne. Around His head is a rainbow; at His feet is a sea of glass. His face is described as shining above the noonday sun.

The books are opened, and He begins to judge them out of the things written therein; and when He has finished, He says, "Depart from me, ye cursed, into everlasting fire. . ." (Matt. 25:41). There is a scurrying hither and yon, and the first thing you know, the big hall is empty, and the big book closes with a jar. The Judge comes down from the throne, and the court of Heaven is adjourned for eternity. The high court of Heaven is adjourned and will never meet again. . . . It will *never* meet again!

Listen to me, my friend! What you do about the salvation of your soul, you will have to do before the wood of the cradle ever bumps the marble of the tomb.

That is my message to you tonight. If you were to cease to breathe where you sit, would you be in Heaven or Hell?

"And as it is appointed unto men once to die, but after this the judgment."—Heb. 9:27.

Those of you listening to me tonight away out yonder across the hills and the valleys, with tears I say, do not come upon this thing unexpectedly or let death take you unaware.

Compiler Urges You to Trust Christ as Saviour

You have read the solemn sermon, ". . . But After This the Judgment," by Dr. B. R. Lakin. What a fearful thing for one to stand before Almighty God in judgment! But, dear friends, Jesus Christ was judged for our sins 2,000 years ago; and if you trust Him as your Saviour, you will never have to stand at the white throne judgment to be judged as a sinner. Jesus Christ bore all your sins in His own body, and God punished Him in your place to pay the debt you owe.

If you will trust Jesus Christ as your Saviour, the Bible promises, "There is therefore now no condemnation to them which are in Christ Jesus" (Rom. 8:1). And again the Bible says in John 5:24, "Verily, verily, I say unto you, He that heareth my word, and believeth on him that sent me, hath everlasting life, and shall not come into condemnation; but is passed from death unto life." The promise is plain and clear; if we trust Jesus Christ as our Saviour, we will not come into condemnation, that is, we will not come into judgment.

Believers will be judged at the judgment seat of Christ for their service, but they will never be judged for sin.

Won't you please trust Jesus Christ today?

XI.

The Great Judgment Day

R. A. TORREY

" [God] *now commandeth all men every where to repent: Because he hath appointed a day, in the which he will judge the world in righteousness by that man whom he hath ordained; whereof he hath given assurance unto all men, in that he hath raised him from the dead.*"—Acts 17:30,31.

Two events in the future are absolutely certain. First, it is absolutely certain that Jesus Christ is coming again to receive His people unto Himself, and to reward them according to their works. Second, it is absolutely certain that Jesus Christ is coming again to judge the world.

When I was on the ocean some time ago, a man asked me one night as we were walking the deck of the great steamer together, "What will be the outcome of this tendency towards great trusts and monopolies in business?" And I replied, "I do not know." Men often come to me with the question, "What will be the outcome of these great combinations of laboring men to resist the encroachments of capital?" And again I reply, "I don't know."

But I will tell you what I do know, and it is infinitely more important: I know that someday the Lord Jesus Christ will come back again and receive His waiting and faithful people unto Himself. And I know that there is going to be a judgment day for the world, and that judgment day is the subject of our thought tonight.

There are five things about the judgment day that are set forth in our text: first, the certainty of it; second, the universality of it; third, the basis of it; fourth, the administrator of it; and last, the issues of it.

I. THE CERTAINTY OF IT

It is absolutely certain that there is to be a judgment day. "God hath

appointed a day, in the which he will judge the world in righteousness."
Men who are living in sin may laugh at it, but they cannot laugh it away.

In the days of Noah, men laughed at his predictions that there was
to be a Flood, but the Flood came and swept them all away.

In the days of Lot, men of Sodom laughed at the idea that God would
rain fire and brimstone out of Heaven and destroy Sodom and Gomorrah and the other cities of the plain; but the fire and brimstone fell, and
these cities were blotted out.

In the days of Jeremiah, the people of Jerusalem laughed at
Jeremiah's predictions that Nebuchadnezzar would come and lay
Jerusalem in the dust and destroy their Temple. But it all came to pass
just as God said and just as Jeremiah believed and predicted.

In the days of Jesus Christ, men laughed at Christ's prediction that
the armies of Rome under Titus and Vespasian would lay Jerusalem's
walls even with the ground and that calamity would overtake that city
such as the world had never seen; but historians outside the Bible tell
us that it all came to pass just as Christ predicted and that Jerusalem
was overtaken with the most appalling siege in the world's history.

All of God's predictions about judgment on individuals and nations
in the past have come true to the very letter in spite of all the false hopes
that were held out by false prophets.

If we are to judge the future by the past—and there is no other way
to judge it—God's predictions about the future with regard to judgment
upon individuals and nations will come true to the very letter, in spite
of all the false hopes held out by the false prophets; that is, by the "liberal
preachers" of the day.

It is absolutely certain that there is to be a judgment day for the world.
God has given us a special guarantee of the judgment day, and that
special guarantee is the resurrection of Christ from the dead. As we
read in the text, "[God] will judge the world in righteousness by that
man whom he hath ordained; *whereof he hath given assurance unto
all men, in that he hath raised him from the dead.*"

The resurrection of Jesus Christ from the dead is an absolutely certain fact of history. It is not a theological fiction nor a poet's dream;
it is an established fact of history. If I had time tonight to go into the
evidence, I could prove to every fair-minded, thinking man that, beyond
question, Jesus Christ rose from the dead.

When we were in Sydney I talked to the businessmen there and members of both Houses of Parliament for four hours, to prove to them that Christ did rise from the dead. Many an agnostic, deist, unitarian and higher critic had his views utterly shattered and turned to the risen Christ.

There is no time, however, tonight to go into the evidence of the resurrection of Jesus Christ. I simply want to say that the evidence is so overwhelming that it is impossible for any honest man to sit down and thoroughly sift the evidence and come to any other conclusion than that Christ did rise from the dead.

Years ago there were two eminent lawyers, one named Lyttleton and the other West. These two were deists; that is, they had faith in a Supreme Being, but did not believe in revelation or in inspiration or in the miraculous. One day they got to talking about their views, and finally one said to the other, "Well, we cannot maintain our position until we disprove two things: first, the reputed conversion of Saul of Tarsus. and second, the reputed resurrection of Jesus Christ from the dead."

Said Lyttleton to West, "I will write a book to prove that Saul of Tarsus was never converted in the way which the Acts of the Apostles records."

Said West to Lyttleton, "I will write a book to prove that Jesus Christ did not rise from the dead as the evangelists say."

Well, they wrote their books; and when they met afterwards, West said to Lyttleton, "How have you got on?"

"I have written my book," said Lyttleton, "but as I have studied the evidence from a legal standpoint, I have become convinced that Saul of Tarsus was converted in just the way the Acts of the Apostles say he was, and I have become a Christian. How have you got on?"

"Well," said West, "I have sifted the evidence for the resurrection of Jesus Christ from the legal standpoint, and I am satisfied that Jesus of Nazareth was raised from the dead just as Matthew, Mark, Luke and John record, and I have written my book in defense of Christianity."

These two books can be seen in our libraries today.

It is absolutely impossible for any man with a legal mind and accustomed to sifting evidence, to sit down and thoroughly investigate the evidence for the resurrection of Jesus Christ, and come to any other conclusion than that Jesus of Nazareth rose from the dead.

Well, that resurrection of our Lord Jesus Christ is a guarantee that a judgment day is coming. When Jesus Christ came upon the earth, He claimed in John 5:22,23, "The Father judgeth no man, but hath committed all judgment unto the Son: That all men should honour the Son, even as they honour the Father. He that honoureth not the Son honoureth not the Father which hath sent him." He claimed that there was a judgment day coming and that He was to be the Judge. Men hated Him for making the claim and the other claim involved in it—the claim of deity. They put Him to death for making this claim, but before they put Him to death He said, "My Father will set His seal to the claim for which you put Me to death."

And when the third day came, the breath of God swept through the sleeping clay and God, by the resurrection of Christ, set His seal to Christ's claims and said in accents that cannot be mistaken and that are a message to all ages, "There is a judgment day coming."

The indisputable resurrection of Jesus Christ in the past points with unerring finger to a certain judgment in the future. If there is any man here tonight who flatters himself that there is to be no judgment day; if there is any man here who fancies that he can go on in sin and never be called to account for it; if there is any man here who believes he can go on trampling under foot the Son of God and not have to suffer for it, O man, throw that hope away tonight, for it is baseless. It is absolutely certain that there will be a day in which Jesus Christ will judge the world in righteousness.

II. THE UNIVERSALITY OF THE JUDGMENT

Please note the universality of the judgment day. "[God] hath appointed a day, in the which he will judge *the world.*" It will be no class judgment; every man and woman on the face of this earth will have to face the Judge in that day. Of course all who are Christians, all who have accepted Christ as their Saviour, will have been caught up to meet Him in the air. But all the rest will have to face the Judge in that day. There will be no escaping that day.

Men often escape human courts. There is many a thief that has never been arrested, there is many a murderer that remains unhung; but when God sends forth His officers to gather the people for that judgment day, they will have to come, and they will have to stay right there until their case is settled.

Men have often escaped me when I am preaching. When the preaching becomes too pointed, they get up and go out and thus escape me. You can't escape God that way. You will have to come there, and you will have to stay there until your case is decided. He is going to judge the world in righteousness.

How you would rejoice if every infidel in London were at this meeting tonight. But most infidels would not dare to come to this meeting. But there will be a meeting where every infidel will be. There will be one meeting where every hypocritical church member will be. There will be a meeting where every unpenitent sinner will be present—the meeting with Jesus Christ at the judgment bar of God.

That man who is sitting in this meeting tonight trying to make light of everything I am saying—you will be at that meeting, and you will not make light of it. You will be there face to face with Jesus Christ. That woman who has come to this meeting tonight for any purpose but a good one, you will meet Christ there at the judgment bar of God.

III. THE BASIS OF THE JUDGMENT

In the third place, note the basis of judgment.

1. *The judgment will be "according to their works."* In Revelation 20:12, 13 we read,

"And I saw the dead, small and great, stand before God; and the books were opened: and another book was opened, which is the book of life: and the dead were judged out of those things which were written in the books, according to their works. And the sea gave up the dead which were in it; and death and hell delivered up the dead which were in them: and they were judged every man according to their works."

"According to their works" is the basis of that judgment. There are preachers who tell us that a man can die in sin and, after he is dead, can have another probation, another chance to repent, that he may repent after his death and turn to God and be saved. The old Book does not hold out any such hope. That kind of teaching contradicts the plain teaching of the Word of God, which says distinctly that "according to their works," in the life that now is, is to determine the issues of eternity.

That man tonight who is living in drunkenness, who is squandering his time, squandering his money, squandering his manhood in a life of dissipation; he will have to answer for it in that day.

That woman tonight who is living a life of frivolity and pleasure instead of living for the God who made her and the Christ who died for her; she will have to answer for it in that day.

That man here who professes to be a Christian but lives like the world; he will have to answer for it in that day.

That man who has made gold his god, overreaching his neighbor in business, oppressing his employee, turning a deaf ear to the cry of the widow and orphan; he will have to answer for it in that day.

That man who knows the truth but will not heed it because it will hurt him in business or politics; he will have to answer for it in that day.

That man who is a libertine, living in lust, living like a beast, scattering ruin wherever he goes; he will have to answer for it in that day.

The wicked things done in the body—they will all come up, things that have been forgotten for years.

There is a man here who years ago did a base, nefarious deed, and tonight he is very comfortable in the thought that no one on earth knows of it. Man, the whole world will know about it in that day unless you repent, and Jesus Christ will know about it and will pass judgment upon it.

There is a woman here tonight who has a very black page in her past history, but of late years she has been very comfortable over that black page. No one now knows anything about it; it is all forgotten; there is no one to bring it up. The whole world will know about it in that day unless she repents and turns to Christ.

2. *"The secret things" will be judged.* In Romans 2:16, we read: "In the day when God shall judge the secrets of men by Jesus Christ." The secret things, the things done in the dark, the things done under the cover of night, the things that nobody saw but God; all will be brought to light on that day.

I remember hearing years ago of an incident that happened here in your own country. A woman had killed her husband by driving a nail into his skull. So successfully had she covered up the wound that he was buried without any suspicion being cast upon her. After several years the woman flattered herself that she would never be found out. One day, however, while the grave digger was at work in the cemetery, he threw up this man's skull and there saw the nail. I do not know that he suspected the woman, but he took it to her and said, "Look there."

She threw up her hands and cried, "My God! Found out at last."

It will all be found out at last, the secret things, the thoughts and imaginations of the heart.

Oh, you men who are boasting of your morality, how would you like to have the thoughts and fancies and desires and the imaginations of the last twenty-four hours photographed and thrown upon a screen before this audience tonight? The whole world will see those secret things in that day, not those of twenty-four hours only, but those of a lifetime, unless you repent.

You, madam, who have boasted of your purity and your nobility of character above others and fancied that you ought to be saved because of your goodness; how would you like to have the hidden things of the chambers of imagery and imagination and desire photographed and thrown on a screen before all this audience? But the whole world will see it in that day unless you repent. The secret things will all come to light.

3. *The Lord tells us again that the basis of judgment will be our WORDS.* In Matthew 12:36 I read, "But I say unto you, That every idle word that men shall speak, they shall give account thereof in the day of judgment." Our careless, thoughtless, unstudied words reveal what we are at heart. Our studied speeches do not reveal what we are but what we would like to be; but our idle words that we drop accidentally are the best revelation of what there is in our hearts. Your impure words, your unkind words, your harsh words, your words of gossip and slander—for them you will give account thereof.

On one occasion, at a service in Minneapolis, one of my workers came to me and said, "Here is an infidel; will you come and speak to him?" I went to him, and in reply to my question, he said, "Yes, I am an infidel."

I asked, "Why are you an infidel?"

He replied, "Because the Bible is full of contradictions."

"Full of contradictions?"

"Yes."

"Will you please show me one?"

"Oh," said he, "it is full of them."

"Well, if there are so many, you ought to be able to show me one."

"Oh, it is just full of them."

"Well," I insisted, "please show me one."

Then he replied, "Well, I don't pretend to know as much about the Bible as you do."

I said, "Then what are you talking about it for in this way?" Then I looked him right square in the eye, and I told him what Jesus said of the idle words that men speak. "Now," I said, "this is God's Word. God is the Author of this Book, and you lightly and thoughtlessly have been slandering the Word of God, and thus slandering God, the Author. I want to say to you, sir, that you will have to give account of your words in the day of judgment."

The man turned pale, and well he might.

I want to say to you men tonight who are pulling the Word of God to pieces because you have been told that some German scholar says so and so; you men who dare to criticize the Book you don't know anything about; you men who are taking up the idle talk of newspapers and reviews and retailing it, slandering God's Word and God, the Author of it—you will have to give an account thereof in the day of judgment. Well may you tremble.

I want to say to you men who have taken the name of the glorious Son of God, in whom dwells all the fullness of the Godhead, lightly on your lips and have been saying flippantly, "I don't believe that Jesus is divine, I don't believe that Jesus is the Son of God"; you men who have been robbing the glorious Son of God of what is His due, you will have to give an account of this in the day of judgment.

4. *But the great basis of the judgment day will be what we do with Jesus Christ.* We are told in John 3:18, "He that believeth on him is not condemned: but he that believeth not is condemned already, because he hath not believed in the name of the only begotten Son of God." God has sent One down into this world to be our Saviour. The rejection of Jesus Christ, the Son of God whom God has appointed to be our Saviour, our King and our Lord, is the most daring and damning of all sins. Light has been sent into the world, and men have loved darkness rather than light because their deeds are evil.

There is nothing that reveals what is in the human heart so clearly as what a man does with Christ. Christ is God incarnate, the light of God come into the world, and the rejection of Jesus Christ proves a wicked heart. The great question in the judgment day will be, "What did you do with Jesus Christ?"

Oh, I can imagine some people in that day. That man who sits in yonder gallery trying to make light of what I am saying tonight, he will be there. I see him standing before the judgment bar. The throng falls back, and there is profound silence. Then comes rolling forth, like the sound of many waters, the majestic voice of the Judge, "What did you do with Jesus Christ?"

IV. THE JUDGE

We now come to the fourth point. Who is to be the judge in that day? Jesus Christ Himself. "[God] hath appointed a day in the which he will judge the world in righteousness *by that man whom he hath ordained;* whereof he hath given assurance unto all men, in that he hath raised him from the dead." Jesus Christ is to be the Judge. That Christ whom you are rejecting is to be the Judge. That same Christ whom you are robbing of the honor which is His due is to be the Judge. That same Christ whose divinity you are denying, not that you have any reason for denying it, but simply you don't want to have to believe it, and want comfort in your sin—that same Christ whom you are trampling under foot will sit as Judge in that day.

That will be a very dark day for some.

It will be a dark day for Annas and Caiaphas, who robbed Jesus of every form of justice. Now they stand before the bar, and Christ sits upon the throne.

I can imagine Pontius Pilate in that day, who knew that Jesus Christ was innocent, yet condemned Him to appease the Jewish mob. Pilate will stand at the bar, and the Christ he so basely wronged will be on the throne.

I can imagine the soldiers who spat upon Him and mocked Him and crowned Him with thorns. The Christ they spat upon, buffeted and crowned with thorns, sits upon the throne, and they stand at the judgment bar.

I can imagine Judas Iscariot, who for thirty pieces of silver sold his Master after three years of close association with Him; now he stands before the bar, and the Christ he betrayed sits upon the throne.

I can imagine that man and woman in this audience tonight who have been telling your friends that you do not believe that Jesus is divine, who have been trampling the Son of God under foot, who have been resisting the invitations of mercy, it may be, for years; you stand before the throne, and the Christ whom you have defamed, slandered, rejected and trampled under foot, sits as Judge.

V. THE ISSUES OF THE JUDGMENT DAY

Once more, please notice the issues of the judgment day. They will be eternal. They will be either eternal joy and life and glory, or eternal death, eternal darkness, eternal despair and eternal shame. O men and women, I would that I had it in my power tonight so to picture to you that great judgment day that every man and woman in this audience would go out from here with the judgment day of Christ before you as a great reality; but it surpasses my power.

There is the judgment throne; its blazing glory, its overwhelming splendor, I cannot describe. There is the Christ upon the throne, His face shining with a glory above the glory of the noonday sun. His eyes like flames of fire piercing men through and through. And there you stand before that awful judgment bar, the eyes of Christ upon you like a flame of fire, piercing you through and through, your whole life laid bare and your secret thoughts revealed.

O men and women, repent, REPENT, *REPENT!* "[God] now commandeth all men every where to repent: Because he hath appointed a day, in the which he will judge the world in righteousness by that man whom he hath ordained; whereof he hath given assurance unto all men, in that he hath raised him from the dead."

Repent, REPENT, *REPENT!*

(Used by permission of Revell Publishers, copyright holders)

TOM MALONE
1915-

ABOUT THE MAN:

Tom Malone was converted and called to preach at the same moment! At an old-fashioned bench, the preacher took his tear-stained Bible and showed Tom Malone how to be saved. He accepted Christ then and there. Arising from his knees in the Isbell Methodist Church near Russellville, Alabama, he shook the circuit pastor's hand; and this bashful nineteen-year-old farm boy announced: "I know the Lord wants me to be a preacher."

Backward, bashful and broke, yet Tom borrowed five dollars, took what he could in a cardboard suitcase and left for Cleveland, Tennessee. Immediately upon arrival at Bob Jones College, Malone heard a truth that totally dominated his life and labors for the Lord ever after—soul winning!

That day he won his first soul! The green-as-grass Tom, a new convert himself, knew nothing of soul-winning approaches or techniques. He simply asked the sinner, "Are you a Christian?" No. In a few minutes that young man became Malone's first convert.

Since that day, countless have been his experiences in personal evangelism.

Mark it down: Malone began soul winning his first week in Bible college. And he has never lost *the thirst* for it, *the thrill* in it, nor *the task* of it since. Pastoring churches, administrating schools, preaching across the nation have not deterred Tom Malone from this mainline ministry.

It is doubtful if young Malone ever dreamed of becoming the man he is today. He is now Doctor Tom Malone, is renowned in fundamental circles for his wise leadership and great preaching, is pastor of the large Emmanuel Baptist Church of Pontiac, Michigan, Founder and President of Midwestern Baptist Schools, and is eagerly sought as speaker in large Bible conferences from coast to coast.

Dr. John R. Rice often said that Dr. Tom Malone may be the greatest gospel preacher in all the world today!

XII.

The Judgment of Sinners

TOM MALONE

"And I saw a great white throne, and him that sat on it, from whose face the earth and the heaven fled away; and there was found no place for them. And I saw the dead, small and great, stand before God; and the books were opened: and another book was opened, which is the book of life: and the dead were judged out of those things which were written in the books, according to their works."—Rev. 20:11,12.

The great white throne judgment deals with the unsaved. No other doctrine in the Bible is more neglected than that of the great white throne judgment. There is a reason for this.

In recent generations, people have gotten some unscriptural ideas about what God is like. For instance, you hear many unsaved people say that God is a God of love, a God of mercy, a God of grace.

God is a God of love. We read in I John 4:8, "He that loveth not knoweth not God; for God is love."

The same Bible that says God is a God of love, says that God is holy: "And one cried unto another, and said, Holy, holy, holy, is the Lord of hosts: the whole earth is full of his glory" (Isa. 6:3).

So not only does the Bible say that God is a God of love, but the Bible says that God is a God of holiness. Anyone who reads the Bible honestly will come to the conclusion that God loves sinners but hates sin. The very nature of God demands that He punish sinners, and that is what this great white throne judgment is about.

In Genesis 18:25 is an all-important question, ". . . Shall not the Judge of all the earth do right?" In order to do right and be consistent with His attributes, God must punish sin. That is what the great white throne judgment is about. This world needs to hear more about the judgment of the unsaved, the great white throne judgment. I will tell you why. The 3rd chapter of Romans gives us an inspired description of the sinfulness and depravity of man.

Verse 10 says, "As it is written, There is none righteous, no, not one."

Verse 12 says, ". . . there is none that doeth good, no, not one."

Verse 23 says, "For all have sinned, and come short of the glory of God."

Then in the midst of this third chapter describing the depravity and sinfulness of man is this statement, "There is no fear of God before their eyes" (vs. 18).

You see this today. You see it in the masses of humanity. There is no fear of God before their eyes. A person who does not have a reverential fear of God is going to live without Christ, without any desire to be saved and without any intention of ever settling this sin question.

You ask, "Should people always be afraid of God?" No. I loved my grandfather. He had as great a part in raising me as any other individual. In fact, he raised me several times! I remember very distinctly! I used to love to sit and look at him. He was a distinct sort of man, an individualist and opinionated, and usually his opinions were right.

He wore high-top shoes and a big broad-brimmed hat and had a big heavy mustache. He was an individualist. I never saw another who even reminded me of him. Though I loved him, yet I had a fear of him. I knew that when he said something, he meant it. I knew if he ever promised punishment, I would get it. I not only loved my grandfather, but I feared him.

I believe that should be the attitude of people toward Almighty God. He is a God of love, but the Bible says in Romans 3:18, "There is no fear of God before their eyes." The Bible says it is a bad thing for people not to fear God.

You wonder why we preach on the great white throne judgment. Because there needs to be a fear of God.

I think it is a misunderstood doctrine—this doctrine of the judgment of the unsaved. Many still have the idea that everyone is going to stand before the Lord at one time and He is going to say, "You are lost, and you are saved; you are lost, and you are saved." That is not how it is going to happen. Some Scriptures people do not know how to rightly divide. They come to the conclusion that all at one time are going to stand before God.

There is no such thing in the Bible as a general resurrection. There is no such thing in the Bible as a general judgment. John 5:28,29 says:

"Marvel not at this: for the hour is coming, in the which all that are in the graves shall hear his voice, And shall come forth; they that have done good, unto the resurrection of life; and they that have done evil, unto the resurrection of damnation."

Some people say, "There it is. People are going to come out of the grave—some unto the resurrection of life, some unto the resurrection of damnation."

True, that verse does say that, but between these two resurrections are more than a thousand years. The first resurrection will take place when Jesus comes, and the dead in Christ are brought out of the graves; the second resurrection, at the end of the millennium when God has His great white throne judgment and the unsaved dead will then be raised to stand before Him. This is a misunderstood doctrine.

This doctrine of the judgment of the unsaved dead helps you to see God's attitude toward Christ rejection. People rejecting Him as God's Son and setting Him at naught, trampling His precious blood under their feet, refusing His offer of mercy—God doesn't take this lightly. John 3:18 says, "He that believeth on him is not condemned: but he that believeth not is condemned already, because he hath not believed in the name of the only begotten Son of God."

Every unsaved person is sitting today under the condemnation of Almighty God.

How important this doctrine is! This is the last great act of God. You can study prophecy and study the Bible and what God is going to do, all in chronological order; but this is the last thing God is going to do. After this great white throne judgment, I read these words,

"And I [John] saw a new heaven and a new earth: for the first heaven and the first earth were passed away; and there was no more sea. And I John saw the holy city, new Jerusalem, coming down from God out of heaven, prepared as a bride adorned for her husband."—Rev. 21:1,2.

After this, time shall be no more. After this, eternity sets in. After this, not one soul is ever saved. After this, there is just Heaven for the saved throughout all eternity. After this, there is nothing but eternal damnation for all those who are not saved. This is God's last great act, and it brings to an end what man calls time. Then the New Jerusalem descends.

This shows God's full execution of the Edenic curse. When you read the history of man and of sin, of when Adam and Eve fell in the garden, you see that God placed a curse on several things.

First, He placed a curse upon a woman. Women, let me say this to you kindly and in love. You find in this opening part of the Bible a woman talking to the Devil. She had no business talking to him. God made man first and made man in His own image and took woman from the side of man and made her. He made her not in God's image but in man's image, and God made man the head of all His creation.

Satan comes and the woman begins to talk to him. As a result, the fall of man comes. God pronounces a curse first upon the woman. Genesis 3:16 says, "Unto the woman he said, I will greatly multiply thy sorrow and thy conception; in sorrow thou shalt bring forth children; and thy desire shall be to thy husband, and he shall rule over thee." That has been true through all the history of the human race.

God pronounced a curse on the Devil. It says in Genesis 3:15, ". . . and between thy seed and her seed; it shall bruise thy head. . . ." God will execute that curse. The Devil, although he is on the loose today, is a defeated foe, and the result of this battle between him and God is an inevitable one.

God someday is going to say to one angel, just one, not a whole legion, "Go bind him with chains and put him in the bottomless pit." He will be there a thousand years, then released for a little time. Then after further war, God will put him back in the bottomless pit.

God said that the Devil would be tormented day and night forever and ever. His smoke shall ascend up and up and up. God is going to torment the Devil forever. There will be no reign, no authority in Hell. Not even the Devil will have it. God will execute His curse upon it.

In that fall in Eden, God placed a curse upon man. In Genesis 3 we read where God said:

"Thou shalt not eat of it: cursed is the ground for thy sake; in sorrow shalt thou eat of it all the days of thy life; Thorns also and thistles shall it bring forth to thee; and thou shalt eat the herb of the field; In the sweat of thy face shalt thou eat bread, till thou return unto the ground; for out of it wast thou taken: for dust thou art, and unto dust shalt thou return."—Vss. 17-19.

God not only placed a curse on man but on the ground and earth. That is why Jesus on the cross was to bear these curses and have a crown of thorns placed upon His brow.

At the close of the Bible we see a holy God who cannot break His word and who always must do as He said. We see that God executes these curses, the one on earth, for instance—". . .the earth and the heaven fled away; and there was found no place for them" (Rev. 20:11). It doesn't just say that the heaven and earth were shaken and moved; it says that the heaven and earth were done away with.

God's curse is being executed. If man will not come to Christ, God executes the curse upon him at that judgment day, and he must stand before God at the great white throne judgment and be judged.

There are many judgments in the Bible. Some say that there are seven—there might even be more. There is the judgment of believers' sins or Calvary. Thank God, the sins of a believer have already been judged. Isaiah 53:6 says, "All we like sheep have gone astray; we have turned every one to his own way; and the Lord hath laid on him the iniquity of us all."

There is a judgment called self-judgment. I believe when a person sits in judgment on himself and settles it with himself, God does not judge that man anymore. Paul said in writing to the Corinthians, ". . .yea, I judge not mine own self. For I know nothing by myself; yet am I not hereby justified: but he that judgeth me is the Lord" (I Cor. 4:3,4).

There is a judgment called the judgment seat. Only Christians stand at that judgment seat and have their works judged.

"For we must all appear before the judgment seat of Christ; that every one may receive the things done in his body, according to that he hath done, whether it be good or bad."—II Cor. 5:10.

There is a judgment called the judgment of angels. Angels fell when Satan was cast out of Heaven; and Peter said in II Peter 2:4, ". . .but cast them down to hell, and delivered them into chains of darkness, to be reserved unto judgment."

There is a judgment for the nation Israel. God is going to judge Israel. He has deposited in Israel His oracles of truth. Her loins, humanly speaking, produced the blessed Christ of God. God has been good to Israel, but He is going to judge her someday.

There is a judgment called the judgment of sinners—the one I am reading about. "And I saw a great white throne" (Rev. 20:11).

I want you to see some truths about the judgment of people who are unsaved and who will not give their heart and life to Christ and receive Him as their personal Saviour.

I. THE JUDGMENT THRONE

First, I would like you to see the judgment throne or the great white throne. It is great in contrast to any other throne the world has ever known and to other thrones mentioned in the Bible. Hebrews 4:16 says, "Let us therefore come boldly unto the throne of grace, that we may obtain mercy, and find grace to help in time of need."

This is a throne of grace. You can come, if you will, to a throne of grace and find mercy. However, there will be no grace at the great white throne. There will be no mercy there, no tolerance there, no second chance there. This is the last throne, and God said it would be a white throne because it stands for justice and purity.

Hundreds of years before Jesus was ever born, Daniel took his prophetic telescope and as God led him, looked down across the centuries unborn and said, "I beheld till the thrones were cast down, and the Ancient of days did sit, whose garment was white as snow, and the hair of his head like the pure wool: his throne was like the fiery flame, and his wheels as burning fire" (7:9).

Daniel had seen a great throne. He had seen that great image which pictured the four great Gentile kingdoms. He saw the kingdom of Babylon, Greece, Media-Persia, then the great Roman Empire. Daniel saw thrones in the making. He saw the throne of Babylon ruled over by Nebuchadnezzar who conquered the whole world. He saw Belshazzar assume that throne and in his pomp and unbelief rule with a rod of iron over the whole world. Daniel said, 'I see a day when thrones like this and every other throne will be destroyed and only one will remain.'

"I beheld till the thrones were cast down, and the Ancient of days did sit, whose garment was white as snow, and the hair of his head like the pure wool: his throne was like the fiery flame, and his wheels as burning fire. A fiery stream issued and came forth from before him: thousand thousands ministered unto him, and ten thousand times ten thousand stood before him: the judgment was set, and the books were opened."—Dan. 7:9, 10.

God's Word says that there will be a great white throne and He who sits upon it will have such fiery indignation in His face against sin that heaven and earth will flee away, but that sinners must stand before Him at the judgment day.

Yes, there will be the judgment throne.

II. THE JUDGE ON THE THRONE

I would not only like you to see the judgment throne but the Judge on the throne.

God is a Trinity—Father, Son and Holy Spirit. Everyone knows that; but John 5:22 teaches that God is going to let Jesus do the judging: "For the Father judgeth no man, but hath committed all judgment unto the Son."

You see, the One on that throne, the Judge on the throne, is the Lord Jesus Christ. The same Jesus who one night with a little infant wail announced His arrival in the little manger among the lowly cattle in a stable in Bethlehem; the same Jesus who walked gently among men and was in privacy for thirty years of His life, then one day walked out in the River Jordan and was baptized of John; the same Jesus who for three and a half years reached out His hands and begged people to come to Him; the same Jesus who said, "All that the Father giveth me shall come to me; and him that cometh to me I will in no wise cast out"; the same Jesus who said, ". . . I am the bread of life: he that cometh to me shall never hunger; and he that believeth on me shall never thirst"; the same Jesus who said, "Come unto me, all ye that labour and are heavy laden, and I will give you rest"—that same Jesus will sit on that throne.

At that coming He is pictured as a Lamb that openeth not His mouth, a Lamb that is led before His shearers and is dumb. A lamb does not offer resistance. He is pictured as a Lamb when He comes to die because He is a sacrificial Lamb.

The same Bible pictures Him as a Lion. When Jesus sits on that throne, He will not sit there as God's Lamb but as God's Lion.

You cannot separate any of the great doctrines of the Bible from the doctrine of the judgment of the unsaved. In fact, it is even connected with the doctrine of the resurrection, with the doctrine of the second coming, with the doctrine of Hell.

Some people who claim to have read the Bible in the original Greek language try to come up with some kind of concoction that there is no such thing as an eternal Hell. They have a battle of semantics and argue about Hades and Sheol. It is true that in the Old Testament Sheol means a great abyss. It could mean a grave, in the sense of the place of the dead, not a literal sepulcher. A grave is not always a great abyss. Sheol in the Old Testament speaks of the bowels of the earth where God imprisons sinners.

The same is true of Hades in the New Testament. It speaks of a place. Jesus talked about this place when He told of the rich man and the poor man in Luke 16—one man begging for food at the gate and the other whose table was full of all the bounties of life.

"And it came to pass, that the beggar died, and was carried by the angels into Abraham's bosom: the rich man also died, and was buried; And in hell he lift up his eyes, being in torments, and seeth Abraham afar off, and Lazarus in his bosom. And he cried and said, Father Abraham, have mercy on me, and send Lazarus, that he may dip the tip of his finger in water, and cool my tongue; for I am tormented in this flame."—Vss. 22-24.

Now remember that Jesus said this. He said the rich man died and begged for a drop of water. When you come to this judgment, God doesn't use the word Hades or Sheol. He says that people are going to be put in a lake of fire. I don't enjoy talking about it any more than talking about a child having to be punished or someone having to suffer surgery. But it is a necessity because it is a divine truth that is unalterable. Sinners are going to have to stand before God. Revelation 20:15 says, "And whosoever was not found written in the book of life was cast into the lake of fire."

Sheol in the Old Testament and Hades in the New is God's jail. God keeps them there until this judgment. The lake of fire is God's penitentiary. Man stays in God's jail until the day of his trial; then he is in God's penitentiary forever. No exit, no end, no water, no relief.

Call me an old-fashioned preacher if you want to; accuse me of using terms that are antiquated if you will, but I am preaching what the Bible says—"And whosoever was not found written in the book of life was cast into the lake of fire."

When the Gospel first went to the Gentiles in the days of Simon Peter and the house of Cornelius, Simon said, "And he commanded us to preach unto the people, and to testify that it is he which was ordained of God to be the Judge of quick and dead" (Acts 10:42).

In Acts 24 we see Paul standing before Felix, and in verse 25 we read, "And as he reasoned of righteousness, temperance, and judgment to come, Felix trembled, and answered, Go thy way for this time; when I have a convenient season, I will call for thee."

It talks about the judgment to come. That is what I am talking about. Felix trembled, but he said, "Go thy way for this time; when I have a convenient season, I will call for thee."

Felix trembled but Felix did not repent. You may be afraid of judgment, but unless you do something about it, you will be as lost as Felix was.

Hebrews 9:27 says, "And as it is appointed unto men once to die, but after this the judgment."

III. THE JUDGMENT ISSUES

Now notice the issues of the judgment. When this resurrection— spoken of in the Bible as the second resurrection—takes place at the end of the millennium, when all the unsaved dead are raised and stand before God, what will be the issues in the judgment day? What will God condemn these unsaved people for?

There are several issues that will be brought into focus at the great white throne judgment. First, the Bible teaches that man shall be judged for his deeds. We read in the Bible where the books will be opened and they shall be judged for their works or their deeds. Romans 2:6 says, "Who will render to every man according to his deeds."

If this Bible be true, no unsaved person will escape meeting his life and his wicked deeds at the judgment bar of God. At the great white throne judgment one of the issues will be the deeds of men.

In speaking of the unsaved, God talks of their wicked work. And everything an unsaved person can do is wicked before God, even if he is religious. If he is not saved, even his religious deeds are an abomination unto God.

Then his words will be brought into focus at the judgment of the unsaved. I don't know of a more heart-searching thing than the fact that the Bible plainly teaches that a man's words will be brought into focus at the judgment.

Sometimes people say, "Well, how can God bring every idle word into judgment, as Jesus declares He will do in Matthew 12:36?"

Listen, God can do anything. There are electronic devices that capture men's words and preserve them for generations. Words can be spoken in secret and amplified to millions. At the judgment day, according to Jesus, every idle word of man shall be accounted for.

If you will examine that 12th chapter of Matthew where Jesus gave that statement, you will find that He talks about one of the most crucial and delicate matters a person could ever contemplate. Jesus talks about a sin for which there is no forgiveness. Jesus says there that if one commits this sin he shall not be forgiven in this life nor in the world to come. That sin is blasphemy against the Holy Ghost.

"Wherefore I say unto you, All manner of sin and blasphemy shall be forgiven unto men: but the blasphemy against the Holy Ghost shall not be forgiven unto men."—Vs. 31.

Then in verse 36 Jesus went on to say, ". . . every idle word that men shall speak, they shall give account thereof in the day of judgment."

You don't have to say it with your lips; just think it with your heart, and if it is against God, it is a wicked thought.

We read in I Corinthians 4:5, "Therefore judge nothing before the time, until the Lord come, who both will bring to light the hidden things of darkness, and will make manifest the counsels of the hearts: and then shall every man have praise of God." God said that even in that judgment day the things that have been made secret in the life of an unsaved person, the unspoken counsels of his heart never spoken by his lips—God said that man will give an account thereof in the day of judgment.

What will be the issues of that judgment day? The secrets of men. "In the day when God shall judge the secrets of men by Jesus Christ according to my gospel" (Rom. 2:16).

The main issue of the judgment day will be your relationship to Jesus Christ, what you have done with Jesus. Recently I was thinking of one of the most wonderful verses about assurance. When people have asked me, "Preacher, how can you know beyond any shadow of doubt that you are saved?" I have often used John 5:24 in answering. There Jesus said,

"Verily, verily, I say unto you, He that heareth my word, and believeth on him that sent me, hath everlasting life, and shall not come into condemnation; but is passed from death unto life."

Many times we have applied that verse to a Christian—that if one hears God's Word and believes on His Son, Jesus said that one shall not come into judgment. That gives him assurance. And what does that verse mean to an unsaved person? If that verse means that one who has believed shall never come to this judgment, it also means that one who has not believed is bound to come to that judgment, for that judgment is for everyone who rejects God's Son. It is like the question asked by Pilate, "What shall I do then with Jesus which is called Christ?" (Matt. 27:22).

So the issue of the judgment day will be what you have done with God's Son, the Lord Jesus Christ.

IV. THE JUDGED

Notice now—who is going to be judged? Revelation 20:12 says, "And I saw the dead, small and great, stand before God"—little people in the eyes of the world, maybe insignificant people. Poor people are going to be at the judgment. Sometimes people get the idea that that man out at the gate in Luke 16 begging for crumbs, went to Heaven when he died because he was poor. No—he went to Heaven because he was saved. Sometimes people think that, if they have it rough in this life and live in poverty here, they are going to escape Hell. The Bible doesn't teach that. It says that those who never had enough to eat here will perish in Hell, with never a drop of water throughout eternity, **if they are not saved.**

Poor people will be there. Oppressed people will be there. Those mistreated will also stand at the judgment bar of God and be condemned for all eternity.

Afflicted people will be there. Persecuted people will be there. The unsaved, whether or not they were poor and afflicted on earth, will be at the judgment throne and be assigned their place in eternal Hell.

In that awful day when men meet God, John said in Revelation 20:12, "And I saw the dead, small and great, stand before God; and the books were opened . . . ." John said little people and he said great people. There will be kings at that judgment. There will be men who have ruled nations at that judgment. There will be senators and judges and lawyers and potentates at that judgment. Perhaps one who has been President of the United States of America will someday stand at the judgment bar of God and hear Jesus say, ". . . I never knew you: depart from me, ye that work iniquity" (Matt. 7:23). Jesus is going to say, 'Depart from Me, ye accursed. I never knew you as one of My own. Depart ye into everlasting fire.'

In a previous chapter John saw a picture of the coming wrath of God and said that in that awful day when God judges the world, captains and mighty men and rich men shall all cry out to the mountains and to the rocks, "Fall on us, and hide us from the face of him that sitteth on the throne, and from the wrath of the Lamb: For the great day of his wrath is come; and who shall be able to stand?" (Rev. 6:16,17).

If I am speaking to one who has never been to Calvary and been born the second time, you will stand in the white light of His holiness and your every word and thought will be in panoramic view across the heavens. That will be an awful day.

I wouldn't want to stand in the sinner's shoes. If God could give me the power to paint that picture from the Bible in regards to what it means to be unsaved, without God, without hope, headed toward a judgment bar and an eternal Hell, there would not be one of you unsaved. If you could see it as it really is—that God is a holy God and a God of wrath who will punish sin—you would come right now to meet Jesus Christ as your personal Saviour.

V. THE JUDGMENT ITSELF

Fifth, the judgment itself proves some things: first, that death doesn't end everything. Every once in awhile I meet someone who thinks it does, but it doesn't. Death does not end all—not for a man. Of all the things God ever made, we are the only thing made like God. We are made in His image. Man is as eternal as God. I am going to live just as long as God lives, somewhere.

I heard Dr. Bob Jones, Sr., say that once while walking along a road in Florida a truth hit him that changed his life, something he had known and believed was true but had never really thought about before: *I am going to live just as long as God lives!* My friends, the judgment proves that death does not end all. Remember—you might die today, tomorrow or ten years from now; but on the judgment day you will be raised to stand before God.

The judgment teaches something else—that God is inescapable. You cannot escape God. You may think you can. You may determine not to listen to a preacher. It may not matter to you if loved ones pray for you, nor do you care how many people knock on your door nor care how many sermons are preached nor how many songs are sung—"I don't have to respond," you say. Right. You don't.

I have had people say to me, "I don't want anyone to force me to be saved." No one could; but one thing you cannot escape is God. Someday you are going to face Him. If there is one here not saved, oh, believe the truth that you are going to meet God someday! The judgment proves that there is no escape. Amos 4:12 warns, "Prepare to meet thy God."

The judgment proves that God is holy and just. He rectifies everything. God Almighty makes everything all right before the end of time. The judgment proves that sin must be reckoned with. Romans 6:23 says, "For the wages of sin is death." Galatians 6:7 reminds us, "Be not deceived; God is not mocked: for whatsoever a man soweth, that shall he also reap."

The judgment proves that sin must be reckoned with. Unsaved, you can't laugh it away. You can't smile it away. You can't keep on ignoring it. Someday you must meet sin head on at the judgment bar of God.

A man told his little boy one time, "Son, when you do something bad, I am going to drive a nail in that post. When you do something good, I will pull one out."

The little fellow did so many things right that soon every nail in that post had been pulled. Then the boy said to his father, "Daddy, the nails are all gone, but the holes are still there."

Maybe you have forgotten, but God never has. If you are not saved and the sins of your life are not under the blood, you will meet God at the judgment bar.

"Be not deceived; God is not mocked: for whatsoever a man soweth, that shall he also reap."—Gal. 6:7.

"For the wages of sin is death."—Rom. 6:23.

God says that sin must be reckoned with, and man will reckon with it at the judgment bar.

The judgment teaches me also that Hell is a reality. There is no way to estimate how many people are in Hell today because of the cults and isms in the world.

A country preacher one time said, "I will be so glad when all the isms are 'wasms.'" I will too.

There is no way to estimate how many millions are already in Hell. People get into a battle of semantics and a bantering with words. As I mentioned before, too many people are arguing that Sheol in the Old Testament and Hades in the New Testament don't mean Hell. They do mean Hell. But forget all that for a moment.

People can argue all they want to, and literally thousands can be engulfed by wicked cults; but they are going to end up in Hell.

The Devil can really sugarcoat his pills so that people will take them. He puts a little truth in with a lot of lies and puts truth in that is misappropriated. I know people who can quote Scripture by the yard who are going to end up in Hell because they are confused about who Jesus is. They say, "There is no Hell. God is too good." Others say we will just be annihilated. The Bible does not teach annihilation, not in the Old Testament nor in the New. There is not one iota of teaching in the Bible that a person will be annihilated and his suffering will be only instantaneous. It is eternal, God says.

One man who engulfed thousands in one of the most wicked cults was once put on a witness stand and asked if he could quote the Greek alphabet. He could not. This one who helped start one of the most wicked cults which literally swept thousands of people around this encircled globe, couldn't even quote the Greek alphabet. He had been deceiving people for almost a generation by saying, "And the Greek says. . . ."

Listen, you can't get into a battle of words on Revelation 20 which says, "And whosoever was not found written in the book of life was cast into the lake of fire." You must take it like it is. God said "lake of fire."

Someone says, "That is figurative language." Listen, if that is a figure, then the truth is far worse than the figure. Every time the Bible uses figurative language the whole context will show that God is using a symbol. Here God's Word plainly says, "And whosoever was not found written in the book of life was cast into the lake of fire."

The judgment itself proves to me that there is a Hell. There is not much said about Hell today. When I was a boy, in a week of revival meetings at least one night out of the seven you would hear a sermon on Hell.

Someone says, "Oh, in this modern age we don't believe in scaring people. You preachers tell deathbed stories and talk about God burning people up and all of that. Fear is not a good motive."

But I read in Hebrews 11:7, "By faith Noah, being warned of God of things not seen as yet, moved with fear, prepared an ark to the saving of his house; by the which he condemned the world, and became heir of the righteousness which is by faith." It is a shame that someone didn't tell Noah about what psychologists believe.

You say, "Fear is not a good motive." Listen, you take your little child to the fire and say, "Hot—burn! Hot—burn! Hot—burn! Don't touch—burn!" You take him out where the cars are going up and down the road and say, "Now you stay out of that street. You get in that street, and a car will hit you."

Why? You want to scare him because you love him. You want to scare him because you don't want to lose him. You want to scare him because he is important to you.

Likewise, God wants people to fear Him enough to be saved. Romans 3:18 says, "There is no fear of God before their eyes."

We need some preaching on Hell. For one thing, it makes us better Christians. I would to God that we believed it. If today we had Christians who believed in Hell like it is taught in the Bible, we would win a lot more people to the Lord. We need that. Hell is just a myth in the minds of many people. Listen, Jesus said,

"And if thy hand offend thee, cut it off: it is better for thee to enter into life maimed, than having two hands to go into hell, into the fire that never shall be quenched: Where their worm dieth not, and the fire is not quenched."—Mark 9:43,44.

Jesus said that one day a Christ rejecter died and lifted up his eyes in Hell and cried being in torments. The great white throne judgment is to settle, finally, everyone who is to be put into Hell.

The judgment teaches me that it is universal. No one will escape. Acts 17:31 says,

"Because he hath appointed a day, in the which he will judge the world in righteousness by that man whom he hath ordained; whereof he hath given assurance unto all men, in that he hath raised him from the dead."

God raised Jesus from the dead to guarantee a day of judgment. If people would believe that there is a judgment day coming, it would affect their behavior here and now. If you are not saved, I think it would cause you to be saved.

VI. THE JUDGMENT IN PROPHECY

The judgment is in prophecy all through the Bible.

Someone says, "Well, I don't believe God is going to judge the world."

Let's look at the past for a moment. Ecclesiastes 12:14 says, "For God shall bring every work into judgment, with every secret thing, whether it be good, or whether it be evil."

You look back across the pages of Holy Writ. One day God judged this world because of its sinful flesh. He looked down on it and said, "The end of all flesh is come before me; for the earth is filled with violence through them; and, behold, I will destroy them with the earth" (Gen. 6:13).

Genesis 6:3 says, "And the Lord said, My spirit shall not always strive with man, for that he also is flesh: yet his days shall be an hundred and twenty years."

God sent a Flood that destroyed the world: "And, behold, I, even I, do bring a flood of waters upon the earth, to destroy all flesh, wherein is the breath of life" (Gen. 6:17). One day God looked down upon two cities and because of their worldliness, Sodom and Gomorrah were destroyed. God used the Flood to destroy the race because of man's flesh, and He destroyed Sodom and Gomorrah because of their worldliness.

Read about that day when Uncle Abraham talked to his nephew Lot. Their herdsmen were arguing because they had so much worldly goods.

Abraham said to Lot, "We do not need to quarrel. We are brethren. You go one way, and I will go the other, and we will still be brethren. If you want to go to the mountains, I will go to the plains. If you want to go to the plains, I will go to the mountains."

Lot began to look around. He saw Sodom and Gomorrah. And the Bible says that the men of those cities were wicked exceedingly, but the plains were well watered. Lot said, "A poor place for me to be, a terrible place for my family, but a wonderful place for my cattle. I can be rich in Sodom," and he was. He became mayor of the city. The Bible says that he was the one who sat in the gate like that of a judge.

One day God looked down on those two cities; and because of their worldliness and materialism, He said He would destroy them, so He rained down fire and brimstone from Heaven.

Some folks wonder if there is real fire in Hell. Sure. God rained it out of Heaven, and He destroyed those cities. Today not one living thing is found in the Dead Sea. Down at the south end, under water, are the remains of the cities of Sodom and Gomorrah. The sulphuric atmosphere still prevails all around that body of water, and not one blade of grass grows there. God destroyed those cities. God did judge the world with a Flood and with fire and brimstone.

One day men were judged because of a bloodless religion. They said, "Go to, let us build us a city and a tower, whose top may reach unto heaven; and let us make us a name, lest we be scattered abroad upon the face of the whole earth" (Gen. 11:4). God said, "Let's go see what the people are doing." God the Father here is speaking to the other Persons of the Trinity. Man said, "Let us build." God said, "Let us go down and look." God went down and saw that tower and the efforts of man to get to Heaven without God. God said, "Man will never be restrained in anything if he is allowed to do this," so He struck it to the ground.

"Go to, let us go down, and there confound their language, that they may not understand one another's speech. So the Lord scattered them abroad from thence upon the face of all the earth."—Gen. 11:7,8.

You say, "Well, God judged the world." Yes, He did.

He judged the land of Egypt. For four hundred long years they kept God's people in bondage, and God said that He would send judgment on the land. I have walked in that land, and I have seen the flies and insects and poverty and blindness and disease and ignorance and sin. There are millions of people still in a land that God judged. Will God judge? Yes, He will.

God judged Babylon. Nebuchadnezzar built the city walls so thick that three chariots could race around them at one time on top of the walls. One night the unseen messenger of God wrote on the walls, *"TEKEL; Thou art weighed in the balances, and art found wanting"* (Dan. 5:27).

The tingling of glasses stopped, and the flying feet on the dance floor and the orchestra hushed, and God spoke in that night, and Belshazzar was slain.

God said, "Babylon will never be rebuilt. It will be the home of owls and jackals and night animals." You can go to those ruins today, and that is just what you find because God is a God of judgment.

You say, "Will God judge the world?" He has judged nations in the past. It says in Proverbs 14:34, "Righteousness exalteth a nation: but sin is a reproach to any people."

I have seen God send judgment on people. I remember a man down in Tennessee whose little daughter died. No one knows why God takes a sweet little child.

The old-fashioned people used to prepare their dead for burial. They would send to town for a casket and bring it back on a wagon. The neighbors would come; they would prepare the body for the casket, leave it in the home and the next day bury it.

Some of those helping about the dead little daughter said to the father, "Go chop some wood so we can heat some water to prepare this child for burial."

He went out, and before picking up the ax he lifted his fist toward God and said, "Yeah, You can kill a little baby, but have You ever tried killing man! Why don't You come down and fight with a man!"

As he reached down to put his hand on the ax handle, a little insect bit him on the end of the finger, and in three days he died of blood poisoning, died blaspheming God.

It is like a young man who said to friends, "None of these things are sacred to me. I don't believe in God nor Jesus nor blood nor Calvary nor the Holy Ghost." He took a sheep and waded out into the creek leaving his three friends on the shore. He said, mockingly, "We are going to have a baptismal service. In the name of the Father, Son and Holy Ghost . . ."; and he put the sheep under water. When it came up struggling, it pushed the man down, and he fell into the stream with the sheep. Not being able to swim, he drowned. His three companions stood like frozen stones and watched. Someone said, "Why didn't you help him?" They answered, "If bands of steel had been around our arms, we couldn't have moved any less. We were bound to our tracks on that day."

Listen, God judges people today. I have seen Him do it. I have seen the intervening hand of God come in judgment.

Proverbs 29:1 says, "He, that being often reproved hardeneth his neck, shall suddenly be destroyed, and that without remedy." God is going to judge the world.

VII. THE JUDGMENT BOOKS

I close by saying that there were judgment books. John said, "And the books were opened." Daniel spoke of the books in Daniel 7:10, ". . .the judgment was set, and the books were opened."

In those books will be a record of every time you have ever heard the Gospel or felt conviction of the Holy Spirit. There will be a record of every time you ever had a contact with a true believer. There will be a record of every time you have procrastinated and said, "Go thy way for this time." In those books will be a record of every promise you ever made to get right with God and didn't. There will be a record of every invitation song you ever heard, of every tear that was ever shed for your salvation. There will be a record of every time you were ever angry at a witness who tried to win you. All will be in the books.

Listen! God is an accurate Bookkeeper. John said, "Hallelujah! A book was opened—the book of life."

Do you know why it is there? Here will come a man like Matthew 7 speaks of who will say, "Lord, I am not unsaved. Why, I did wonderful works in Your name." God will say to a recording angel, "Get the little book out and look up the name of this man." The angel will look, then say, "There is no such name here." Jesus will then say, "Depart from me ye accursed into everlasting fire. I never knew you."

The book of life always has been. God has always had it. He had it in Moses' day. When the children of Israel sinned, Moses prayed and sobbed and broke in his statement and said, "Yet now, if thou wilt forgive their sin—; and if not, blot me, I pray thee, out of thy book which thou hast written" (Exod. 32:32).

Oh, yes, the books will be there. They will be at the judgment. Every word, every deed, every thought, every wasted opportunity, every moment of procrastination, every gospel song you have ever heard, every verse of Scripture you ever heard read or quoted will be written in that book.

But, thank God, there will be another book there! Thirty-five years ago I saw that my name was written in that book. When I believed in the blood of Christ, God wrote it down forever. The judgment holds no fear for me, for I was judged at Calvary when Jesus died.

"And I saw a great white throne, and him that sat on it, from whose face the earth and the heaven fled away; and there was found no place for them. And I saw the dead, small and great, stand before God; and the books were opened: and another book was opened, which is the book of life: and the dead were judged out of those things which were written in the books, according to their works."—Rev. 20:11,12.

JACK HYLES
1926-

ABOUT THE MAN:

If we could say but one thing about Dr. Hyles, I guess we would call him MR. SOUL WINNING.

Born in Italy, Texas, he began preaching at age nineteen. He pastored several churches in that state, most notably the Miller Road Baptist Church in Garland that was no doubt the fastest growing church in the world for many years. In seven years it grew to the astounding number of 4,000 members.

Then on to the formal downtown First Baptist Church in the Calumet area of Hammond, Indiana. There, after fighting for separation in the church, he won victory after victory. Now that church is the largest Sunday school in the world. Attendance of over 25,000 is common on a Sunday.

Hammond Baptist Schools, Hyles-Anderson College, Hyles-Anderson Publications, and many other gospel projects have come forth from his fantastic ministry.

His best friend, the late Dr. John R. Rice, said about this giant: *"Jack Hyles is a tornado of zeal. He is pungent in speech, devastating in sarcasm. You will laugh and cry — and repent! Preachers who are not dead will preach differently after hearing him. Thousands point to a message from Jack Hyles as the time of a transformed life. He is simply beyond description, with a unique anointing from God."*

Dr. Hyles is the author of many books, including *Hyles Church Manual, Hyles Sunday School Manual, Kisses of Calvary,* and a great series of *How to. . .* books. He also has a large cassette ministry.

Place Dr. Jack Hyles among the giants of this generation!

XIII.

The Great White Throne

JACK HYLES

The Second Resurrection
The Second Judgment
The Second Death
The Second Adam
The Second Birth

"And I saw a great white throne, and him that sat on it, from whose face the earth and the heaven fled away; and there was found no place for them. And I saw the dead, small and great, stand before God; and the books were opened: and another book was opened, which is the book of life: and the dead were judged out of those things which were written in the books, according to their works. And the sea gave up the dead which were in it; and death and hell delivered up the dead which were in them: and they were judged every man according to their works. And death and hell were cast into the lake of fire. This is the second death. And whosoever was not found written in the book of life was cast into the lake of fire."—Rev. 20:11-15.

Herein you find the story of what is known in doctrinal terminology as the great white throne judgment.

In all my ministry I have never thought there was anything as important as keeping folks out of Hell. That is why Jesus left Heaven. That is why He came and lived on earth for thirty-three years. That is why He went to Calvary. That is why He rose again. In Heaven He is interceding for us, that people might go to Heaven.

That is the biggest thing the church has to do. That is the greatest job of the preacher. That is the most important job of the Christian. Jesus said, "The Son of man is come to seek and to save that which was lost." He said again, "As the Father hath sent me, even so send I you."

Years ago the famous preacher, J. Wilbur Chapman, took a poll of people in his campaigns as to what age they were when they were saved. He found by far the great majority who come to Christ are saved before the age of twenty. The greatest majority are saved between the ages of twelve and sixteen. How many here received Christ somewhere between ten and fifteen? You see the huge response.

He took also a poll and found that, when one passes 25 years of age, he has one chance in 1,000 to get saved. Only one person in 1,000 is saved after he is 25. If a person passes 35, he has one chance in 50,000 to be saved. If a person passes 45 without Jesus Christ, he has one chance in 200,000 to get saved. If a man passes 55 without Christ, he has one chance in 300,000 to get saved. And if a man passes 75 without Jesus, he has one chance in 700,000 to be saved, or one chance in almost a million.

Now you can see why it is tremendously important that we stay after sinners, that we try to get folks saved.

Now a word of introduction. We are looking for the rapture of the church, the event when the Lord Jesus Christ will come, the trumpet of God shall sound, the dead in Christ shall be raised, those who are alive and remain shall be caught up to meet the Lord in the air. For seven years we will be with Him in the air.

While that seven years transpires, on earth will be what is known as the Great Tribulation period, the time of suffering, of war, of famine, of death, of bloodshed. On earth—a seven-year period known as the Great Tribulation; in Heaven—the judgment seat, the marriage of the Lamb for seven years. Remember: the saved—seven years in Heaven while the Tribulation is going on for seven years on earth.

At the end of that time we will come back with Jesus to establish a kingdom on the earth. For one thousand years, we as God's children shall rule and reign with the Lord Jesus Christ upon this earth. We shall be priests of God.

Now at the end of that thousand years will take place what is known as the great white throne judgment. Have you ever heard anybody pray thus, "Dear Lord, help me to live so as someday I may appear before the great white throne"? I don't want to pray like that. I don't intend to appear before the great white throne, for that judgment is for the unsaved dead.

Now tonight for our message I will use the word *seconds* and show you a series of second things that will summarize the study of the great white throne judgment found in Revelation, chapter 20, verses 11 through 15.

First, I call your attention to the second resurrection. Second, I call your attention to the second judgment. Third, I speak on the second Adam. Fourth, the second death. And fifth, the second birth.

We look first at

The Second Resurrection.

Turn to Revelation 20:5:

"But the rest of the dead lived not again until the thousand years were finished. This is the first resurrection."

In this verse we find the resurrection of the saved, when those of us who are saved shall be caught up to meet the Lord Jesus Christ in the air. I remind you that all peoples will not be raised at the same time. I hear such talk as, "At the last day," "the resurrection." There will be no such thing as *the* resurrection, one general resurrection. The Bible says when Jesus comes, two shall be grinding at the mill. One shall be taken; the other left. Two shall be in bed. One shall be taken; the other left. And so at the first resurrection—which takes place at the rapture of the church—only Christians will be resurrected. For our message we speak on the second resurrection.

Now, after the Christians are gone, the Bible says the unsaved will be left. Those who die in their sins will still be in the grave. "They lived not again until the thousand years were finished."

Just suppose tonight, here is a man who is saved; here is a wife who is lost. They die, they are buried. Now that man, that saved person, will be raised from the dead when Jesus comes for His own. But this lost wife over here in the grave, right beside the saved person, won't rise at the second coming of Christ but will stay in the grave one thousand and seven years longer than the saved. The saved rise before the millennium; the lost rise after the millennium. There are two separate resurrections.

Look at verses 12 and 13:

"And I saw the dead, small and great, stand before God; and the books were opened: and another book was opened, which is the book

*of life: and the dead were judged out of those things which were writ-
ten in the books, according to their works. And the sea gave up the
dead which were in it; and death and hell delivered up the dead which
were in them: and they were judged every man according to their
works."*

Now at the second resurrection, at the end of the thousand-year reign
of Christ upon the earth, the unsaved dead will be raised—the drunkards,
the harlots, the whoremongers, the liars, the thieves, the sorcerers, the
adulterers, the idolaters—all unbelievers; those who rejected the Gospel
of Christ, those who, in services like this, said no to Jesus Christ; those
who believed they knew more than God—the infidels, the liberals, the
modernists—all the people who laughed at the Bible and thought they
were too smart for the Word of God, will be raised at the second
resurrection.

Now notice the words *death* and *Hell*. This says that death and Hell
will deliver up the dead which were in them. At death a lost man's body
goes to the grave while his soul goes to Hades. Actually the word *Hell*
in verse 23 is translated from "Hades." Hades is the place where the
rich man of Luke 16 is, who lifted up his eyes, being in torments, and
said, "Father Abraham. . .send Lazarus, that he may dip the tip of his
finger in water, and cool my tongue; for I am tormented in this flame."
His body was in the grave; his soul was in Hades.

At the second resurrection, the soul of that rich man and the soul
of all the unsaved will come from Hades while their bodies will come
from the graves. Both soul and body shall be reunited, and both shall
be cast into the final lake of fire.

Let me say again: I believe in a burning, literal Hell of fire. If the
Bible is not true on Hell, we have no reason to believe it is true on
anything else. If it is not fire in Hell as Jesus said it was, we can say
salvation does not mean exactly what it says. Heaven is not real if we
do not believe the Scriptures on Hell. Jesus said Hell was fire. We
modern folks have gotten too educated. We are too scientific.

My friends, the Bible **IS** true. The Bible says, "Let God be true, but
every man a liar." And so the souls of people who die in their sins are
in conscious torment in Hell tonight.

But at the end of the millennium, the souls shall come from Hades,
the body shall come from the grave, and both body and the soul of
the unsaved shall be reunited. Then Jesus Christ Himself shall take both

body and soul and cast them into the lake of fire.

My precious friend, if you are hoping that maybe you will go to purgatory and somebody will pull you out of purgatory, you have your eggs in the wrong basket. My Bible says there is a place called Heaven, there is a place called Hell; and between the two a great gulf is fixed whereby no one can pass from one to the other. Death seals your destiny. People can call prayer meetings and pray for your departed spirit; they can call a high mass or a low mass, but if you have not received Christ, you are lost forever in the pit of an eternal Hell.

So the body of the unredeemed will come from the grave, the soul from Hades; then Jesus will later cast both body and soul back into Hell.

Now we have seen the second resurrection. We hasten on to what is known as

The Second Judgment.

This takes place after the second resurrection. Look in verse 13 again:

"And the sea gave up the dead which were in it; and death and hell [hades] *delivered up the dead which were in them* [the second resurrection]*: and they were judged every man according to their works* [the second judgment]*."*

We have preached to you before about the judgment seat of Christ. I told you about a time coming when all believers shall receive their rewards. Not a single lost person will be at that judgment. Do not forget this: there will never in this world nor in the world to come be a time when all people, saved and unsaved, will be brought before the same judgment of God. Our sins were judged in Jesus on the cross of Calvary. That takes care of that. I will never stand before God as far as salvation is concerned. We will, before the millennium, before the thousand years, stand before God to get our rewards. At the end of the thousand years will be the second judgment when the unsaved are judged.

Before the second judgment, verse 11 says, "And I saw a great white throne, and him that sat on it, from whose face the earth and the heaven fled away. . . ." Did you see that? At the great white throne judgment, when all the redeemed are resurrected and stand before God, then "the earth and the heaven shall flee away."

There is coming a time when the earth shall flee away. The Scripture says it shall melt with a fervent heat. Even Heaven itself shall flee away. In the Sermon on the Mount given in Matthew, Jesus said that heaven shall pass away, earth shall pass away, but the Word of God abideth forever. So before the great white throne judgment, heaven and earth shall pass away.

Now why will the earth pass away? Because God will not have anything contaminated by sin. So He is going to give us a new earth and a new heaven—the starry heaven. When this time comes, somewhere in the skies, in the third Heaven maybe, when Jesus Christ sits on the great white throne and all the unredeemed stand before Him, heaven and earth shall flee away; then shall be a new heaven and a new earth.

May I say again: this judgment in Revelation 20 is not for the saved; it is only for the unsaved. Dear friend, if you are saved, you are not going to stand before God.

I have heard folks say, "Well, I hope I get saved in the end." Brother, if you don't get saved in the beginning, you won't get saved in the end. If you don't get saved this side of death, you won't get saved at all. There will never be a time when God will take us and decide then whether we go to Heaven or Hell. That was decided the moment you received Christ as your Saviour.

These people this morning who came down these aisles and by faith received Jesus Christ as their Saviour, once and for all settled their going to Heaven. When they accepted Him, they got a release from this great white throne judgment of God. Only the unsaved will be present at that judgment.

And this great white throne judgment of God is not a judgment of salvation, but a judgment for degrees of punishment. Some are going to burn hotter than others. (That is not a very good way to put it, but that is about the way it is.) Just as some at the judgment seat shall receive more rewards than others, at the great white throne judgment some shall receive more punishment than others. Let me say this, too: those who reject and reject and reject Jesus Christ, those who say no to the Gospel, will receive greater punishment in Hell.

Here is a good man who lived where there was no gospel preaching. Only once did he ever hear the Gospel. He is a good husband, a good father; but he rejected the Gospel of Christ. Yes, he will go to Hell because he received not the Saviour, but he will not burn as much as this fellow who heard the Gospel every Sunday and rejected it. Some of you belong to a church but have never been born again—you come to church regularly and are reminded every Sunday, "Do you know if you died tonight, you would go to Heaven?" Again and again and again and again the preacher says that, and your conscience is pricked. You know you are not saved. You know you are lost. The Bible says those people who have received much shall be punished more. And people who have heard the Gospel much and rejected many, many times the story of Christ, those who have lived in awful sin, shall get more punishment than those who have not heard it so often.

And so the white throne judgment is not for salvation, but for degrees of punishment.

Let's picture it for you. Here is the great throne over here. On it is the Lord Jesus Christ. Ken, can you and John imagine you are lost, for a minute? I will have you both stand before the throne. Ken is standing before the throne. He has been a bootlegger; he has beaten his wife. He is a first-class crook. He has come to church all his life but never believed the Gospel of Christ. He does not believe the Bible is the Word of God. He does not believe that Jesus Christ is God's Son. His wife carried the children to church all her life while Ken laughed, mocked and made fun of the old-time religion and the Bible being the Word of God and Jesus being the Son of God.

When Ken stands before God, he will suffer more Hell than will somebody else who didn't have the opportunities that he had. His Fahrenheit will be 640 degrees.

Here is John. He is a good man. Soda is the very strongest drink John drinks. John stands before God.

God says, "John, have you ever heard the Gospel?"

"Yes, sir. When I was a little boy, I heard the Gospel one time."

"Did you receive it?"

"No, I didn't."

"John, have you been a good husband?"

"Yes."

"Have you been a good father?"

"Yes."

"Have you been a good citizen?"

"That's right."

"Have you lived a pretty clean life?"

"That's right."

"John, you will still have to go to Hell, but yours will be 190 degrees Fahrenheit."

Don't tell me that the drunkard in the gutter, the wife-beater, the man who made light of the Word of God, will not suffer more than a fifteen-year-old who died without trusting Christ. The Word of God says they shall be judged **every man according to his works.**

The second resurrection, when the unsaved are raised from the dead. The second judgment, when the unsaved stand before God.

Now we come to what is known as

The Second Adam.

In I Corinthians, chapter 15 and verse 22, it is mentioned. Jesus Christ is called the second Adam. In the first Adam, all died. In the second Adam, all became alive. Whereas through the first Adam, sin came into the world; through the second Adam, righteousness came into the world. So Jesus is called the second Adam.

Who is going to judge? In verse 11 of Revelation 20:

"And I saw a great white throne, and him that sat on it, from whose face the earth and the heaven fled away; and there was found no place for them."

John, chapter 5, says all judgment is given to Jesus Christ. The second Adam will sit on the throne.

May I say this: in that day Jesus Christ will not be the loving, tender Saviour wanting to save. Tonight He is. Tonight Jesus says, "Him that cometh unto me, I will in no wise cast out." In that day He will not give you a chance to come to Him. Now Jesus, the Son of God, the One you rejected, the One who tried to save you, the One who died for you, sits on the throne, and He calls your name. Here is Jesus, and here you are. For the first time in your life you must stand face to face with Jesus Christ and give an account for why you rejected the Gospel.

Here is an unsaved one standing before Jesus. Too late to get saved then. You will have to get saved now, for it will be too late then.

It is said a judge in a large city was walking along near some water one day. Seeing a young man drowning, he rushed to his rescue, took off his coat, jumped in the water and brought the man to safety. The man, so grateful, expressed his gratitude to the judge. The judge literally had saved him from death.

A few months passed, and this same young man committed some crime against society and was brought before this same judge. The judge sentenced him to whatever the penalty was.

The man said, "But judge, you remember me, don't you?"

Sternly the judge answered, "Sir, I don't recall."

He said, "Judge, remember a few months ago you were walking near the water and I was drowning? You pulled off your coat, jumped in and pulled me to safety. You saved my life, judge. Now you don't want to send me to jail."

The judge looked at him and said, with steely eyes, "Young man, that day I was your saviour; today I am your judge."

Jesus Christ is your Saviour tonight. He will save any child, any man, any woman who will come to Him by faith. He will forgive your sins. He will make you a home in Heaven. He will save you from the fires of Hell. He will make you His child. All that belongs to Him shall belong to you. And you can leave this building tonight saying, "I know that I know that I know that I am a child of God." But in that day the loving Saviour will be your Judge.

But you say, "Dear Lord, I am on the prospect file down at the First Baptist Church in Hammond. They always beg me. I thought about coming when I got around to it."

"I was your Saviour then; now I am your Judge," He will answer back.

Jesus, the second Adam, shall be the Judge.

We have seen the second resurrection, the second judgment, the second Adam; now may I remind you of

The Second Death.

Look at verse 14:

"And death and hell [hades] were cast into the lake of fire. This is the second death."

The second resurrection shall take place first. After the second resurrection, the unsaved will be judged at the second judgment. They will be judged by the second Adam, and then they will suffer the second death. Here it is. They call the names...

John Peabody!

Mary Smith!

Jack Johnson!

Joe Jones!

They call the names! They stand before God, and God opens the books. The books are opened, and another book which is the book

of life, and Revelation 20:15 says those not found written in the book
of life were cast into the lake of fire. This is the second death.

Do you know what America needs? A generation of Hell-fire-and-
brimstone preachers.

Listen to me tonight. Every religious revival this world has ever known,
every spiritual revival, has been built on preaching the judgment and
the wrath and the fury of a righteous and holy and just God. I am not
discounting God's love. I believe in preaching about the love of God.
But as Billy Sunday used to say, "You can't love flowers unless you
hate weeds." You can't love God unless you hate sin. For it was sin
that nailed the Saviour to the cross. And the more you love and appreciate Him, the more you hate that which caused Him to suffer on
the cross of Calvary.

Billy Sunday, D. L. Moody, R. A. Torrey, Paul Rader, Gypsy Smith,
George Truett, Bob Jones, John Rice—how many more names we
could call; men of yesterday—Savonarola, Martin Luther, John Wesley,
John Calvin, John Huss—were men who realized our God is a con-
suming fire.

My precious friend, you hear me tonight! Someday you will stand
before God; and if you are not saved, you will hear Him say, "Cast
him into outer darkness. Bind him hand and foot, for he has not received
the invitation to come to My supper."

The second death. Chapter 21, verse 8, says the same thing:

*"But the fearful, and unbelieving, and the abominable, and murderers,
and whoremongers, and sorcerers, and idolaters, and all liars, shall have
their part in the lake which burneth with fire and brimstone: which is
the second death."*

Nowadays theology says, "Don't tell folks about Hell. Don't tell them
they are going to Hell if they die and are lost. Tell them that in Jesus
they have the more abundant life."

That is right. You do have the more abundant life. But brother, lost
people are going to have an abundant death, and you had better tell
them about that, too. I believe Jesus does give abundant life. Thank
God, I have been happy ever since I came to Christ. Now I am happy
in the Lord. I love the prayer life, the Bible study, the fellowship with
God. But I do know that the same God who accepts sinners also con-
demns them to Hell if they receive not the Gospel of Christ.

The second death; the fires of Hell. Some of you folks will say, "Well,

I just don't believe Hell is real fire." You have a right not to believe what you do not want to believe, but you can't say you believe the Bible and not believe Hell is real fire.

You have a right to believe what you want to believe, but don't you call yourself a Christian, don't you call yourself a Bible-believer, don't call yourself a fundamental believer in the Gospel of Christ if you don't believe what Jesus said about Hell being fire. He said, "Then shall he say also unto them on the left hand, Depart from me, ye cursed, into everlasting fire. . . ."

But you say, "He didn't mean fire." But He said fire, didn't He? And as the little girl said, "Mama, if Jesus didn't mean what He said, why didn't He say what He means?"

Again He said in Mark 9:44, "Where their worm dieth not, and the fire is not quenched." Over and over and over again we are reminded that those who reject the Gospel of Christ must suffer the second death.

My friends in the balcony, on the lower floor, up here—I beg you tonight, if you have never by faith received Jesus Christ, flee to the Son of God who alone can save you from the fires of Hell.

After the great white throne judgment will come the second resurrection. After the second resurrection will come the second judgment. On the throne shall be the second Adam, and there shall be a second death.

But you say, "Preacher, how can I escape the second resurrection? How can I escape the second judgment? How can I escape facing, at the awful time, the second Adam? How can I escape the fires of the second death?"

I am glad you asked me. You can escape by being participants in the second birth.

The Second Birth

The Lord Jesus said, "Ye must be born again." Those who have the second birth will not have to suffer the second death. If you have not received the second birth, you have to suffer the second death. Jesus stands, the books are opened, another book is opened, the book of life. You stand before God. God looks at you.

Jesus Christ asks, "Is your name in the book?"

You say, "Dear Lord, it must be. I was a good church member."

He says, **"Is your name in the book?"**

204 GREAT PREACHING ON JUDGMENT

"Well," you say, "I guess so. I was baptized."

"But is your name in the book?"

"Well," you say, "I imagine it is. I had an attendance pin. I didn't miss in Sunday school for fourteen years."

"But is your name in the book?"

"Well, I think so. I gave to the United Way every year."

"But is your name in the book?"

"Well, I think so. I was a good husband."

"Is your name in the book?"

"Well, I guess so. I was a good father."

"Is your name in the book?"

"Well, I paid my debts."

"IS YOUR NAME IN THE BOOK?"

There is only one way: by being born again. If you have trusted Christ, you will go to Heaven. If you haven't, you will go to Hell regardless of all the good things you have done. Only one determining question: have you been born again? If you have, you will miss all of this. If you haven't, you will stand before God as the books are opened.

In Philadelphia, Pennsylvania, Ethan Allen stood up to testify at a Christian meeting. Ethan Allen was for years an officer in the United States Army. Allen gave this testimony at a businessmen's luncheon:

> I married the girl of my dreams. We were so in love, so happy. But she was a Christian; I was an infidel. I watched her go to church Sunday after Sunday. I looked at her life, listened to her prayers. I saw her Bible stained with tears. I was an infidel. I laughed at her as she walked off to church, made fun of her as she prayed. I thought she was foolish for reading the Word of God. I was an infidel.

Ethan Allen said:

> After awhile, gentlemen, God gave us a baby, a precious little girl. Oh, we loved her! How we loved her! When she was an infant, her mother carried her to Sunday school *every* Sunday. When she was a beginner—four, five, six—*every* Sunday she was at church. Every Sunday night—back to the Sunday night service. Every Wednesday night—to mid-week prayer service. She never missed. Every week she went with her mother.

Then said Ethan Allen:

> When she was six—to church with mother. Seven—to church with mother. Eight, nine, ten, eleven—to church with mother. But when

she got to be about twelve, I began taking her with me to nightclubs, to dance halls, to high balls. She had a good time.

Finally she began to tell her mother, "Mother, I don't want to go to church today. I am too sleepy. Daddy and I stayed out so late last night."

Ethan Allen continued:

I would laugh under my breath and say, *She is not going to follow the old-time religion of her mother. I am so happy about that.* Her mother would plead and beg, "Honey, please go with mother. Please go with mother." But I would say, "Honey, you stay home if you want to." So she would say no to her mother.

Finally on Sunday nights I would take her out to the dance halls or some nightclub with me, and we would have a big time painting the town red while mother was at the church house weeping her eyes out because her daughter had gone into sin.

He said:

Finally our daughter quit going to church. She never went with her mother. She was a beautiful girl, fifteen or sixteen years of age. We loved her dearly. Her mother was a Christian; I an infidel. She was following daddy's footsteps.

But one night she was out with a gang of kids in a carriage. They had been swimming, and she caught cold. After awhile it went into pneumonia. In those days we didn't have penicillin and all the other cures we have now. So before long she was at the point of death.

The doctor called me in and said, "Mr. Allen, your girl is dying."

Allen looked at those businessmen and said:

I went in and looked at my little girl—just a teenager. Her mother had served Jesus Christ; I was an infidel. I looked at her, and my daughter said to me, "Daddy, I am dying, am I not?"

I replied, "Yes, honey. You are going to die." Then I began to weep. Her mother was crying. But there was not a tear in our little girl's eyes. She said, "Daddy, I want to know one thing. All my life mother has gone one way, and you have gone the other way. Now daddy, since I am dying, I have got to know the answer. I have got to know. I love you, daddy. I love you and I trust you and believe what you say. Daddy, while I am dying, should I die mommy's way or your way?"

Ethan Allen said:

I began to cry. Then I threw my body on hers and said, "Honey, choose mother's way! Choose mommy's way! Quickly, honey! Choose mommy's way!"

Ethan Allen said:

> Before I could get it said, she had gone off to meet the Lord Jesus.
> I will never know until I face God whether or not she chose mommy's
> way or daddy's way!

Oh, in Jesus Christ tonight is escape from judgment. There is salvation forever. Heaven with Christ and the saints. That is the best way. Choose mommy's way!

Thomas Paine thought he could live without God. When Paine came to die he said, "I wish I had never lived!"

Voltaire laughed and mocked at God. When Voltaire came to face death, he said, "O Jesus Christ, O Jesus Christ! It is hell to be left alone!"

Thomas Hobbs wrote book after book denying the efficacy of the Gospel of Christ. When Thomas Hobbs came to die, he said, "I am taking a fearful leap into the dark! O Christ! O Jesus!"

My precious friends, in Christ tonight, in the second birth, you can know the second Adam; you can escape the second death, the second resurrection and the second judgment, if you know Christ in the second birth.

Do you know Him tonight? Will you be at the first resurrection, or at the second? Will you be at the first judgment, or the second? Will you choose the second birth, or suffer the second death? Do you know what it is to receive Christ by faith and know that your sins are forgiven? If you don't, you can, just as easy as a lifted prayer to God, saying, "God, be merciful to me, a sinner." I recommend Him to you tonight. Oh, how wonderful! Oh, how marvelous is our Saviour's love for me!

> **I stand amazed in the presence**
> **Of Jesus the Nazarene,**
> **And wonder how He could love me,**
> **A sinner, condemned, unclean.**

He loves you tonight. He will save you. Do you know that, if you die, you will go to Heaven? Are you sure you are saved? Have you been born again? Have you had the experience of the second birth? If you have, you don't have to worry about the second resurrection. You don't have to worry about the second judgment. You don't have to worry about the second death, because you have the second Adam in your heart by experiencing the second birth.

A famous artist was teaching one of his pupils. The pupil painted a beautiful scene, a beautiful forest scene. The trees were lovely, the forest was beautiful. The master came and looked at the picture. The young man was so proud, so happy. The master, as he observed the picture, made this criticism, "Young man, never paint a forest without a path leading out."

I think I can say that to every preacher: never preach about Hell, never preach about the judgment, without a path leading out.

Thank God, there is a path! That path is Jesus who said, "I am the way, the truth, and the life."

Do you know Him tonight? Have you trusted Him? Is He your Saviour?

PRAYER:

Our Father, we come tonight in this sober thought, realizing some-day the unsaved must stand before God. Someday those who have not received the Saviour must face Him. Oh, what an awful day! When the books are opened, and death and Hades deliver up their dead, and the people who are unsaved shall be judged according to their works and cast in the lake of fire! We thank Thee that we have a refuge in Thee.

RUSSELL ISAAC HUMBERD
1893-1965

ABOUT THE MAN:

Humberd's parents moved to Flora, Indiana, a few months after Russell was born. He did not know exactly when he was saved, but he did know that from an early age he wanted to serve the Lord. He had gone forward in a revival meeting; he was baptized at age 12.

In 1915 he married his sweetheart, and they had seven children.

Answering the call for help in a mountain mission, Humberd went to Kentucky for a time, then on to Moody Bible Institute, where he graduated in 1921. More schooling followed. In 1926 he graduated from college with an A.B. degree.

After taking a church in Michigan, he went to Pennsylvania and was pastor there for thirteen years. He also taught at the Altoona Bible Institute, wrote for several magazines and brought forth many of his booklets while there.

Circumstances necessitated a move to Akron, Ohio, then back to his birthplace, where permanent headquarters were established.

His most well-known books were: *Humberd's Bible Charts, The Card With a Red Border* (fiction), and *The Book of Revelation.*

He was a member of the Grace Brethren Church.

He spoke on 66 different radio stations in 25 states, as well as the Panama Canal Zone and Canada, and in 112 colleges, seminaries and Bible institutes.

Several of his articles were used in THE SWORD OF THE LORD.

He died in 1965 in Flora, Indiana, at age 72.

XIV.

Judgment at the Great White Throne

R. I. HUMBERD

"It is appointed unto men once to die, but after this the judgment."—
Heb. 9:27.

Everyone who ever lived will sometime stand before the judgment
bar of God. If he is a Christian, he will appear before the "judgment
seat of Christ" to "receive the things done in the body, according to
that he hath done, whether it be good or bad" (II Cor. 5:10). "But the
rest of the dead [the unsaved] lived not again until the thousand years
were finished" (Rev. 20:5).

Great White Throne

Then "I saw a great white throne." This throne is "great" and it is
"white." Not white like ivory, but white hot with the wrath of God. In
chapter 4 we see another throne, but there is a rainbow about it (vs.
3). The rainbow denotes mercy, but there is no rainbow here about
this throne. It is judgment of absolute justice for those who have spurned
the mercy of God.

"And him that sat on it" (Rev. 20:11). Do we wonder who sits upon
that throne? "The Father judgeth no man, but hath committed all judgment unto the Son" (John 5:22). This is the same Person who once
lay as a babe in Bethlehem's manger—none other than our Lord Himself.

And why is He the Judge? Why not an angel or a cherub? "And hath
given him authority to execute judgment also, BECAUSE he is the Son
of man" (John 5:27).

While holding meetings in Pennsylvania, I stayed in a home where
a young man had recently returned from China. He had been in a large
city when they put the penalties in force. A great crowd gathered. If

a man had stolen, they might cut off a hand, or maybe two hands or maybe a head.

If the Chinese thus judged their fellowmen, what might be the fate of an American if he fell into the clutches of their law! Thus the United States government put a court in China where an American in trouble could be tried by his own countrymen. Thus he would receive more sympathy than in a foreign court.

And so is our Lord the final Judge "because he is the Son of man." He is a man, a member of the human race. He has more sympathy with mankind than an angel might have or a cherub; for He was "touched with the feeling of our infirmities," for He was "in all points tempted like as we are, yet without sin" (Heb. 4:15).

John saw a great white throne and Him that sat on it "from whose face the earth and the heaven fled away" (Rev. 20:11). Imagine, if we can, a face so terrible that this old earth speeds through space like a cannon ball. And then to think, men one time spit into that face. Verily they will never spit in that face again.

The Unrighteous Dead

"And I saw the dead, small and great, stand before God." These are the unrighteous dead who are raised one thousand years after the first resurrection. "And the books were opened: and another book was opened, which is the book of life. . . . And whosoever was not found written in the book of life was cast into the lake of fire" (vss. 12-15).

This raises a question. If these are not saved, then why is the book of life there? Verily, this brings us probably the saddest verse in the Bible. Many thousands of church members are not saved, and they will say in that day, "Lord, Lord, I was a preacher. I did many wonderful works"; but alas, the book of life is there, and where their name should have been is a fearful blank (Matt. 7:22). "And the dead were judged out of those things which were written in the books, according to their works" (Rev. 20:12).

Three little boys might pick strawberries. They are to receive twenty-five cents a quart. One picks five quarts, another ten and the third twenty. When they come in to get their pay, they cannot blame the owner of the patch, for they are paid according to their works.

And so will there be weeping and wailing when the lost ones learn of their fate and see the folly in their own life that is passed. And so will "every mouth" be stopped, and there will not be one word of blame, not one cry of injustice to their Judge (Rom. 3:19).

I. OPENING THE BOOKS

These books will cover every angle of life. Let us just see what might be in some of these books.

1. The Book of Memory

Memory is a heartless thing. You cannot get around it. The rich man in Hades was crying for an act of mercy; but Abraham said, "Son, remember that thou in thy lifetime. . . ." And so strong was his memory that not a word of injustice for his fate was uttered.

Joseph's brethren sold him into Egyptian bondage. Years passed and those same brethren went into Egypt to buy food. They were brought in before the prime minister of the land, and things looked dark indeed. They got into a huddle, as memory reached her hard cold fingers far back into the dark avenues of their minds and turned the pages of her book. Back—back—until it came to the day they had sold their brother into Egypt.

It revealed a face bathed in tears and distorted in agony; a voice crying for mercy and finding none. Now justice in their own hearts decreed that, since they had showed no mercy, they can expect none; and they said, "We are verily guilty concerning our brother, in that we saw the anguish of his soul, when he besought us, and we would not hear; therefore is this distress come upon us" (Gen. 42:21).

2. The Book of Motives

The book of motives will ruin the value of many a noble deed. Just why did you sing that song? Just why did you give that money to foreign missions? To be seen of men? Then you have your reward, and you cannot get two rewards for the same thing.

Only one life, 'twill soon be past;
Only what's done for Christ will last.

When I was a little fellow, an old woman lived in our town who had never married. She had no near relation, but she had quite a bit of money. And the man on her farm had his eyes on that farm—and he was such a good man. What can rejoice the heart of a city dweller more than to see a buggy from the farm come in with fresh eggs, fresh butter and a hen or two—he was such a good man.

Sometimes he would come in and get her in his buggy and take her to his country home where he would lavish every kindness upon her—he was such a good man. One time he took her to his farm home—he was such a good man—and as she was sitting in the room enjoying his boundless hospitality, a little babe toddled up to the old woman and "spilled the beans." *"When Old Mag dies, we will have lots of money."*

Verily, those few words nigh cost that man a farm. For when Old Mag learned his motive; when she learned that all his kindness was lavished upon her, not because he cared a snap for her, but because he wanted her farm, she "blew up."

And so at the great white throne, the book of motives will ruin the value of many a noble deed.

3. The Book of Works

"The dead were judged out of those things which were written in the books, according to their works."—Rev. 20:12.

In our day of cameras and photo equipment, it may not be hard for us to realize that God has the deeds of our entire life photographed somewhere on the film of the universe.

Light travels at the rate of 186,000 miles a second. And at that fearful rate, it takes eight minutes for it to reach us from the sun. Thus when we see the sun, we see what happened up there eight minutes ago. The north star is so far away that it takes fifty years for it to reach our earth. So if you are about fifty years old, you go out some night and hunt the big dipper. Then follow those two stars over to the north star. Then you just imagine. The light you see tonight has been traveling at the rate of 186,000 miles a second, ever since that morning when your father told the neighbors that you had just been born—speeding through space all your life.

Thus when you see the north star, you see what happened fifty years ago. Now if you could be suddenly transferred to the north star and your vision enlarged, you would see what had happened here on earth fifty years ago. You might see yourself being born; later see yourself going on your first day of school. All the events of your life are there to the minutest detail.

4. The Book of Secrets

There is coming a time when "God shall judge the secrets of men" (Rom. 2:16). Not only the words we say and the acts we do, but those we do not do.

But someone will say, "I'll just say I didn't do it." But God will have wisdom to bring the very secrets of our heart out into the open, for "there is nothing covered, that shall not be revealed; neither hid, that shall not be known . . . and that which ye have spoken in the ear in the closets shall be proclaimed upon the housetops" (Luke 12:2,3).

Two women lived together in the same house. Both had babies. One night one mother overlaid her baby, and it died. She took her dead babe and exchanged it for the living babe. Next morning the controversy raged so strong they called King Solomon to decide.

"Well," said Solomon, "both women claim the living babe. About the fairest way to settle the case is to cut the living babe in two and give half to one and half to the other."

"That is very fine," said the false mother.

"Oh," cried the real mother, "give her the living child, and in no wise slay it!"

"Give her the living child," cried King Solomon; for "she is the mother of it" (I Kings 3:26,27).

Solomon had enough wisdom to bring out the secrets of their hearts. So will God, in His omniscience, know how to bring out the secrets of every heart.

When I was a little lad, one day big boys brought a very large crayfish to school and threw it down by the schoolhouse door. I had never seen such a dangerous-looking creature, with its many legs and big pincers.

Finally someone suggested it would be a joke to put the thing in the chalk box up on the teacher's desk. I thought so too, so they showed me how to carry it without getting into the big pincers. I dropped it in the chalk box, fully intending to take it out before school took up, but for some reason I forgot all about it.

School took up, and I was studying as innocent as could be, when suddenly I was startled by a burst of laughter. I looked up, and to my extreme horror, saw just ahead of me a little girl with her feet on her desk and the tears rolling down her cheeks and that horrible creature just beneath her desk. To make matters worse—it was the teacher's own little daughter!

The teacher looked around from the blackboard, but he made no mistake. All the secrets of my heart came right out on my face. It was easy to pick me out as the guilty culprit.

And so, when God shall judge the secrets of men's hearts, there will be nothing hidden; for "all things are naked and open unto the eyes of him with whom we have to do" (Heb. 4:13).

5. The Book of Influence

Influence is a real thing. How well we know how a little click of response resounds in our own heart one way or another as we walk down the street of our home town and meet people we know. And so is our own daily walk an influence to those about us, "For none of us liveth to himself" (Rom. 14:7).

A person one time got in to ride with me. I could smell pumpkins. Later I learned they kept their pumpkins in the clothes closet. And so it is that our garments will take on the odor about us. When we travel on the train, ofttimes people who meet us at the depot are puzzled, for our clothes have taken on the odor of cigarette smoke.

Years ago the magazines often carried a series of cartoons. The first was of a young woman in great distress. Last fourth of July, someone took her to the dance and never asked to come back. On Thanksgiving, a young man took her to the show, and he never came back. Last night another took her out, and it was the same story. She is in deep dismay. The second cartoon shows a kindhearted friend who tells her that she has B.O. or body odor.

Verily, we all have exactly the same thing, only it is S.O.—or spiritual odor. Just as her body odor was obnoxious to the young men, so is our spiritual odor obnoxious to the world.

The holy place in the Tabernacle in the wilderness was some thirty feet long by fifteen feet wide. It was at the little golden altar where they burned the incense. If we were to burn incense in so small a room, the odor of the incense would be clinging to our garments as we walked down the streets of our home town. And since that incense speaks of the merits of Christ, thus we would smell like Christ. That is exactly what Paul says about it:

"For we are unto God a sweet savour of Christ, in them that are saved, and in them that perish: To the one we are the savour of death unto death; and to the other the savour of life unto life."—II Cor. 2:15, 16.

Thus if we have been burning incense at the altar of prayer and nourishing our hearts at the table of shewbread, as we walk down the street of our home town, we will smell like Christ. But alas, like the B.O., our S.O. is an offence to the world, for we are a savour of death to them.

How true! Let a good old man walk down the street of his home town. Everyone knows that he spends time in deep communion with his Lord. Here is a group of ungodly men with their filthy stories and boisterous laughter, but p-s-s-s-s. All is quiet as the old man trudges past. He smells like Christ, and it is a kill-joy to them.

But the old man trudges on down the street. He turns a corner. There is a group of Christians. To them he is a savour of life and encouragement.

Influence is a mighty force for good or ill and is such a subtle power that it stands us in hand to beware. I speak from charts, and since they are fifteen feet long, it is difficult for me to fold them by myself, so I usually get a little boy or girl to help me fold them.

I was holding meetings in Pennsylvania, and a little girl about twelve years old was helping me fold my chart, and I asked, "Did you ever take Jesus as your Saviour?"

"No," she said with a fearful jerk.

"Wouldn't you like to take Him as your Saviour?"

"No." She fairly threw the word at me and ran to the back of the room. Later I learned her father was kicking the preacher. What a terrible influence that father is to his daughter!

6. The Book of Words

"But I [the Judge Himself is speaking] *say unto you, That every idle word that men shall speak, they shall give account thereof in the day of judgment."*—Matt. 12:36.

Words influence lives, and even those thoughtless utterances may cause great havoc in a tender heart.

When I was a little lad, a preacher held a tremendous place in my thinking. Even today, I may be traveling on the train; and when I hand out a tract, the person may ask if I am a preacher. It came to my attention some time ago that I seldom answer with a positive "yes," for I never felt that I measured up to the high place where I thought preachers trod.

Let us use our imagination and see the possibilities of an idle word.

"Well, I hear that Elijah went to Heaven today," said the father as he drew his chair up to the table and reached for a piece of bread.

"Yes," said the mother, "I hear there were horses and chariots of fire."

"Well," drawled father, "I hope he has a better welcome up there than he had down here. Seems like he couldn't make it down here. He was always making famines and complaining how people lived. I'm right glad he's gone."

"But I am not real sure that we are through with him," she replied. "I hear that the spirit of Elijah rests upon Elisha."

"Well, I wish that fellow would take his bald head and go up too," he said vehemently. "A chariot ride would do him good."

But neither the father nor mother had noted that two bright eyes were sparkling with interest, that two little ears were tuned to every word and a little heart was throbbing with distrust and disrespect for the man of God.

A few days later Elisha came to Bethel and walked slowly down the street. There was a whispered conversation in the alley.

"You're afraid to say that out loud."

"No, I ain't either."

"I dare you to say it."

"Go up, thou bald head."

And just where did that young lad hear those words? Did he not hear his father utter them in disgust?

"Go up, thou bald head." Ah, that was fun! Other children joined in—"Go up, thou bald head."

Elisha moved slowly down the street, and the children followed him—dozens of them, scores of them—"Go up, thou bald head."

It was evident there was little welcome in Bethel for the man of God that night, so he moved on and out into the open country, with the children following him—"Go up, thou bald head."

Suddenly the man of God stopped; he turned; he uttered a few short words, and there was sorrow in the homes of Bethel that night; for "there came forth two she bears out of the wood, and tare forty and two children of them" (II Kings 2:24).

II. THE STANDARD OF JUDGMENT

Few people are aware that we set the standard of our own judgment.

"Judge not, that ye be not judged. For with what judgment ye judge, ye shall be judged" (Matt. 7:1). "Blessed are the merciful, for they shall obtain mercy" (Matt. 5:7).

This world is teeming with creatures that are so susceptible to pain and suffering. And who knows how much our own judgment may be bound up in the way we may cause unnecessary suffering among the creatures that are so helpless below us?

The barns of Pennsylvania are so well constructed that they are warm even in the coldest weather. I used to try to change the ways of a stock buyer. He would take a tender veal calf out of a warm barn and haul it over the country in an open truck in the coldest of weather, with its little body shaking terribly from the cold. Verily, "a righteous man regardeth the life of his beast, but the tender mercies of the wicked are cruel" (Prov. 12:10). There is one "that is higher than the highest," and He regardeth it all (Eccles. 5:8).

I called in the home of one of my members. The high school girl took me into the front room and proudly showed me her collection of little creatures with pins through their bodies. Then, flipping a big grasshopper, she said carelessly, "Oh, he's not dead yet." That poor creature had been suffering for two days. If you mount creatures with pins through their bodies, they should certainly not be made to suffer unnecessarily. Verily, "He shall have judgment without mercy, that hath shewed no mercy" (James 2:13).

"Therefore thou art inexcusable, O man, whosoever thou art that judgest: for wherein thou judgest another, thou condemnest thyself; for thou that judgest doeth the same things."—Rom. 2:1.

While holding meetings in Iowa, I went out into a field to talk to a man who was shucking corn. He would not accept the Lord, but in course of the conversation, he said with dismay, "I have a son up there in the house. For over twenty years I have clothed and fed that boy, but he won't help me back. He should be out here right now helping me with the corn."

I said, "You are right. He should appreciate what you have done for him and be out here helping you get your corn in." "But," I said, "for forty years you have been breathing God's air, drinking God's water, enjoying God's sunshine and refusing to serve Him." The farmer then realized that he had set the standard of his own judgment.

As I travel coast to coast in meetings, I am often ashamed as I ride with some preachers who disregard the traffic laws and even joke about it. If anyone on earth should obey the laws, it should be a Christian, "not only for wrath [fear of the police], but also for conscience sake" (Rom. 13:5).

I was riding with a minister in California who kept up a continual gripe at everyone about him. That person was going too slow; "get out of my way"; "look at that fellow." But he was inexcusable for, in that he judged another, he broke the law himself and drove through two stop signs.

David

"David, there is a man in your kingdom who had a pet lamb. It lay in his lap. It ate from his hand. It was like a daughter to him. His neighbor in the big mansion on the hill had an abundance of flocks and herds. A few days ago the man in the big mansion had company; and instead of taking a lamb from his own flock, he tore the little pet lamb out of the bosom of the poor man and served it to his guests."

"The rascal," cried King David, as righteous indignation blazed in his eyes. "He will die for that."

But there was a strange light in the eye of the old prophet as he pointed his finger into the face of the king and cried, "David, thou art the man. The God of Heaven has given you an abundance of everything, and you killed Uriah to get his wife." David went down in terrible conviction as he saw that he had set the standard of his own judgment.

Judah

"Judah, Tamar, thy daughter-in-law, has played the harlot and is with child" (Gen. 38). "Bring her forth and let her be burnt," cried Judah, as self-righteous indignation blazed in his eyes.

Tamar came forth. But the self-righteous pride died within his breast as Judah saw her with a bracelet and a staff in her hand. And his mind went back to that day when he had gone to shear his sheep. He had seen a woman along the way with her face covered. Judah thought she was a harlot; but in fact, it was Tamar, his daughter-in-law. "By the man, whose these are, am I with child," said Tamar. "She hath been more righteous than I," cried Judah as he realized he had set the standard of his own judgment.

III. JUSTICE

So just will this judgment be that even the righteous will recognize the just condemnation of the lost. No wife will ever sorrow for an unsaved husband. Rather, will "much people in heaven" cry "Hallelujah!" as the "great whore" slips into her final doom, and will rejoice that a righteous judgment has been wrought.

Some feel that a wife cannot be happy in Heaven knowing that her husband is in Hell. If any husband feels thus, let him try this: go to Niagara Falls, lay a pile of your clothing at the top where the water flows over the falls, write a note, then leave the country.

Your wife weeps and sorrows, and her distress is real, for she thinks you are in Hell. But you come back at the end of three years and go down to your old home and peep in at the half-drawn shade. Yes, there she is. Your wife thinks you are in torment, but she is not worrying about you now. Rather, she is enjoying the love of a new husband, and you seldom come into her mind.

If a wife can be so taken up with the love of a new husband, think ye that the love of her Lord will not erase all thoughts of you from her mind?

The Modernist

One of the most awful things of our day is modernism. Many preachers today do not even believe the Bible, but stand in the pulpit and deny the very essentials of our salvation. Of course, they are not saved. But their condemnation is sure and certain; and as they slip into an eternal Hell, the righteous will put on a hallelujah chorus, and her smoke will rise up "for ever and ever" (Rev. 19:3).

Suppose you are walking down the street some summer's evening; and as you near the parsonage of an apostate preacher, you hear a little "boom." You go on and as you near the house, you find that his house is on fire. His hot water tank exploded, and you can see through a big window that the explosion threw the piano over and pinned him to the floor. And as you see him writhing in helpless agony, just roasting to death, you stand in the street and cry, *Good! You are getting just what you deserved!*

Verily, are any of my readers so mean as to do that? Of course, no one would do that now, for the time is not yet. But the time will come when you will stand upon the battlements of Glory and cry "Hallelujah!" as that very same preacher slips into an eternal Hell. It is the voice of "much people in heaven" who cry "Hallelujah!" as the smoke of that old harlot, the church of the apostates, rises up "for ever and ever" (Rev. 19:3).

What Did He Do?

But why should he receive such a fearful penalty? He was a wonderful man. We met him in the supermarket one day, and he was so friendly and nice. He even carried a big bag of groceries out to our car. How can he merit such a decree from the great white throne?

One Sunday morning a high school girl came to him after church and said, "Pastor, the teacher said last week that we all came into being through evolution, but I told him that the Bible says that God created us. He just smiled and said the Bible is not to be trusted, for science has proven that it is merely a collection of myths. What shall I do?"

Her pastor smiles and, giving her a fatherly pat on the cheek, says, "Well daughter, remember, your teacher has spent many years in the school room, and he has many degrees. In fact, they do find many difficulties in the Bible and things contrary to scientific truth." And that girl turns and enters a life of darkness and despair.

One day he is called to the hospital. A pair of earnest eyes meet his own as he enters the hospital room, and a weak trembling voice says, "Preacher, the doctor says I cannot live two weeks. Now I have always paid my debts and lived a good life, but I was never a religious man. What can I do?"

"Ah," says the modernistic preacher, "you are all right. I can see that you have lived a good, clean life. Remember—we are all the children of God, and God loves us all. Now don't worry, for I know all is well." And the man clings to a false hope and goes out into eternity a lost man.

Verily, dare we think that preacher can escape the righteous judgment of an outraged God? Dare we think that the heart of a long-suffering God will never burn with righteous indignation at his faith-destroying errors? Nay, verily, rather to him "is reserved the blackness of darkness for ever" (Jude 13).

What a judgment this will be! Acres and acres of humanity; millions and millions of sinful creatures standing before their God. Just how it will be, I do not know, but the men of Nineveh will point a finger of scorn at the men of Israel and shall condemn them; "for they repented at the preaching of Jonah; and behold, a greater than Jonah" was there (Luke 11:32).

Nineveh worshiped Dagon, a part-fish, part-man god. They thought he sent a messenger from time to time from the sea. Thus when Jonah came that way, they accepted him as a messenger from God. Israel was looking for a messenger from God out of Bethlehem. He came, but they rejected Him. And as these men stand at the last judgment, the men of Nineveh will condemn the men of Israel for their unrighteous act.

Degrees of Punishment

Some have difficulty with Hell because they cannot see why a good, honest person should be put in the same place as a heartless rascal. But position in Hell is determined by light rejected. The people of Sodom gave themselves over to fornication and became so wicked that God burned them off the face of the earth. Capernaum was a self-righteous city of Christ's own time. Yet "I say unto you [the Judge Himself is speaking], That it shall be more tolerable for the land of Sodom in the day of judgment, than for thee" (Matt. 11:24).

Verily, there are mysteries here, "for if the mighty works, which have been done in thee [Capernaum], had been done in Sodom, it would have remained until this day" (Matt. 11:23). God had the Gospel preached where He knew it would not be accepted and did not have it preached where He knew it would have been accepted. However, God knows the heart, and in the judgment all will be made absolutely right.

People so often are urged to pray, just as though everyone is on praying grounds with God, and anyone can do wonders if he can only string out a long line of words and keep it up long enough. But the first need in a human heart is to let God do the speaking. Let a man read and meditate upon the Word of God that he may grow thereby. It is even possible to make long prayers for a pretense: "Therefore ye shall receive the greater damnation" (Matt. 23:14).

IV. THE PENALTY

And right here is where we get into trouble, for there is a great dislike for the truth of such a thing as Hell. I get letters like the following concerning my booklet, The Lake of Fire:

"I note you are also a red-hot, Hell-fire-and-torment preacher, and just blindly follow in the trend of others, perpetuating this delusion, not using reason and good judgment."

On the other hand, a missionary in Alaska wrote me that it had helped three or four to accept the Lord. A man in Cheyenne, Wyoming, started to read it but wanted to get right with the Lord before he finished. If a little boy or girl has money to buy one of my books, almost always will they get *The Lake of Fire*.

Verily, how I wish there were some way around it, for my mind cannot dwell upon its horrors; but our Lord was the greatest Hell-fire preacher of all time. Thus there are two reasons why I believe in Hell. First, Christ said so, and He would not lie. Second, would the Creator of all the universe have come to this earth and let men spit in His face and nail Him to a cross to save us from an imaginary place?

Verily, there is more in the Bible about Hell than about Heaven. So when we come to the penalty meted out at the judgment of the great white throne, almost everything we have to say is based upon the words of our Lord, Himself the final Judge.

Gnashing of Teeth

"There shall be weeping and gnashing of teeth, when ye shall see Abraham, and Isaac, and Jacob, and all the prophets, in the kingdom of God, and you yourselves thrust out."—Luke 13:28.

Gnashing of teeth speaks of great anger. For long ages the ungodly have had their own way as they persecuted, tormented and killed the godly. But when they see those same godly people welcomed into Heaven and they themselves cast out, they will gnash their teeth in blinding rage.

I started to walk across a big field in Pennsylvania. Soon I saw, away out in the middle of the field, a very large ground hog busily digging in the ground. I thought I would have some fun if I could slip up on him and see him run. As I got closer and closer, I began to laugh within myself as I imagined he would fairly fall all over himself to get away when he would see me.

But as I drew near and he still had not seen me, I began to wonder if things might not go as I had expected; and since he was such a large animal, I thought it might be wise to make a noise. So I did, and he looked up—and run? Not at all. Rather did he sit upon his haunches and gnash his teeth, the like of which I had never heard before nor since. It seemed the chips and sparks must surely fly in his terrible rage at me.

And so when the ungodly see the righteous welcomed into Heaven and they themselves sent to Hell, they will gnash their teeth in blinding rage.

Furnace of Fire

"And shall cast them into a furnace of fire."—Matt. 13:42.

Verily, those words fell from the lips of our Lord, the final Judge, and let not mortal men joke about Hell.

I was in a conference in Ohio when a lull in the program gave opportunity for an old man to get up on the platform and give a funny story about Hell.

A small city had a new fire department. A public-spirited old man was giving an address on its merits, when finally he stopped and blurted out, "I wish that whole fire department was in Hell." His audience sat aghast until they realized that what he meant was that, if such an efficient fire department were in Hell, they could put out all the fire. But such a story is not funny, and let no child of God treat the subject lightly.

Walking down the street in Phoenix, Arizona, I passed a gasoline filling station, and a man drove in who was cursing and calling upon God to damn something to Hell. I went over and said, "Man, what if God would answer your prayer?"

I was standing in a blacksmith shop in Michigan watching a man shoe a horse. He was cursing with all the speed his tongue could utter. I moved over carefully and said, "Did you know that God will not hold him guiltless that takes His name in vain?"

He stopped with a jerk and looked up at me. The elements of that look bore mute evidence that those words had found their mark.

The Worm That Dieth Not

"If thy hand. . . foot. . . eye offend thee, cut it off: it is better for thee to enter into life maimed, than having two hands. . . feet. . . eyes to go into hell, into the fire that never shall be quenched: Where their worm dieth not, and the fire is not quenched."—Mark 9:43-48.

Three times did our Lord warn of a place where the worm never dies.

Verily, it is better to go to Heaven with one eye, than to go to Hell with two, into a place where the worm never dies.

When I was a little boy, a man in our community had only one arm. He had lost the other in the Andersonville prison, a fearful stockade where thousands of war prisoners were crowded in, to die of starvation, scurvy and the most awful deaths.

A stream ran through the middle of the prison, and along the edge was a small swamp. As time passed, the filth of the camp washed into that swamp, and it became a living mass of maggots or worms.

One man told how to get the only semblance of fresh water was to go down to that stream just before daylight before the camp was astir. As he would pass that swamp, he would see men, living skeletons of men, who had attempted to crawl down for a cooling drink in the night, but were too weak. And there they lay—living men with the maggots crawling in their eyes, nose and mouth.

Why remind ourselves of so terrible a sight? Verily, those worms have been dead a whole century, but our Lord warns of a place where the worm never dies. And again we say, Let not mortal men joke about that place.

Some time ago as I stopped for gas, I asked the woman who got the gas where she would be in one hundred years. Then I told her that the Bible says there are two places, a Heaven and a Hell. Then she told me a "funny" story and said her pastor got a good laugh out of it. She did not think she would mind being in Hell the first few years, for she would be shaking hands with those she knew and would be too busy to mind it. But I told her that it is no matter to joke about.

Everlasting Fire

"Depart from me, ye cursed, into everlasting fire, prepared for the devil and his angels."—Matt. 25:41.

"And these shall go away into everlasting punishment: but the righteous into life eternal."—Vs. 46.

When I was in college, I became aware that things were not going right. So I innocently turned to this verse and read it and said that Hell must be as long as Heaven for it is the same word. But I was soon to learn that the professor did not agree.

I was changing buses in Walla Walla, Washington. As I sat in the depot I saw some literature. I read two or three big pages proving that Hell is not eternal. Verily, such a display of printer's ink ought to do some good; but when I come back to the Bible—it is still there—"forever."

Thirst

It was our Lord who told of the rich man in Hell who called for an act of mercy, "that he may dip the tip of his finger in water, and cool my tongue" (Luke 16:24).

Fearful indeed is the torment of thirst. I know little about thirst, but I have not forgotten that hot afternoon I went to cultivate corn and forgot to take any water along. Verily, the torment of a few hours was fearful indeed; but that poor man in Hell has not had a drink for two thousand years, and the prospects for relief ahead are utterly void.

Stripes

"That servant, which knew his Lord's will, and prepared not himself, neither did according to his will, shall be beaten with many stripes."— Luke 12:47.

I do not know much about stripes, but I have not forgotten those welts my father produced on my legs. And then when I went to my mother for sympathy, I got none. To be punished is bad enough, but to be punished in the presence of someone else and get no sympathy is worse.

Can you imagine yourself, writhing in agony, being tormented in fire and brimstone, and Jesus just standing there with arms folded and doing nothing to help you! Yet that is the fate of some who will be "tormented with fire and brimstone in the presence of the Lamb," and that Lamb is Christ (Rev. 14:10).

The Millstone

*"Whoso shall offend one of these little ones which believe in me, it were better for him that a millstone were hanged about his neck, and that he were drowned in the depth of the sea."—*Matt. 18:6.

One evening Luella Mabbit walked out across the lawn, got into the buggy and drove away with Amer Green. It was just another evening— another time together. But home folks never saw Luella again. The strong arm of the law brought Amer out of his hiding place and lodged him in the county jail. But the midnight air of that small city vibrated with sledge hammer blows; the iron bars gave way; the mob rushed in, and the next morning Amer Green's body was hanging from a tree some two miles from where I used to live.

Verily, it is a fearful thing to put a rope about a man's neck and take his life. It is a fearful deed. But there is something worse than that. To break the faith of a little child is worse than that. And yet, thousands of preachers are doing just that with their faith-destroying messages; teachers with their evolution and other God-dishonoring errors; parents with their careless and ungodly behavior in the home. What fearful judgment awaits those who would dare to offend a little one!

Wandering Stars

"Wandering stars, to whom is reserved the blackness of darkness for ever."—Jude 13.

Our earth moves around the sun, and the sun around another star and so on. A wandering star is one that has broken away from its center and speeds through space with no goal in sight.

The center of a Christian's life is Christ, and a person who has rejected Christ is a wandering star, and to him it is reserved to wander in absolute darkness throughout the ceaseless ages of eternity. Imagine traveling a thousand years this way and a thousand years that way and never seeing anyone and never coming to a desired haven.

We can hardly imagine the fearful heartlessness of an Assyrian king. Their delight was to kill and destroy. One king took a city and punched out the eyes of the people and made three big piles of human eyes. Imagine thousands of children and fathers and mothers screaming and calling for loved ones they cannot see. Imagine them, bumping into trees and falling over stones as they wandered about in blackness of darkness. But it would not last forever, for a few weeks and the last poor victim would find relief in death. But for the apostate, there is no relief; but as a wandering star will he be forever.

The Lake of Fire

The trumpet has blown. The earth has vomited out her unrighteous dead, and there they stand before the great white throne. Bleary-eyed drunkards; withered old hags; men once proud and influential; ladies once cultured and beautiful. But earth's distinctions have faded now, and there they are all huddled together in one vast sea of humanity.

There goes the earth as we know it today, shooting through space like a cannon ball. Gladly would they also flee from the face of Him who sits upon that throne; but such is not for them, for each must meet the issues of a misspent life. They must endure the penetrating blaze of those eyes as they search out the very secrets of their hearts.

The earth is gone, the stage on which they played their brief part in life's great drama, the place where they bought and sold, the place where the rich held their possessions and the poor cursed their Creator, the place where the frivolous rejoiced in their pleasures and the foolish passed up their opportunities.

The judgment is over—"Depart!" The thunderous tones of that voice jar the very foundation upon which they stand; and quivering and quaking, it falls apart. Cries of fear and groans of agony escape every lip as they gnaw their tongues for pain. There is weeping and wailing and gnashing of teeth as they slip toward their certain doom.

Do not be deceived: in the end sin will demand its wages. Your own conscience tells you that, if you transgress the laws of God, somehow, someday, somewhere you will have to pay.

But a new horror looms up ahead. Directly in their path is a lake of fire shimmering like molten metal in the distance, its liquid flames lashing and washing the shores of their eternity. Great blisters of heat, bubbling and sending out little eddies over the seething surface. Lurid tongues of flame leaping from the surface, snapping and darting with ten thousand furies and falling again in whirlpools of liquid fire, writhing and whipping the surface into a sulphurous foam.

The Final Plunge

Sin's long war with God must end; and as the last shriek of despair is choked beneath those fiery waves, a shout of triumph peals from heavenly portals and echoes and re-echoes upon the battlements of Glory, "Hallelujah; salvation, and glory, and power belong to our God, for true and righteous are his judgments."

The Dumb Mule

"Be not as the horse, or as the mule, which have no understanding." —Ps. 32:9.

A human being has understanding, but many ten thousands are acting as dumb as a mule which has no understanding.

A farmer awakens some night. There is a peculiar flicker of light upon his bedroom wall. Oh, his barn is on fire! He dashes out into the midnight air. The fire is still in this corner. The horses are in the opposite corner. There is plenty of time to get them out. But prod and coax and push and pull—those horses will not budge. Sometimes if they throw on a set of harness, the horse will go out; but close the door quick, or he will run around the lot and back again in the barn and perish in the flames.

But that poor horse has no understanding. And yet many a man is acting like a dumb horse and is running right into Hell-fire with both eyes open. Verily, be not like a horse which has no understanding.

The whole issue of our eternity rests upon our attitude toward one Person today. "He that believeth on the Son hath everlasting life: and he that believeth not the Son shall not see life" (John 3:36). God's Son has been to this earth. Some loved Him and some hated Him. What will you do with Jesus?

In the First World War, Germany overran Belgium in a very disgraceful manner. One Sunday morning a man in a little Belgium town was on his way to church when he saw that a large group of people had gathered down the street.

He went over and found that an automobile had attempted to dash through their town but had stalled, and two young German men were working frantically to get it started. But the Belgians were gathering a mob, intending to kill the two young Germans. The Christian man quieted the mob, reminding them that they all had loved ones on the firing line. He asked them to treat these young men like they would hope they would treat their loved ones in a similar position. He quieted the mob. The two young German men repaired their car and went on in peace.

A few days later, a letter arrived in that small town, bearing all the marks of the Royal court of Germany; it was from the Kaiser himself, assuring the citizens of that town that, as long as the war would last, no foot would tread their streets to do them harm. And why? Verily, one of those young men was the Kaiser's own son.

And so has God's Son been to this earth. What will you do with Jesus?

JONATHAN EDWARDS
1703-1758

ABOUT THE MAN:

Jonathan Edwards was only twelve when he attained a working knowledge of Latin, Greek and Hebrew. He graduated from Yale University when he was seventeen. At nineteen he began preaching and was ordained as a Congregational minister five years later.

He pastored at Northampton, Massachusetts, 1729-1750, then at Stockbridge, Massachusetts, until 1757, followed by a brief few weeks as president of Princeton Seminary where he died March 22, 1758, as a result of a smallpox vaccination, at age fifty-four.

Edwards profoundly influenced George Whitefield, Thomas Chalmers and David Brainerd. A notable philosopher and deep thinker, Edwards ranks as one of the great preachers of colonial America.

The following sermon is his most celebrated, and one of the most famous ever preached by anyone. It was a powerful impetus to the great revival in New England. As Edwards preached (actually, he read the manuscript to the congregation), strong men and women held onto the pews and cried out for mercy, pleading with the preacher, "Is there no way of escape?"

Hundreds were converted as they heard that sermon—a subpoena from the skies.

XV.

Sinners in the Hands of an Angry God

JONATHAN EDWARDS

"Their foot shall slide in due time."—Deut. 32:35.

There is nothing that keeps wicked men at any one moment out of Hell but the mere pleasure of God.

By the mere pleasure of God, I mean His sovereign pleasure, His arbitrary will, restrained by no obligation, hindered by no manner of difficulty any more than if nothing else but God's mere will had, in the last degree, or in any respect whatsoever, any hand in the preservation of wicked men one moment.

The truth of this observation may appear by the following considerations:

1. There is no want of power in God to cast wicked men into Hell at any moment. Men's hands cannot be strong when God rises up. The strongest have no power to resist Him, nor can any deliver out of His hands.

He is not only able to cast wicked men into Hell, but He can most easily do it. Sometimes an earthly prince meets with a great deal of difficulty in subduing a rebel, who has found means to fortify himself, and has made himself strong by the number of his followers. Not so with God. No fortress is any defense from the power of God. Though hand join in hand, and a vast multitude of God's enemies combine and associate themselves, they are easily broken in pieces. They are as great heaps of light chaff before the whirlwind, or large quantities of dry stubble before devouring flames.

We find it easy to tread on and crush a worm that we see crawling on the earth; so it is easy for us to cut or singe a slender thread that anything hangs by: thus easy is it for God when He pleases, to cast His enemies down to Hell. What are we, that we should think to stand before Him, at whose rebuke the earth trembles, and before whom the rocks are thrown down?

2. They deserve to be cast into Hell, so that divine justice never stands in the way; it makes no objection against God's using His power at any moment to destroy them. Yea, on the contrary, justice calls aloud for an infinite punishment of their sins. Divine justice says of the tree that brings forth such grapes of Sodom, "Cut it down; why cumbereth it the ground?" (Luke 13:7). The sword of divine justice is every moment brandished over their heads, and it is nothing but the hand of arbitrary mercy and God's mere will that holds it back.

3. They are already under a sentence of condemnation to Hell. They do not only justly deserve to be cast down thither, but the sentence of the law of God, that eternal and immutable rule of righteousness that God has fixed between Him and mankind, is gone out against them and stands against them so that they are bound over already to Hell. John 3:18—"He that believeth not is condemned already."

So every unconverted man properly belongs to Hell; that is his place; from thence he is. John 8:23—"Ye are from beneath"; and thither he is bound; it is the place that justice and God's Word and sentence of His unchangeable law assign to him.

4. They are now the objects of that very same anger and wrath of God that is expressed in the torments of Hell; and the reason why they do not go down to Hell at each moment is not because God, in whose power they are, is not at present very angry with them, as He is with many miserable creatures now tormented in Hell, who there feel and bear the fierceness of His wrath. Yea, God is a great deal more angry with great numbers that are now on earth, yea doubtless with some who may read this book who, it may be, are at ease, than He is with many of those who are now in the flames of Hell.

So it is not because God is unmindful of their wickedness and does not resent it that He does not let loose His hand and cut them off. God is not altogether such a one as themselves, though they may imagine Him to be so. The wrath of God burns against them; their damnation does not slumber; the pit is prepared; the fire is made ready; the furnace is now hot, ready to receive them; the flames do now rage and glow. The glittering sword is whetted and held over them, and the pit hath opened its mouth under them.

5. The Devil stands ready to fall upon them and seize them as his own, at what moment God shall permit him. They belong to him; he has their souls in his possession and under his dominion. The Scripture represents them as his goals (Luke 11:21). The devils watch them; they are ever by them, at their right hand; they stand waiting for them, like greedy hungry lions that see their prey and expect to have it, but are for the present kept back. If God should withdraw His hand, by which they are restrained, they would in one moment fly upon their poor souls. The old serpent is gaping for them; Hell opens its mouth wide to receive them; and if God should permit it, they would be hastily swallowed up and lost.

6. There are in the souls of wicked men those hellish principles reigning that would presently kindle and flame out into Hell fire if it were not for God's restraints. There is laid in the very nature of carnal men a foundation for the torments of Hell. There are those corrupt principles in reigning power in them and in full possession of them that are seeds of Hell fire. The principles are active and powerful, exceedingly violent in their nature; and if it were not for the restraining hand of God upon them, they would soon break out; they would flame out after the same manner as the same corruption, the same enmity, does in the hearts of damned souls, and would beget the same torments as they do in them.

The souls of the wicked are in Scriptures compared to the troubled sea (Isa. 57:20). For the present, God restrains their wickedness by His mighty power, as He does the raging waves of the troubled sea, saying, "Hitherto shalt thou come, and no further"; but if God should withdraw that restraining power, it would soon carry all before it.

Sin is the ruin and misery of the soul; it is destructive in its nature; and if God should leave it without restraint, there would need nothing else to make the soul perfectly miserable.

The corruption of the heart of the man is immoderate and boundless in its fury; and while wicked men live here, it is like fire pent up by the course of nature; and as the heart is now a sink of sin, so, if sin were not restrained, it would immediately turn the soul into a fiery oven, or furnace of fire and brimstone.

7. It is no security to wicked men for one moment that there are no visible means of death at hand! It is no security to a natural man that he is now in health and that he does not see which way he should now immediately go out of the world by any accident, and that there is no

visible danger, in any respect, in his circumstances. The manifold and continual experience of the world, in all ages, shows this is no evidence that a man is not on the very brink of eternity and that the next step will not be into another world.

The unseen, unthought-of-ways and means of persons going suddenly out of the world are innumerable and inconceivable. Unconverted men walk over the pit of Hell on a rotten covering, and there are innumerable places in this covering so weak that they will not bear their weight, and these places are not seen. The arrows of death fly unseen at noonday; the sharpest sight cannot discern them.

God has so many different, unsearchable ways of taking wicked men out of the world and sending them to Hell that there is nothing to make it appear that God had need to be at the expense of a miracle, or to go out of the ordinary course of His providence to destroy any wicked man, at any moment. All the means that there are of sinners going out of the world are so in God's hands and so universally and absolutely subject to His power and determination that it does not depend at all the less on the mere will of God whether sinners shall at any moment go to Hell, than if means were never made use of, or at all concerned in the case.

8. Natural men's prudence and care to preserve their own lives, or the care of others to preserve them, do not secure them a moment. To this, divine providence and universal experience do bear testimony.

There is this clear evidence that men's own wisdom is no security to them from death; that, if it were otherwise, we should see some difference between the wise and politic men of the world and others, with regard to their liableness to early and unexpected death; but how is it in fact? "How dieth the wise man? as the fool" (Eccles. 2:16).

9. All wicked men's pains and contrivances which they use to escape Hell while they continue to reject Christ and so remain wicked men, do not secure them from Hell one moment. Almost every natural man who hears of Hell flatters himself that he shall escape it; he depends upon himself for his own security; he flatters himself in what he has done, in what he is now doing, or what he intends to do; everyone lays out matters in his own mind, how he shall avoid damnation, and flatters himself that he contrives well for himself, and that his schemes will not fail. They hear indeed that there are but few saved, and that the greater part of men who have died heretofore are gone to Hell;

but each one imagines that he forms plans to effect his escape better than others have done. He does not intend to go to that place of torment. He says within himself that he intends to take effectual care and to order matters so for himself as not to fail.

But the foolish children of men miserably delude themselves in their own schemes and in confidence in their strength and wisdom; they trust to nothing but a shadow. The greater part of those who heretofore have lived under the same means of grace, and are now dead, are undoubtedly gone to Hell; and it was not because they were not as wise as those who are now alive; it was not because they did not lay out matters as well for themselves to secure their own escape.

If we could come to speak with them and inquire of them, one by one, whether they expected, when alive and when they used to hear about Hell, ever to be subjects of that misery, we, doubtless, should hear one and another reply, "No, I never intended to come here: I had arranged matters otherwise in my mind. I thought I should contrive well for myself. I thought my scheme good. I intended to take effectual care. But it came upon me unexpectedly; I did not look for it at that time and in that manner; it came as a thief. Death outwitted me. God's wrath was too quick for me. O my cursed foolishness! I was flattering and pleasing myself with vain dreams of what I would do hereafter; and when I was saying peace and safety, then sudden destruction came upon me."

10. God has laid Himself under no obligation, by any promise, to keep any natural man out of Hell one moment. God certainly has made no promises either of eternal life, or of any deliverance or preservation from eternal death, but what are contained in the covenant of grace, the promises that are given in Christ, in whom all the promises are yea and amen.

But surely they have no interest in the promises of the covenant of grace who are not the children of the covenant, who do not believe in any of the promises and have no interest in the Mediator of the covenant.

So that, whatever some have imagined and pretended about promises made to natural men's earnest seeking and knocking, it is plain and manifest that whatever pains a natural man takes in religion, whatever prayers he makes, till he believes in Christ, God is under no manner of obligation to keep him a moment from eternal destruction.

So that thus it is that natural men are held in the hand of God over the pit of Hell. They have deserved the fiery pit and are already sentenced to it. God is dreadfully provoked. His anger is as great towards them as those who are actually suffering the execution of the fierceness of His wrath in Hell; and they have done nothing in the least to appease or abate that anger; neither is God in the least bound by any promise to hold them up for one moment. The Devil is waiting for them; Hell is gaping for them; the flames gather and flash about them, and would fain lay hold on them and swallow them up. The fire pent up in their own hearts is struggling to break out. They have no interest in any Mediator. There are no means within reach that can be any security to them. In short, they have no refuge, nothing to take hold of. All that preserves them every moment is the mere arbitrary will and uncovenanted, unobliged forbearance of an incensed God.

APPLICATION

The use of this awful subject may be for awakening unconverted persons to a conviction of their danger. This which you have heard is the case of everyone out of Christ. That world of misery, that lake of burning brimstone, is extended abroad under you. There is the dreadful pit of the glowing flames of the wrath of God; there is Hell's wide gaping mouth open; and you have nothing to stand upon, nor anything to take hold of; there is nothing between you and Hell but the air; only the power and mere pleasure of God hold you up.

You are probably not sensible of this. You find you are kept out of Hell, but do not see the hand of God in it. You look at other things as the good state of your bodily constitution, your care of your own life, and the means you use for your own preservation. But indeed these things are nothing. If God should withdraw His hand, they would avail no more to keep you from falling than the thin air to hold up a person who is suspended in it.

Your wickedness makes you, as it were, heavy as lead, and to rend downwards with great weight and pressure towards Hell; and if God should let you go, you would immediately sink and swiftly descend and plunge into the bottomless gulf; and your healthy constitution, your own care and prudence and best contrivance and all your righteousness would have no more influence to uphold you and keep you out of Hell than a spider's web would have to stop a falling rock. Were it not for the sovereign pleasure of God, the earth would not bear you one moment, for you are a burden to it. The creation groans with you. The creature is made subject to the bondage of your corruption not willingly. The sun does not willingly shine upon you to give you light to serve sin and Satan. The earth does not willingly yield her increase to satisfy your lusts, nor is it willingly a stage for your wickedness to be acted upon. The air does not willingly serve you for breath to maintain the flame of life in your vitals, while you spend your life in the service of God's enemies.

God's creatures are good and were made for men to serve God with; they do not willingly subserve any other purpose. They groan when they are abused to purpose so directly contrary to their nature and end. And the world would spew you out were it not for the sovereign hand of Him who hath subjected it in hope.

There are the black clouds of God's wrath now hanging directly over your heads, full of the dreadful storm and high with thunder; and were it not for the restraining hand of God, they would immediately burst forth upon you. The sovereign pleasure of God, for the present, stays His rough wind; otherwise it would come with fury, and your destruction would come like a whirlwind and would be like the chaff of the summer threshingfloor.

The wrath of God is like great waters that are restrained for the present; but they increase more and more, and rise higher and higher, till an outlet is given; and the longer the steam is stopped, the more rapid and mighty is its course when once it is let loose.

It is true that judgment against your evil works has not been executed hitherto; the floods of God's vengeance have been withheld, but your guilt in the meantime is constantly increasing, and you are every day treasuring up more wrath. The waters are constantly rising and waxing more and more mighty; nothing but the mere pleasure of God holds the waters back that are unwilling to be stopped, and press hard to go forward. If God should only withdraw His hand from the floodgate, it would immediately fly open, and the fiery floods of the fierceness and wrath of God would rush forth with inconceivable fury and come upon you with omnipotent power. If your strength were ten thousand times greater than it is, yea, ten thousand times greater than the strength of the stoutest, sturdiest devil in Hell, it would be nothing to withstand or endure it.

The bow of God's wrath is bent and the arrow made ready on the string. Justice directs the bow to your heart, and strains at the bow. Nothing but the mere pleasure of God—that of an angry God—without any promise or obligation at all, keeps the arrow one moment from being made drunk with your blood.

Thus all you who never passed under a great change of heart by the mighty power of the Spirit of God upon your souls; all you who were never born again and made new creatures and raised from being dead in sin, to a state of new and before altogether unexperienced light and life, are in the hands of an angry God. However you may have reformed your life in many things—and many have had religious affections— and may keep up a form of religion in your families and closets and in the house of God, it is nothing but His mere pleasure that keeps you from being this moment swallowed up in everlasting destruction.

However unconvinced you may now be of the truth of what you hear, by and by you will be fully convinced of it. Those who are gone from being in the like circumstances with you, see that it was so with them. Destruction came suddenly upon most of them, when they expected nothing of it and while they were saying, "Peace and safety." Now they see that those things on which they depended for peace and safety were nothing but thin air and empty shadows.

The God who holds you over the pit of Hell much in the same way as one holds a spider or some loathsome insect over the fire, abhors you and is dreadfully provoked. His wrath towards you burns like fire. He looks upon you as worthy of nothing else but to be cast into the fire. He is of purer eyes than to bear to have you in His sight. You are ten thousand times more abominable in His eyes than the most hateful venomous serpent is in ours. You have offended Him infinitely more than ever a stubborn rebel did his prince; yet, it is nothing but His hand that holds you from falling into the fire every moment.

It is to be ascribed to nothing else that you did not go to Hell the last night; that you were suffered to awake again in this world after you closed your eyes to sleep; there is no other reason to be given why you have not dropped into Hell since you arose in the morning, but that God's hand has held you up. There is no other reason to be given, while you have been reading this address, but His mercy; yea, no other reason can be given why you do not this very moment drop down into Hell.

O sinner, consider the fearful danger you are in! It is a great furnace of wrath, a wide and bottomless pit, full of the fire of wrath that you are held over in the hand of that God whose wrath is provoked and incensed as much against you as against many of the damned in Hell. You hang by a slender thread, with the flames of divine wrath flashing about it and ready every moment to singe it and burn it asunder; and you have no interest in any Mediator, and nothing to lay hold of to save yourself, nothing to keep off the flames of wrath, nothing of your own, nothing that you have done, nothing that you can do, to induce God to spare you one moment.

1. Consider here more particularly whose wrath it is. It is the wrath of the infinite God. If it were only the wrath of man, though it were of the most potent prince, it would be comparatively little to be regarded. The wrath of kings is very much dreaded, especially of absolute monarchs who have the possessions and lives of their subjects wholly in their power, to be disposed of at their mere will.

Proverbs 20:2—"The fear of a king is as the roaring of a lion: whoso provoketh him to anger sinneth against his own soul." The subject who very much enrages an arbitrary prince is liable to suffer the most extreme torments that human art can invent, or human power can inflict.

But the greatest earthly potentates, in their greatest majesty and strength and when clothed in their greatest terrors, are but feeble, despicable worms of the dust, in comparison with the great and almighty Creator and King of Heaven and earth. It is but little that they can do, when most enraged and when they have exerted the utmost of their fury. All the kings of the earth, before God, are as grasshoppers; they are nothing, and less than nothing. Both their love and their hatred are to be despised. The wrath of the great King of kings is as much more terrible than theirs as His majesty is greater.

"And I say unto you my friends, Be not afraid of them that kill the body, and after that have no more that they can do. But I will forewarn you whom ye shall fear: Fear him, which after he hath killed hath power to cast into hell; yea, I say unto you, Fear him."—Luke 12:4, 5.

2. It is the fierceness of His wrath that you are exposed to. We often read of the fury of God—as in Isaiah 59:18, "According to their deeds, accordingly he will repay, fury to his adversaries." So Isaiah 66:15, "For, behold, the Lord will come with fire, and with his chariots like a whirl-

wind, to render his anger with fury, and his rebuke with flames of fire."
So also in many other places.

Thus we read of "the winepress of the fierceness and wrath of Almighty
God" (Rev. 19:15). The words are exceedingly terrible. If it had only
been said, "the wrath of God," the words would have implied that which
is unspeakably dreadful; but it is said, "the fierceness and wrath of
God"—the fury of God! the fierceness of Jehovah! Oh how dreadful
must that be! Who can utter or conceive what such expressions carry
in them?

But it is also "the fierceness and wrath of Almighty God." As though
there would be a very great manifestation of His almighty power in what
the fierceness of His wrath should inflict; as though Omnipotence should
be, as it were, enraged and exerted, as men are wont to exert their
strength in the fierceness of their wrath.

Oh, then, what will be the consequence? what will become of the
poor worm that shall suffer it? whose hands can be strong? whose heart
can endure? To what a dreadful, inexpressible, inconceivable depth of
misery must the poor creature be sunk who shall be the subject of this!

Consider this, you that yet remain in an unregenerate state: That God
will execute the fierceness of His anger implies that He will inflict wrath
without any pity. When God beholds the ineffable extremity of your
case and sees your torment to be so vastly disproportioned to your
strength, and sees how your poor soul is crushed and sinks down, as
it were, into an infinite gloom, He will have no compassion upon you.
He will not forbear the execution of His wrath, or in the least lighten
His hand. There shall be no moderation or mercy, nor will God then
at all stay His rough wind. He will have no regard to your welfare, nor
be at all careful lest you should suffer too much in any other sense,
than only that you shall not suffer beyond what strict justice requires.
Nothing shall be withheld, because it is so hard for you to bear.

*"Therefore will I also deal in fury: mine eye shall not spare, neither
will I have pity: and though they cry in mine ears with a loud voice,
yet will I not hear them."*—Ezek. 8:18.

Now, God stands ready to pity you. This is the day of mercy. You
may cry now with some encouragement of obtaining mercy. But when
once the day of mercy is passed, your most lamentable and dolorous
cries and shrieks will be in vain. You will be wholly lost and thrown
away of God as to any regard to your welfare. God will have no other

use to put you to, but to suffer misery; you may be continued in being to no other end! For you will be a vessel of wrath fitted to destruction, and there will be no other use of this vessel, but only to be filled full of wrath.

God will be so far from pitying you when you cry to Him that it is said He will only "laugh and mock."

" Because I have called, and ye refused; I have stretched out my hand, and no man regarded; But ye have set at nought all my counsel, and would none of my reproof: I also will laugh at your calamity; I will mock when your fear cometh; When your fear cometh as desolation, and your destruction cometh as a whirlwind; when distress and anguish cometh upon you. Then shall they call upon me, but I will not answer; they shall seek me early, but they shall not find me: For that they hated knowledge, and did not choose the fear of the Lord: They would none of my counsel: they despised all my reproof. Therefore shall they eat of the fruit of their own way, and be filled with their own devices. For the turning away of the simple shall slay them, and the prosperity of fools shall destroy them." —Prov. 1:24-32.

How awful are those words of the great God:

"I will tread them in mine anger, and trample them in my fury; and their blood shall be sprinkled upon my garments, and I will stain all my raiment." —Isa. 63:3.

It is, perhaps, impossible to conceive of words that carry in them greater manifestations of these three things—namely: contempt, hatred and fierceness of indignation. If you cry to God to pity you, He will be so far from pitying you in your doleful case, or showing you the least reward or favor, that instead of that, He will only tread you under foot. And though He will know that you cannot bear the weight of Omnipotence treading upon you, yet He will not regard that; but He will crush you under His feet without mercy. He will crush out your blood and make it fly, and it shall be sprinkled on His garments so as to stain all His raiment. He will not only hate you, but He will have you in the utmost contempt. No place shall be thought fit for you but under His feet, to be trodden down as the mire of the streets.

3. The misery you are exposed to is that which God will inflict, to the end that He might show what the wrath of Jehovah is. God hath had it on His heart to show to angels and men, both how excellent

His love is, and also how terrible His wrath is.

Sometimes earthly kings have a mind to show how terrible their wrath is by the extreme punishments they would execute on those who provoked them. Nebuchadnezzar, that mighty and haughty monarch of the Chaldean empire, was willing to show his wrath when enraged with Shadrach, Meshach and Abednego; and accordingly gave order that the burning, fiery furnace should be heated seven times hotter than it was before. Doubtless, it was raised to the utmost degree of fierceness that human art could raise it.

But the great God is also willing to show His wrath and magnify His awful majesty and mighty power in the extreme sufferings of His enemies.

"What if God, willing to shew his wrath, and to make his power known, endured with much longsuffering the vessels of wrath fitted to destruction." —Rom. 9:22.

And seeing this is His design and what He has determined, even to show how terrible the unmixed, unrestrained wrath, the fury and fierceness of Jehovah is, He will do it to effect. There will be something accomplished and brought to pass that will be dreadful with a witness.

When the great and angry God hath risen up and executed His awful vengeance on the poor sinner, and the wretch is actually suffering the infinite weight and power of His indignation, then will God call upon the whole universe to behold the awful majesty and mighty power that is to be seen in it.

"And the people shall be as the burnings of lime: as thorns cut up shall they be burned in the fire. Hear, ye that are afar off, what I have done; and, ye that are near, acknowledge my might. The sinners in Zion are afraid; fearfulness hath surprised the hypocrites. Who among us shall dwell with the devouring fire? who among us shall dwell with everlasting burnings?" —Isa. 33:12-14.

Thus it will be with you who are in an unconverted state, if you continue in it. The infinite might and majesty and terribleness of the omnipotent God shall be magnified upon you in the ineffable strength of your torments. You shall be tormented in the presence of the holy angels and in the presence of the Lamb. And when you shall be in this state of suffering, the glorious inhabitants of Heaven shall go forth and look on the awful spectacle, that they may see what the wrath and fierceness of the Almighty is. And when they have seen it, they will fall down and adore that great power and majesty.

"And it shall come to pass, that from one new moon to another, and from one sabbath to another, shall all flesh come to worship before me, saith the Lord. And they shall go forth, and look upon the carcases of the men that have transgressed against me: for their worm shall not die, neither shall their fire be quenched; and they shall be an abhorring unto all flesh." —Isa. 66:23, 24.

4. It is everlasting wrath. It would be dreadful to suffer this fierceness and wrath of Almighty God one moment, but you must suffer it to all eternity. There will be no end to this exquisite, horrible misery. When you look forward, you shall see a long forever, a boundless duration before you, which will swallow up your thoughts and amaze your souls. You will absolutely despair of ever having any deliverance and end, any mitigation, any rest at all. You will know certainly that you must wear out long ages—millions of millions of ages—in wrestling and conflicting with this almighty merciless vengeance. Then when you have so done, when many ages have actually been spent by you in this manner, you will know that all is but a point to what remains. So that your punishment will indeed be infinite.

O, what can express what the state of a soul in such circumstances is! All that we can possibly say about it gives but a very feeble, faint representation of it. It is inexpressible and inconceivable, for, "Who knoweth the power of God's anger?"

How dreadful is the state of those who are daily and hourly in danger of this great wrath and infinite misery! But this is the dismal case of every soul that has not been born again, however moral and strict, sober and religious, they may otherwise be.

Oh, that you would consider it, whether you be young or old! There is reason to fear that there are many who will read this book, or who have heard the Gospel, who will actually be the subjects of this very misery to all eternity. We know not who they are, or what thoughts they now have. It may be they are now at ease and hear all these things without much disturbance and are now flattering themselves that they are not the persons, promising themselves that they shall escape.

If we knew that there was one person, and but one, of those that we know, who was to be the subject of this misery, what an awful thing would it be to think of! If we knew who it was, what an awful sight would it be to see such a person! How might every Christian lift up a lamentable and bitter cry over him!

But alas! instead of one, how many is it likely will remember these solemn reflections in Hell! And some may be in Hell in a very short time—before this year is out. And it would be no wonder if some readers who are now in health and quiet and secure, may be there before tomorrow morning.

Those of you who finally continue in a natural condition who may keep out of Hell longest, will be there in a little time! Your damnation does not slumber; it will come swiftly and, in all probability, very suddenly, upon many of you. You have reason to wonder that you are not already in Hell. It is doubtless the case of some whom you have seen and known, who never deserved Hell more than you, and that heretofore appeared as likely to have been now alive as you. Their case is past all hope. They are crying in extreme misery and perfect despair. But here you are in the land of the living, blessed with Bibles and Lord's days and ministers, and have an opportunity to obtain salvation. What would not those poor damned, hopeless souls give for one day's opportunity such as you now enjoy?

And now you have an extraordinary opportunity, a day wherein Christ has thrown the door of mercy wide open and stands calling and crying with a loud voice to poor sinners, a day wherein many are flocking to Him and pressing into the kingdom of God. Many are daily coming from the east, west, north and south. Many who were very lately in the same miserable condition that you are in are now in a happy state with their hearts filled with love to Him who has loved them and washed them from their sins in His own blood, and rejoicing in hope of the glory of God.

How awful is it to be left behind at such a day to see so many others feasting while you are pining and perishing! To see so many rejoicing and singing for joy of heart while you have cause to mourn for sorrow of heart and to howl for vexation of spirit! How can you rest one moment in such a condition? Are not your souls as precious as the souls of those who are flocking from day to day to Christ?

Are there not many who have lived long in the world, who are not to this day born again, and so are aliens from the commonwealth of Israel, and have done nothing ever since they have lived but treasure up wrath against the day of wrath? O sirs! your case, in an especial manner, is extremely dangerous. Your guilt and hardness of heart are extremely great. Do not you see how generally persons of your years are passed over and left, in the dispensations of God's mercy? You had need to consider yourselves and wake thoroughly out of sleep: you cannot bear the fierceness and wrath of the infinite God.

And you, young man and young woman, will you neglect this precious season which you now enjoy, when so many others of your age are renouncing all youthful vanities and flocking to Christ? You especially have now an opportunity; but if you neglect it, it will soon be with you as it is with those persons who spent all the precious days of youth in sin and are now come to such a dreadful pass in blindness and hardness.

And you children who are unconverted, do not you know that you are going down to Hell to bear the dreadful wrath of that God who is now angry with you every day and every night? Will you be content to be the children of the Devil, when so many of the children of the land are converted and are becoming the holy and happy children of the King of kings?

And let every one who is yet out of Christ and hanging over the pit of Hell, whether they be old men and women, or middle aged, or young people, or little children, now hearken to the loud calls of God's Word and providence. This acceptable year of the Lord, a day of great mercy to some, will doubtless be a day of as remarkable vengeance to others. Men's hearts harden, and their guilt increases apace at such a day as this, if they neglect their souls.

Never was there a period when so many means were employed for the salvation of souls; and if you entirely neglect them, you will eternally curse the day of your birth. Now, undoubtedly it is, as it was in the days of John the Baptist, the axe is laid at the root of the trees, and every tree which brings not forth good fruit may be hewn down, and cast into the fire.

Therefore, let every one who is out of Christ now awake and flee from the wrath to come. The wrath of Almighty God is now undoubtedly hanging over every unregenerate sinner. Let every one flee out of Sodom: "Escape for your lives, look not behind you, escape to the mountain, lest you be consumed."

For a complete list of books available from the Sword of the Lord, write to Sword of the Lord Publishers, P. O. Box 1099, Murfreesboro, Tennessee 37133.